Burnout Syndrome - Recognizing the Signs and Finding Solutions

Edited by Nilgun Ulutasdemir

Published in London, United Kingdom

Burnout Syndrome - Recognizing the Signs and Finding Solutions
http://dx.doi.org/10.5772/intechopen.1010510
Edited by Nilgun Ulutasdemir

Contributors
Aashish Baniya, Alexander Schorb, Bikram Bhandari, Clarine Jacobs, Dulce Milagros Razo-Blanco-Hernández, Edith Araceli Cano-Estrada, Erick Ordoñez-Villordo, Fani Villa-Rivas, Helena H. Heydenreich, Jamuna Das, José Ángel Hernández-Mariano, Juan Carlos Fernando Sánchez-Velázquez, Manika Bose, María Alicia Mejía-Blanquel, Miguel Trujillo-Martínez, Nadia Velázquez-Hernández, Neslişah Gürel Köksal, Nevin Günaydın, Nilgün Ulutaşdemir, Nongluck Manowaluilou, Ram Prasad Subedi, Rocío Castilllo-Díaz, Sagun Ghimire, Suraj Thulung, Suresh Bishokarma

First published in London, United Kingdom, 2026 by IntechOpen
IntechOpen is the global imprint of INTECHOPEN LIMITED, registered in England and Wales, registration number: 11086078, 167-169 Great Portland Street, London, W1W 5PF, United Kingdom

For EU product safety concerns: IN TECH d.o.o., Prolaz Marije Krucifikse Kozulić 3, 51000 Rijeka, Croatia, info@intechopen.com or visit our website at intechopen.com.

British Library Cataloguing-in-Publication Data
A catalogue record for this book is available from the British Library

Burnout Syndrome - Recognizing the Signs and Finding Solutions
Edited by Nilgun Ulutasdemir
p. cm.

This title is part of the Public Health Book Series, Volume 14
Series Editor: José Antonio Mirón Canelo

Print ISBN 978-1-80631-007-4
Online ISBN 978-1-80631-006-7
eBook (PDF) ISBN 978-1-80631-008-1
ISSN 3049-8872

IntechOpen Book Series
Public Health
Volume 14

Aims and Scope of the Series

Public health is what we as a society do collectively to contribute to and ensure the health and social conditions for the enjoyment of health as a resource for life. It can also be defined as science and research that promotes health, prevents disease, and improves populations' well-being and quality of life. Its objective is to know the risk factors that determine and condition the populations' health levels at present. At the end of the 20th century and the beginning of the 21st century, it is unjustifiable and regrettable that morbimortality according to age plays a leading role when the causes are mostly well known and therefore preventable, such as obesity, AIDS, cirrhosis, diabetes mellitus, addictions and cancer associated with the consumption of tobacco and alcohol, etc. In short, public health is science based on epidemiology and biostatistics, and currently, new technologies and artificial intelligence must be incorporated to identify patterns and trends in what we do collectively as a society to ensure living conditions and prevent risk factors that affect individual and population health. For all these reasons, it is essential to scientifically investigate and act on the determinants that impede the well-being and quality of life related to the health of people, patients, and populations in general, given that to control the determinants of diseases, it is important to control the environment and genetics. Consequently, the current fight for public health must prioritize the control of the environment, such as atmospheric and biological pollution and environmental and social biodiversity, promoting the sensitivity and training of society and its individuals by empowering them to make free and appropriate decisions about these aspects to lead healthy lifestyles based on motivation and responsibility in the face of the challenges they cope with from an individual point of view, such as dealing with the addictions that exist in today's complex world. Public health also requires an ethical vision and incorporates strategies to reduce social inequality.

Meet the Series Editor

José Antonio Mirón Canelo is a physician, doctor, and professor of Preventive Medicine and Public Health at the Faculty of Medicine and Dentistry of the University of Salamanca with over 30 years of experience. He is the director of the USAL's Expert Degree in Health Management, currently in its 13th edition. Prof. Mirón Canelo directs a research group at the Research Institute of Biomedical Sciences (IBSAL) of the University of Salamanca focused on addressing the challenges and care needs of vulnerable people and patients such as the elderly with multiple pathologies and people with disabilities and dependence. As a teacher, he has been recognized for excellence in teaching three times in a period of five years.

Meet the Volume Editor

Nilgün Ulutaşdemir graduated with a Ph.D. degree from Fırat University Faculty of Medicine, Department of Public Health in 2012. She became an Assistant Professor in 2012, an Associate Professor in 2019, and a Professor in 2024. Since October 2024, he has been working as a Professor at Ordu University Faculty of Medicine, Department of Public Health. She has served as an executive and researcher on many international and national projects. She has served in the organizing and scientific committees of various international and national conferences. She has published many articles and books in various countries. Her current research interests include public health, occupational health and safety, health management, disaster management, first aid, burnout, work stress, anxiety, elderly health, school health, disabilities, and infectious diseases.

Contents

Preface

The study of burnout syndrome has evolved significantly, with a growing body of literature addressing its complexities and effects in the workplace, family, and friendship relationships. Findings on the physical and emotional symptoms of burnout, including depression and interpersonal difficulties, provide important insights into the wider impact of burnout on personal, family, friendship, and professional life. The need for interventions to address burnout in high-stress professions has increased, particularly amid the growing demands placed on healthcare workers during crises such as COVID-19. Although many ideas have been proposed for addressing burnout, few have been implemented or systematically evaluated. With the right treatment and support, you can overcome burnout, feel more hopeful, and regain your energy and enthusiasm.

A paradox increasingly defines the contemporary professional landscape. As our technological and clinical capabilities reach unprecedented heights, the human infrastructure supporting these systems is facing an exhaustion crisis. Burnout is no longer merely a peripheral occupational hazard; it has emerged as a central challenge to public health, organizational stability, and individual well-being. This edited volume seeks to dissect this phenomenon through a multidisciplinary lens, moving beyond mere symptom identification toward cultivating psychological resilience as a vital, protective resource. By integrating diverse perspectives, ranging from the high-stakes environment of the operating theater to the developmental pressures of the classroom, this work underscores that while burnout manifests individually, its roots are often systemic. The transition from depletion to recovery requires not just personal grit but a fundamental shift in how leadership, technology, and organizational culture interact with the human psyche.

The chapters within this volume are organized to provide a logical progression from foundational theory to specific sectoral analyses and global systemic inquiries: The journey begins with Chapter 1, *Burnout Syndrome in Modern Life: A Psychological Perspective,* which establishes the theoretical groundwork by examining how the accelerating pace of the 21st century reconfigures our stress responses and mental health boundaries. This is followed by Chapter 2, *The Heart of Resilience: Trauma-Informed Leadership in a Burnout Era*, which argues for a paradigm shift in management, emphasizing that resilience must be fostered through empathetic and psychologically informed institutional guidance. The core thesis of our collection is articulated in Chapter 3, *Burnout and Psychological Resilience in Healthcare Professionals: A Protective Psychosocial Resource*. This pivotal study identifies specific psychosocial assets that serve as a bulwark against occupational exhaustion in clinical settings. The book then transitions to specialized medical discourse, beginning with Chapter 4, *Burnout Syndrome in Neurosurgeons: Prevalence, Determinants and Prevention Strategies,* which offers a granular look at one of the most demanding specialties in medicine. This focus continues in Chapter 5, *Burnout Syndrome in Family Medicine Practice*, which highlights the unique pressures of primary care, where the volume of patient interaction and administrative burden create a distinct risk profile. Broadening the scope beyond traditional medicine, Chapter 6, *Burnout and Depression in Sports*, explores the intersection of physical excellence and mental fragility in the competitive athletic arena. We then turn our attention to the next generation in Chapter 7, *Academic Burnout and School Performance Among Adolescents: Concepts, Measurement and Evidence*, which examines how the pressures of achievement take root early in the life cycle. The final section of the volume addresses the global and systemic nature of this crisis. Chapter 8, *Sustaining the Vocational Teaching Workforce in Thailand: Burnout, Modernization Pressures and Technological Transformation*, provides a critical regional case study on how rapid digital shifts can destabilize a traditional workforce. Finally, the volume concludes with Chapter 9, *The Missing Link in Burnout Research: Teacher Wellness and Systemic Recovery across Six Continents*, a comprehensive global survey that calls for an international, systemic approach to recovery and wellness.

In closing, I would like to extend my deepest gratitude to the contributing authors, whose expertise and dedicated efforts have transformed this work into a truly global and multidisciplinary resource. Their rigorous research and commitment to understanding the complexities of the human condition form the very foundation of this book. I would also like to thank the IntechOpen team for their invaluable support and professional guidance throughout the publication process. It is my sincere hope that this work serves as a catalyst for institutional change and guides the construction of a more psychologically sustainable future for healthcare professionals, educators, and leaders. To understand burnout, recognize its symptoms, and identify solutions, a holistic approach that considers both individual experiences and societal pressures is essential. Resilience is not an inexhaustible resource; it is an asset that must be nurtured, protected, and prioritized.

Nilgün Ulutaşdemir
Ordu University Faculty of Medicine,
Department of Public Health,
Ordu, Türkiye

Chapter 1

Burnout Syndrome in Modern Life: A Psychological Perspective

Jamuna Das and Manika Bose

Abstract

Burnout syndrome has emerged as a significant psychological concern in contemporary society, driven by increasing professional demands, digital connectivity, and performance-oriented cultural norms. This article reveals burnout from a psychological point of view, exploring its core dimensions, underlying mechanisms, contributing factors, consequences, and prevention strategies. Conceptually defined by emotional exhaustion, depersonalization, and reduced personal accomplishment, burnout develops gradually as a result of chronic, unmanaged stress. Modern life intensifies vulnerability to burnout due to a busy schedule, work–life ambience, technological overload, perfectionistic tendencies, social comparison, and limited recovery time. Psychologically, prolonged stress disrupts emotional regulation, cognitive functioning, and self-perception, potentially leading to anxiety, depressive symptoms, and diminished overall well-being. The condition also affects physical health through sustained physiological stress responses. Effective intervention requires both individual and systemic approaches. Strategies such as self-awareness, cognitive restructuring, boundary-setting, social support, and value alignment contribute to resilience and recovery. At the organizational level, supportive leadership, manageable workloads, and mental health awareness are essential in reducing risk. Understanding burnout as a multidimensional, context-dependent phenomenon underscores the need for a balanced lifestyle and structural change. Promoting sustainable engagement rather than constant productivity is central to protecting psychological health in modern life.

Keywords: burnout, psychological, treatment, modern life, stress

1. Introduction

Our fast-paced society has changed the way we operate, including how we socialize. Workplace demands, academic competition, financial pressures, and the omnipresence of digital media are reshaping how we work, relax, and socialize. Because of this high-pressure lifestyle, awareness of burnout syndrome has dramatically increased. Burnout used to be seen primarily as a condition experienced in traditional high-stress work environments, but it is now recognized that burnout can also commonly afflict students, caregivers, entrepreneurs, and telecommuters

[1–3]. Burnout, as a phenomenon, was first introduced by psychologist Herbert Freudenberger in the late 1970s, when he noted that many people working in the helping professions were experiencing extreme fatigue and a lack of motivation to do their jobs [4–6]. According to researcher Christina Maslach, burnout can be defined through three basic components: emotional fatigue, increased feelings of detachment or cynicism toward their work (or clients), and reduced levels of personal achievement [1]. The World Health Organization (WHO) currently defines burnout as an occupational phenomenon resulting from chronic stress in the workplace that has not been properly treated, as included in the International Statistical Classification of Diseases (ICD) [7–9].

In contemporary life, burnout is not limited to traditional employment or offices. When workers are under constant pressure to produce, respond, and succeed – all while regularly being compared to others who have done well (thanks to technology) – they don't have enough opportunities for psychological recovery. Burnout develops (and continues to develop) over time, whereas stress is typically referred to in its acute or temporary form. It usually develops due to chronic stress. When people cannot cope with the level of outside demand placed on them, they become burned out. When there is a mismatch between how much energy someone has in terms of emotional energy (internally) versus how much emotional energy they are putting out (externally), and when people consistently expend their emotional resources without the opportunity for adequate rest, support, or recognition, they will experience emotional exhaustion and become ineffective. When this occurs, it affects a person's self-esteem, cognitive performance, relationship quality, and overall mental health. Therefore, from a psychological standpoint, burnout can be thoroughly examined in terms of its causative factors and effects on an individual. By identifying how lifestyle choices contribute to chronic stress and/or emotional imbalance, we can create ways to help people build resilience, maintain a sense of equilibrium, and promote their long-term well-being.

2. Understanding burnout: Core dimensions and psychological mechanisms

Burnout Syndrome can only be fully understood by looking at its psychological makeup and the factors that cause it. Burnout is not just an individual reaction to fatigue; rather, it is a collection of factors arising from long-term exposure to stress that eventually leads to changes in how someone thinks, feels, and behaves [10].

3. Early clinical conceptualization

Burnout is considered a condition experienced by emotionally depleted individuals who volunteer at free clinics. Freudenberger used clinical terms to describe burnout as feelings of exhaustion, irritability, and a lack of motivation among those affected [11]. Maslach and Jackson took Freudenberger's [11, 12] definition from the clinical perspective in 1981 and defined burnout in three parts or dimensions (**Figure 1**), such as:

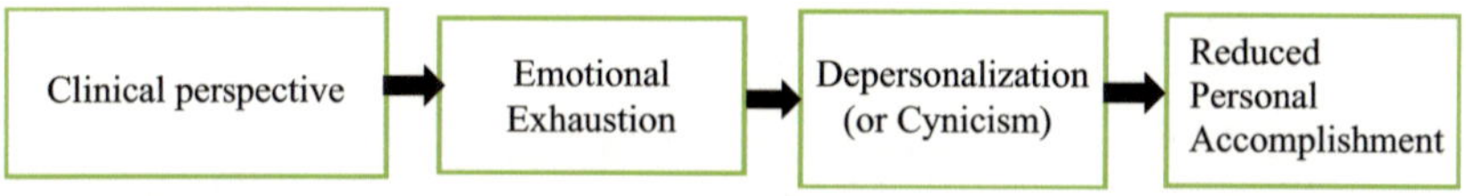

Figure 1.
Clinical dimensions of burnout, illustrating the three core components: emotional exhaustion, depersonalization (or cynicism), and reduced personal accomplishment [13–15].

Psychologist Christina Maslach conceptualized burnout through three interrelated components:

3.1 Emotional exhaustion

Emotional exhaustion is at the heart of burnout. Emotional exhaustion includes the persistent experience of an emotional void and the inability to give of oneself anymore. An individual may feel completely overwhelmed, exhausted, and drained, despite being able to obtain some time off to rest. This emotional exhaustion does not just include physical exhaustion; it indicates a chronic overuse of emotional resources. When considering stress and burnout from a psychological standpoint, emotional exhaustion develops as stress continues to occur with little or no time to recover from it. The sustained activation of the body's nervous system over a long period of time negatively impacts a person's emotional resilience and coping ability [13, 16–18].

3.2 Depersonalization (cynicism)

Depersonalization is marked by feelings of disconnection or cynicism toward one's job, other responsibilities, and other people. People may emotionally distance themselves from others as a protective measure. The emotional distance can manifest as irritability, a lessening or lack of empathy toward those around them, and/or a feeling of disconnection from meaningful work. In a psychological sense, depersonalization is a coping mechanism. When demands placed on the individual feel too much, the individual subconsciously detaches emotional investment to protect themselves. Although, in the short term, this emotional detachment may provide some relief, it will increase one's dissatisfaction and sense of alienation in the long run [14, 19–21].

3.3 Reduced personal accomplishment

People who are burnt out often have very low feelings of competence and achievement in the third dimension. Their self-perception of performance or productivity is lower than actual performance, as shown by objective data. They experience some self-doubt and increased difficulty staying motivated. The cognitive aspect of the third dimension is closely associated with negative self-evaluation patterns. Those who experience chronic stress may develop distorted perceptions of themselves. They tend to dwell on their past mistakes rather than celebrate their successes. Over time, this leads to decreased intrinsic motivation and an increase in feelings of inadequacy [15, 22–28].

4. The stress–burnout continuum

The onset of burnout does not occur over a short period of time; rather, it develops over an extended period and is a function of the individual's experience with stress. The experience of manageable stress (short-term) can actually improve one's level of performance and alertness; however, when long-term stress is combined with inadequate recovery, it ultimately develops into chronic stress that will eventually exhaust your psychological resources, causing you to burn out. Burnout initially has a highly context-specific component associated with the workplace and/or the academic arena. When the individual remains burned out for too long, they are at risk of experiencing an increase in their vulnerability to other mental health issues outside of the original work context. Understanding the characteristics of burnout gives us the ability to differentiate between the two types of fatigue, as well as show that recovery from burnout will take more than just resting; it will require some type of structural, cognitive, and emotional changes in order to successfully recover from the effects of burnout [10, 23, 29, 30].

Stress, burnout, and depression are related but distinct psychological conditions that differ in several key aspects, including duration, scope, emotional tone, and energy levels. As shown in **Table 1**, stress is often short-term and situation-specific, characterized by over-engagement and heightened arousal. In contrast, burnout develops gradually as a chronic condition, primarily associated with work-related exhaustion and emotional depletion. Depression, however, is more pervasive, affecting multiple areas of life and marked by persistent feelings of sadness, hopelessness, and a loss of motivation or pleasure.

While burnout may overlap with depressive symptoms, it remains context-dependent and is typically linked to occupational or role-related stress.

5. Multidimensional models of burnout

Integrative theories are a useful tool for understanding burnout, as they take into account environmental demands, psychological resources, and the motivational processes they elicit, enabling the examination of how these factors interact. Three widely recognized models of burnout include the Job Demands-Resources (JD-R) Model, Conservation of Resources (COR) Theory, and Self-Determination Theory (SDT). These complementary theories assist in explaining the process by which chronic stress develops to create emotional exhaustion, disengagement, and decreased efficacy [31–33].

Feature	Stress	Burnout	Depression
Duration	Often short-term	Chronic	Persistent across contexts
Scope	Situation-specific	Primarily work-related	Pervasive life domains
Emotional tone	Over-engagement	Emotional depletion	Hopelessness, sadness
Energy	Hyperarousal	Exhaustion	Low motivation and pleasure

Table 1.
Burnout vs. Stress vs. Depression.

Burnout has been conceptualized through several integrated multidimensional theoretical frameworks that explain its development and impact across different contexts. As shown in **Table 2**, models such as the Job Demands–Resources (JD-R) Model, Conservation of Resources (COR) Theory, and Self-Determination Theory (SDT) provide complementary perspectives on how burnout emerges. The JD-R model emphasizes the imbalance between job demands and available resources, leading to exhaustion and disengagement. COR theory focuses on the loss of valuable personal and social resources, which creates a cycle of depletion and reduced coping capacity. Meanwhile, SDT highlights the role of unmet psychological needs – autonomy, competence, and relatedness – in diminishing motivation and overall well-being. Together, these models offer a comprehensive understanding of the mechanisms that contribute to burnout and its key dimensions.

6. Causes of burnout in modern life

Burnout does not arise in isolation; it develops through the interaction between environmental pressures and individual psychological vulnerabilities. In modern society, several interconnected factors contribute to the increasing prevalence of burnout [33].

6.1 Chronic workplace stress

The modern workplace usually focuses on productivity, efficiency, and continuous performance evaluation. Heavy workloads, unrealistic deadlines, job insecurity, and little control over how you do your job can create a long-term stress

Theoretical model	Core assumption	Key constructs	Mechanism leading to burnout	Burnout dimension most affected
Job Demands–Resources (JD-R) Model	Burnout results from an imbalance between job demands and job resources	Job demands (workload, time pressure, emotional labor); Job resources (autonomy, support, feedback)	Chronic high demands, combined with insufficient resources, initiate a **health impairment process**, leading to energy depletion and disengagement	Emotional exhaustion; Cynicism
Conservation of Resources (COR) Theory	Stress occurs when valued resources are threatened or lost	Time, energy, self-efficacy, status, social support	Resource depletion creates a **loss spiral**, reducing coping capacity and accelerating further resource loss	Emotional exhaustion; Reduced personal accomplishment
Self-Determination Theory (SDT)	Psychological well-being depends on the satisfaction of basic needs	Autonomy, Competence, Relatedness	Frustration of basic psychological needs undermines intrinsic motivation, leading to disengagement and diminished efficacy.	Reduced personal accomplishment; Depersonalization

Table 2.
Integrated multidimensional models of burnout.

response. Based on occupational models of stress, the risk of experiencing burnout is higher when you experience high demand at work and have low autonomy and/or a lack of recognition for the work you do. Additionally, due to the increase in remote work and the ability to connect with people around the world, many employees may feel obligated to respond to emails and messages outside normal business hours, thereby decreasing their ability to mentally recover and leading to greater emotional exhaustion [31, 34].

6.2 Digital overload and constant connectivity

Although technology has revolutionized communication and information access, it has also increased psychological stress. With our phones, email notifications, and social media, we live in an environment where people are always accessible to us. Non-stop stimulation like this deprives us of cognitive rest and creates unrealistic expectations for instant responses. Additionally, social media helps create a culture of comparison and idealized images of success. When people consistently compare themselves to carefully constructed portrayals of success on social media, it leads to increased feelings of inferiority and self-doubt, which further contribute to the third aspect of burnout: feeling less competent at work or having lower levels of accomplishment [35].

6.3 Perfectionism and internal pressure

Burnout can be caused by both internal and external stressors. The pressure of one's environment is certainly one of those factors; however, an individual's internal psychological traits, such as perfectionism, a high achievement orientation, and a need for affirmation from others, may exacerbate the stress an individual feels. Individuals who possess these psychological characteristics often place extreme expectations on themselves (unrealistic) that will create a scenario where an individual cannot accept making a mistake, resulting in self-criticism and chronic self-criticism. The greater the distance between their expectations and the actual outcome, the more it will continue to result in increased levels of emotional exhaustion and/or dissatisfaction. If an individual's effort does not meet their (or their supervisor's) expectations, motivation will decrease, leading to increased cynicism [10].

6.4 Lack of social support

Social support has been demonstrated to act as a protective buffer against stress. Supportive relationships provide emotional validation, support, and a sense of belonging. In reference to isolation, whether it results from remote work, urban living, or being in a competitive setting, it decreases one's ability to cope. Without sufficient social support, individuals may become overwhelmed by the demands placed on them and internalize stress, leading them to believe they are solely responsible for managing it. This feeling of isolation can quickly increase the time it takes to go from stress to burnout [35].

6.5 Value conflict and loss of meaning

Feeling disconnected from one's core beliefs due to external demands can lead to a loss of motivation and emotional detachment. As this disconnection continues, individuals also begin to erode their sense of connection and become increasingly detached from their coworkers, friends, and family. In today's fast-paced life, there is greater emphasis on productivity than on fulfilment. When accomplishments no longer align with one's intrinsic values, the individual experiences a sense of hollowness or unfulfillment, even when there is an outward display of success [36–38].

7. Psychological and physical consequences of burnout

The impact of stress may be experienced in various ways. In particular, long-term, unresolved stress can produce negative effects across multiple areas, including mental health and the ability to function at optimum levels in one's life.

8. Psychological consequences

Emotional well-being can be severely affected by burnout. Constantly feeling emotionally empty can cause you to be short-tempered, unstable in your mood, and hopeless. Eventually, you may also experience symptoms similar to those of anxiety or depression. Burnout has been classified as an occupational phenomenon by the World Health Organization (WHO). Regardless, if you experience burnout over an extended period of time, it may increase your risk of developing different types of clinical conditions, such as major depressive disorder and/or generalized anxiety disorder. From a verifiable cognitive perspective, burnout can leave you unable to concentrate, remember things, or make decisions as effectively as you did before it set in. Chronic stress is well known to decrease a person's ability to focus, control attention, and perform at their highest level of executive function, which, in turn, leads to greater difficulty accomplishing tasks and feeling more inadequate the longer you remain burnt out [1, 2, 7, 10, 12, 15, 39].

8.1 Behavioral consequences

Burnout leads to withdrawal from work and social activities. As a result, a person will accomplish fewer things, put off completing tasks, and lose most of their energy for their work. Sometimes, individuals suffering from burnout develop maladaptive coping techniques. Some of these include excessive use of technology or screens, overeating, substance abuse, or avoiding emotional experiences. Interpersonal relationships may also be negatively impacted. People who experience burnout may develop depersonalization, which can diminish their ability to empathize or be patient with other people. This depersonalization can create conflicts in work, family, and friendship relationships. As a result, social withdrawal may lead to further isolation and increased psychological distress over time [10].

8.2 Physical health effects

Physiological effects of burnout can also manifest in how we feel physically. The stress response system continually fires due to chronic stress, leading to increased production of stress hormones, including cortisol. Continued elevation of stress hormones can interfere with sleep, weaken our immune system, and cause headaches, as well as digestive and cardiovascular problems. Among the disruptions to sleep are symptoms such as difficulty falling asleep, insufficient sleep, frequent awakenings throughout the night, and feeling unrefreshed upon awakening. These problems create a perpetual cycle where difficulty sleeping increases emotional exhaustion [40–42].

8.3 Impact on identity and self-concept

Burnout can affect a person's perception of themselves beyond just the symptoms. If work or accomplishments are a significant part of one's identity, being unable to perform as usual may impact one's confidence in oneself. A person may begin to doubt their abilities and purpose, as well as their long-term goals. This struggle for self-identity is a significant turning point; burnout now becomes not only about being exhausted but also about losing meaning and direction in life [32, 43, 44].

9. Neurobiological mechanisms

Burnout reflects chronic dysregulation of the stress response system, particularly the hypothalamic–pituitary–adrenal (HPA) axis. A neurobiological explanation of burnout can be framed as an adverse outcome of being under chronic allostatic pressure for a long period of time. Allostatic load represents a physiological adaptation that helps maintain homeostasis (balance) over time. To adapt to the allostatic load, the body will change how it functions, but if the body is chronically exposed to environmental stressors with no (or very little) opportunity to recover, it will become incapable of making any further adaptive changes over time, and this will lead to cumulative biological damage as a result [10, 18, 38].

9.1 Hypothalamic-pituitary-adrenal (HPA) axis dysregulation and allostatic load

The HPA axis constitutes the central neuroendocrine system regulating stress responses. Upon exposure to stressors, whether psychosocial (e.g., workload pressure, evaluation anxiety) or environmental (e.g., time scarcity), the hypothalamus releases corticotropin-releasing hormone (CRH), stimulating adrenocorticotropic hormone (ACTH) release from the pituitary gland. This cascade culminates in the secretion of cortisol by the adrenal cortex.

Under acute stress, cortisol facilitates adaptive responses:

- Increased glucose availability
- Heightened vigilance
- Temporary suppression of non-essential systems

However, chronic occupational stress leads to:

- Blunted diurnal cortisol rhythms
- Hypercortisolism or hypocortisolism patterns
- Impaired feedback inhibition of the HPA axis

Empirical findings indicate that individuals with severe burnout often exhibit altered cortisol awakening responses and flattened diurnal slopes, reflecting dysregulated stress responsivity rather than simple hyperactivation [43, 45, 46].

10. Prefrontal cortex dysfunction and executive control

The prefrontal cortex (PFC), particularly the dorsolateral and ventromedial regions, is critical for executive functioning, emotional regulation, and decision-making. Chronic cortisol exposure compromises synaptic plasticity within the PFC, resulting in:

- Reduced working memory capacity
- Impaired attentional control
- Decreased cognitive flexibility
- Poor inhibitory regulation

These neurocognitive deficits correspond to subjective reports of "brain fog," cognitive fatigue, and diminished productivity, which are frequently described by individuals experiencing burnout. Functional neuroimaging studies suggest decreased activation in executive control networks among chronically stressed individuals, alongside weakened top-down regulation of limbic structures [47–51].

11. Amygdala hyperreactivity and emotional dysregulation

The amygdala plays a central role in threat detection and the processing of emotional salience. Prolonged stress exposure is associated with heightened amygdala reactivity and increased dendritic arborization in stress-sensitive circuits.

In burnout, amygdala hyperactivation may manifest as:

- Irritability
- Heightened emotional sensitivity
- Increased perception of workplace threat
- Reduced tolerance for ambiguity

This hyperreactivity, combined with diminished prefrontal inhibitory control, contributes to emotional exhaustion and interpersonal detachment [48, 52–54].

12. Hippocampal impairment and memory disruption

The hippocampus is particularly vulnerable to chronic exposure to cortisol. Sustained stress reduces neurogenesis within the dentate gyrus and may contribute to the volumetric reductions observed in stress-related conditions.

Functional consequences include:

- Memory consolidation deficits
- Reduced contextual processing
- Impaired learning capacity

These alterations help explain the cognitive inefficiency and attentional fragmentation frequently reported in advanced burnout states [52, 53, 55–57].

13. Neuroinflammation and autonomic imbalance

Emerging research highlights the role of systemic inflammation in chronic stress syndromes. Elevated pro-inflammatory cytokines (e.g., IL-6, TNF-alpha) have been observed in individuals experiencing prolonged occupational stress. Neuroinflammation may contribute to fatigue, mood dysregulation, and cognitive slowing.

Additionally, burnout is associated with autonomic nervous system imbalance, characterized by:

- Reduced heart rate variability (HRV)
- Sympathetic dominance
- Impaired parasympathetic recovery

This physiological profile reflects a diminished capacity for restorative processes [58–62].

Burnout is not only a psychological phenomenon but also involves significant neurobiological alterations across multiple systems in the body. As shown in **Table 3**, dysregulation in key systems such as the hypothalamic–pituitary–adrenal (HPA) axis, prefrontal cortex, amygdala, and hippocampus contributes to the cognitive, emotional, and physiological symptoms of burnout. Chronic activation or blunting of the HPA axis affects stress tolerance and leads to emotional exhaustion. Similarly, reduced executive functioning in the prefrontal cortex impairs decision-making, while heightened amygdala reactivity increases emotional volatility. In addition, hippocampal dysfunction affects memory and learning, and imbalances in the autonomic nervous and immune systems contribute to persistent arousal, poor recovery, fatigue, and mood disturbances. Together, these neurobiological correlates highlight the complex, system-wide impact of burnout.

System	Dysregulation	Functional consequence
HPA axis	Chronic cortisol activation or a blunted response	Emotional exhaustion, stress intolerance
Prefrontal cortex	Reduced executive function and top-down regulation	Cognitive fatigue, impaired decision-making
Amygdala	Heightened reactivity to stress cues	Irritability, emotional volatility
Hippocampus	Stress-related neuroplasticity impairment	Memory disruption, reduced learning
Autonomic nervous system	Reduced HRV, sympathetic dominance	Poor recovery, persistent arousal
Immune system	Elevated inflammatory markers	Fatigue, mood disturbances

Table 3.
Neurobiological correlates of burnout.

14. Treatment

Burnout treatment needs to be conceived as a multi-level, biopsychosocial process of intervention rather than a brief treatment approach to alleviate stress. Burnout has been found to result from long-term exposure to chronic demands, identity-performance fusion, and lack of recovery. Therefore, treatment needs to address restoration at multiple levels, including cognitive, emotional, physiological, behavioral, and structural levels. What is important to highlight at this juncture is that, while burnout has not been categorized as a psychopathological disorder, it has been categorized as an occupational phenomenon.

14.1 Conceptual foundations of burnout treatment

The treatment of burnout syndrome must be viewed as a process of restoring balance across the psychological, physiological, and structural domains. Unlike other forms of stress reactions, burnout syndrome tends to develop over time as a result of prolonged exposure to excessive demands, insufficient recovery time, and emotional pressure. The treatment of burnout syndrome, therefore, cannot be viewed as a process of merely alleviating symptoms of fatigue and irritability. It involves recalibrating stress response systems, restructuring maladaptive thinking patterns, rebuilding depleted psychological resources, and addressing environmental factors. The treatment of burnout syndrome also involves recognizing the interplay between the individual and the systems in which they function (**Figure 2**) [63, 64].

14.2 Individual-level psychological interventions

Figure 2.
Conceptual relationship between therapeutic approaches, showing the progression from cognitive behavioral therapy (CBT) to mindfulness-based interventions (MBI) and acceptance and commitment therapy (ACT) [65–67].

15. Cognitive behavioral therapy (CBT)

Cognitive behavioral therapy specifically focuses on changing negative thought processes that contribute to burnout. People experiencing burnout tend to have absolute beliefs about productivity, accountability, and self-worth. Perfectionism, fear of failure, and excessive negative self-talk contribute to perceived stress levels and make it difficult to disconnect psychologically from work. Cognitive behavioral therapy helps individuals become more aware of negative thought processes and change them into more realistic, balanced ways of thinking. By changing negative thought processes, individuals can shift unrealistic performance expectations and combat burnout [65, 68].

16. Mindfulness-based interventions (MBT)

Mindfulness has been shown to improve our capacity to be aware of what is happening right now and to manage our emotions. Burnout is often related to ruminating on our task completion and worrying about how we will perform in the future. Mindfulness can help break this cycle of rumination by helping people observe their thoughts and feelings without judgment. Additionally, those who practice mindfulness regularly tend to experience decreased physiological stress, increased parasympathetic activation, and improved ability to control their attention. As people practice mindfulness, they gain a greater ability to resist workplace stressors and a stronger sense of psychological detachment [66, 69].

17. Acceptance and commitment therapy (ACT)

Acceptance and Commitment Therapy targets the motivational and existential aspects of burnout. There are people who over-identify with their professional roles and equate success with their identity. ACT focuses on psychological flexibility and living in accordance with intrinsic values rather than extrinsic success factors. It aims to help individuals clarify their values and take meaningful action to transform their professional roles [67, 70–72].

18. Physiological restoration and stress regulation

- Sleep rehabilitation
- Physical activity and neurobiological recovery
- Autonomic nervous system regulation

18.1 Sleep rehabilitation

Burnout is closely associated with sleep disturbances due to chronic stress activation. Restoring healthy sleep patterns is essential for emotional stability and cognitive functioning. Structured sleep hygiene interventions, such as maintaining consistent sleep schedules and reducing evening digital exposure, help regulate circadian rhythms and reduce cortisol dysregulation [73].

18.2 Physical activity and neurobiological recovery

Regular physical activity contributes to stress reduction and neurobiological resilience. Exercise promotes endorphin release, enhances mood regulation, supports hippocampal neurogenesis, and stabilizes the hypothalamic–pituitary–adrenal (HPA) axis. Incorporating moderate aerobic exercise into weekly routines can significantly improve energy levels and reduce fatigue associated with burnout [74, 75].

18.3 Autonomic nervous system regulation

Chronic burnout is associated with sympathetic nervous system dominance. Techniques such as diaphragmatic breathing, progressive muscle relaxation, and heart rate variability (HRV) biofeedback support parasympathetic activation. Improved autonomic balance enhances recovery capacity and reduces persistent physiological arousal [76, 77].

19. Behavioural and lifestyle restructuring

- Boundary reconstruction
- Workload management and task prioritization
- Rebuilding self-efficacy

Restoring boundaries between work and personal life is a key aspect of treating burnout. Digital hyperconnectivity and working remotely can often make it difficult to achieve these boundaries, and as a result, people may experience difficulty in psychologically detaching themselves from their jobs. Some of the most important steps to reduce chronic exposure to demands are: clearly defining work hours; setting limits on after-hours communication; and scheduling restorative activities. Chronic stress and overly ambitious expectations can lead to increased burnout. By using a structured approach to analyzing workloads, individuals can identify non-essential tasks; delegate tasks or responsibilities; and determine which activities deliver the most value. Setting realistic goals reduces mental overload and achieves a restored sense of control. The experience of burnout is characterized by diminished personal accomplishments. Using therapeutic strategies that focus on achieving incremental goals and attaining mastery can help to improve self-confidence and feelings of personal accomplishment after experiencing burnout. Achieving small, easily achievable goals can undermine feelings of incompetence and restore a sense of professional efficacy [78–81].

20. Organizational-level interventions

- Work design and demand reduction

- Leadership and support systems
- Recovery-oriented organizational culture

Burnout Recovery requires accountability from an organization. The potential for burnout will increase significantly when there is too much work, unclear job responsibilities, and no latitude in one's duties. Companies need to redesign the jobs they create by defining what is reasonable to expect from each role, distributing work equitably among employees, and giving them control over how they make decisions.

Supportive leadership has a protective function to prevent and/or recover from burnout. Transparent communication, recognition of employee effort, and participatory decision-making create a sense of psychological safety for employees. When employees feel supported by their leaders and valued as part of an organization, this leads to decreased emotional exhaustion and increased engagement in the workplace.

A possible way for institutions to promote sustainable performance is to create policies that protect the length of recovery by following guidelines such as restricting after-hour emails, creating expectations for employees to take vacations, and providing access to mental health support. The organization's overall culture must shift from one focusing on continuous productivity toward a long-term sustainable future [78, 80–82].

21. Stages of burnout recovery

To acknowledge both our physical and emotional exhaustion is an honest first step toward recovery. Many people who are suffering from prolonged stress or burnout tend to dismiss their experiences as being due to temporary fatigue or weakness. In order for these individuals to take realistic action to recover, they need to recognize that they are experiencing real physical and/or emotional depletion; recognition of being depleted serves as a foundation for recovery. Increased awareness allows us to reduce our denial and break maladaptive ways of coping, such as overworking, avoidance behaviors, or suppressing emotions. An increase in our ability to identify symptoms (chronic fatigue, irritability, poor focus, sleep problems, repeated physical complaints, etc.) is likely to result in seeking the help we need to recover. Shifting from simply enduring the negative impacts to actually acknowledging them represents the true start of recovery.

After one has recognized their current state, one must provide a period of limited/temporary exposure to stress. The continued experience of strain will not allow the nervous system to properly recalibrate. Therefore, an individual may have to pursue short-term stabilization through the following types of modifications to their work/tasks: medical leave, decreased hours, delegating responsibility, or modifying their job assignment, and they may need to move out of high-stress areas if they are going to make progress and not deteriorate further. This is not an example of avoidance but rather is establishing a temporary 'time-out' from which healing may occur. Reducing/removing stressors enables cortisol levels to decrease, improved sleep, and decreased emotional reactivity. Without intentional reduction in demands, recovery further down the path will be impeded.

The psychological and physiological systems are gradually calibrated during stabilization, and therapy often plays a prominent role in this process by providing clients with opportunities to process accumulated stress, detect negative thoughts, and develop more effective ways to deal with life's difficulties. A variety of cognitive-behavioral techniques, mindfulness exercises, and trauma-informed approaches may all play a part in achieving emotional regulation through stimulation of the neurotransmitter system that regulates emotions, as well as providing emotional support through healthy lifestyle changes. Creating healthy habits through sleep, proper nutrition, moderate exercise, and healthy restorative practices (i.e., relaxation training and breathing exercises) all increase the body's ability to heal from an emotional standpoint. Additionally, developing social connections with trusted individuals decreases the degree of social isolation and provides additional support for regaining resiliency. After combining the effects of psychosocial support with the positive impact of making lifestyle changes, eventually, a person's sense of stability and resiliency will be restored.

The last, and often most complicated, piece of a person's recovery process is going back to their job or taking on some of their prior responsibilities, which calls for an intentional plan for how best to accomplish this task. There is a significant risk of repeating prior behaviors that resulted in being depleted if there are no changes made to the structure of the workplace. Thus, an effective reintegration process should include well-defined boundaries, realistic expectations for performance, and improved workload management. In some circumstances, employees may need to openly communicate with their supervisors and/or teammates about the long-term sustainability of their demands. To maintain limits, employees may need to develop assertive communication skills. Continued self-monitoring will allow for early identification of warning signs.

During this phase, it is critical to establish a relapse prevention plan. An effective way to help prevent relapse is to identify personal stress triggers, acknowledge the early signs of being overwhelmed, and create a solid action plan for how you will cope with stress. Continued counseling and/or periodic check-ins may also help provide some extra support during this process. Recovery is not an even or linear process, nor do occasional setbacks equal failure; they are merely ways to improve your coping strategies and continue strengthening your protective behaviors. Through ongoing awareness, flexible boundaries (adapting to changes in the environment), and proactive stress management, individuals can return to their positions with improved balance, resiliency, and long-lasting health.

22. Integrated multilevel treatment approach

Burnout is not solved by a single method. A comprehensive approach to treating burnout must recognize that both personal and organizational intervention strategies are needed to address this issue. Burnout arises when repeated excessive demands on one's structure (psychological/emotional/physical) build to exceed their limits. Recovery will take extended time frames to complete, using a combination of personal and organizational support functions. An individual coping mechanism can help provide cognitive restructuring (i.e., the thought process that leads to excessive internal pressure, such as perfectionism or self-criticism) by creating balanced, realistic thinking that can be carried into other routine activities.

There are also physiological interventions; promoting healthy sleep habits, exercise, and stress-reduction activities will contribute to restoring physiological stability and increasing emotional resilience. There are a variety of behavioral strategies that can be implemented to minimize excessive demands on oneself (e.g., establishing boundaries, setting priorities, and taking restorative breaks). Through these efforts, it is expected that the individual will reduce the time they remain exposed to excessive demands on themselves. While all three components of a multi-level intervention will assist an individual in recovering from burnout, systemic change within an organization must also be addressed if true and sustainable change is to endure long-term. Systemic changes such as manageable workloads, support from leadership, clarified expectations regarding capabilities and achievement, and an overall culture of well-being will offer individuals opportunities to learn and instill coping techniques within the organization, with long-term effects in mitigating excessive demands made on them and in creating sustainable recovery and prevention of burnout.

23. Prevention and intervention: Psychological strategies for addressing burnout

Burnout must be addressed through more than a "break" because you must restore the balance between the demands placed on you and the resources you have to meet those demands. The use of effective prevention and intervention practices can occur at both the individual and organizational levels. These practices can help people change their cognitive patterns, regulate their emotions, develop a structured lifestyle, and create a supportive environment.

24. Strengthening self-awareness

Recognizing early warning signs of burnout is the first step in preventing it. Emotional exhaustion, irritability, decreased motivation, and chronic fatigue are not "normal" parts of being productive. Self-awareness helps individuals detect stress patterns before they escalate. Tools for building psychological awareness (such as writing/journaling, reflection, and mindfully practicing) can help individuals know what to avoid and how to respond to emotional states and stress triggers. Once individuals understand their limitations, they can create boundaries around them [83].

25. Establishing healthy boundaries

Many people today have trouble separating work from their time away from work. Also, it is important for people to be able to set healthy boundaries around their work and life by limiting after-hours communications, scheduling regular breaks, and protecting their time for rest, as these activities allow individuals to achieve recovery by enabling their nervous systems to return to normal and avoid chronic activation of the stress response. Part of the process of setting boundaries to maintain a work-life balance is learning to say no to excessive work. Although the initial discomfort of saying no may be challenging, over time it helps increase resilience and reduce one's overall work-related overload [84, 85].

26. Cognitive restructuring

When someone is suffering from burnout, it can often be due to negative or unhelpful thought patterns – perfectionism, self-criticism, and/or 'all-or-nothing' thinking. Cognitive-behavioral therapy is a method of cognitive restructuring that can help an individual reframe unrealistic expectations by challenging them. Instead of saying, "I need to do everything perfectly," someone experiencing burnout can instead say, "I can work toward excellence without having to be perfect." This allows for less internal pressure and provides sustainable motivation [86].

27. Reconnecting with meaning and values

A strong protective aspect against burnout is having a purpose. The more someone can connect their actions to their values, the more meaningful the work will be to them. Reflecting on both long-term goals and core motivations can help restore a sense of engagement and satisfaction in one's work and reduce feelings of cynicism. If there is an ongoing disconnect between values and environment, you typically need to make a larger change to maintain psychological well-being, such as changing your career or adjusting your role [87, 88].

28. Enhancing social support

Stress can be reduced by strong social support. Having a network of friends, co-workers, or family provides opportunities to share experiences and validate feelings of isolation and emotional pain. If you experience more extreme levels of stress, you can find assistance through professional psychological counseling. In addition to external social supports, your workplace can provide support to individuals experiencing significant stress. Supporting individuals with adequate organizational structures, such as distributing workloads fairly, either using rewards/recognition systems, mental health programs, or flexible schedules, can greatly help reduce the chance of burnout [89].

29. Toward a balanced modern life

Burnout is a result of extended periods of imbalance between demands and recovery from those demands, rather than a sign of weakness. Our culture has a tendency to idolize constant productivity; therefore, prioritizing psychological well-being is an act of self-preservation. Resilience against chronic stress can be developed by building self-awareness, establishing boundaries, creating new cognitive patterns, and enhancing social connections. While it's still necessary to understand systemic and organizational/accountability in developing cultures that embrace value-based performance, along with an individual's well-being [90].

Learning how to properly define and address burnout is not only about preventing human exhaustion but also about fostering sustainable engagement with your work, ensuring meaningful work, and preserving your long-term psychological health in our modern world.

30. Conclusion

Burnout Syndrome has emerged as one of the major psychological problems in today's world; and it has become increasingly difficult for individuals to discover the line between healthy ambition and harmful over-exertion. In an age filled with perpetual connectivity, unrealistic expectations, and excessive demands for performance, the ability to distinguish between the two (healthy ambition and excessive ambition) has decreased. Stress that starts off as manageable can progress to emotional and physical fatigue, leading an individual to feel less capable of achieving his/her goals.

Burnout is caused by ongoing mismatches between demands and coping resources that exceed the individual's ability to manage. In addition to colleagues, job performance, and employers' expectations, burnout is influenced by cultural values that emphasize long hours, competition, and productivity more than rest and emotional well-being. Individual characteristics, such as perfectionism and the tendency to set high goals and have unrealistic expectations, may make people vulnerable to developing burnout, but systemic and environmental factors have just as strong an influence. Burnout is not an indication of weakness and/or a lack of ability; rather, it is a natural human response to various forms of long-lasting stress without a sufficient recovery (re-energization) period. The first step toward addressing burnout is awareness of its symptoms and the development of psychological resilience through supportive, positive social and organizational structures. To prevent burnout, we need a shift in mindset (thinking) and in the structures (physical/digital requirements). To be successful (sustainable) is not about producing (constantly) but about balance (work and personal life), having a purpose, and being psychologically healthy. If our society valued rest as much as production and meaning as much as achievement, it would move toward a healthier, more sustainable society and a better life.

To treat burnout syndrome in the modern world, a holistic and systematic (holistic/systemic) approach is necessary. Burnout recovery requires more than simply reducing stress; it entails changing cognitive and emotional regulation systems, physical systems in the body, behavior, and organizational structure. Recovery from burnout occurs when individuals rebuild their internal resources and external structures to reduce chronic over-stress. In a digital age and performance-oriented environment, the treatment for burnout should be a combination of psychological knowledge and structural changes that support individuals in maintaining well-being and being engaged in their work in the long term.

Acknowledgments

The author acknowledges the use of artificial intelligence (AI) tools for language editing and grammar correction to improve the clarity of the manuscript. The AI tools were used only for linguistic support. All generations of original research content, interpretations, analyses, and conclusions presented in this chapter are solely the responsibility of the author.

DOI: http://dx.doi.org/10.5772/intechopen.1015422

Author details

Jamuna Das[1] and Manika Bose[2]*

1 Department of Psychiatry, IMS and SUM Hospital (Siksha 'O' Anusandhan), Bhubaneswar, India

2 Department of Pharmacology, IMS and SUM Hospital (Siksha 'O' Anusandhan), Bhubaneswar, India

*Address all correspondence to: manikabose@soa.ac.in

IntechOpen

References

[1] Maslach C, Leiter MP. Understanding the burnout experience: Recent research and its implications for psychiatry. World Psychiatry. 2016;**15**(2):103–111. DOI: 10.1002/wps.20311

[2] Stress FG. Definitions, Mechanisms, and Effects Outlined: Lessons from Anxiety. Stress: Concepts, Cognition, Emotion, and Behavior: Handbook of Stress. 2016;3–11. DOI: 10.1016/B978-0-12-800951-2.00001-7

[3] Demerouti E, Nachreiner F, Bakker AB, Schaufeli WB. The job demands-resources model of burnout. Journal of Applied Psychology. 2001;**86**(3):499–512. DOI: 10.1037/0021-9010.86.3.499

[4] Oakley BA. Concepts and implications of altruism bias and pathological altruism. Proceedings of the National Academy of Sciences of the United States of America. 2013;**110**(SUPPL2):10408–10415. DOI: 10.1073/pnas.1302547110

[5] Schaufeli WB, Leiter MP, Maslach C. Burnout: 35 years of research and practice. Career Development International. 2009;**14**(3):204–220. DOI: 10.1108/13620430910966406

[6] Samra R. Brief history of burnout. BMJ. 2018;**363**. DOI: 10.1136/bmj.k5268

[7] Bianchi R, Schonfeld IS. Examining the evidence base for burnout. Bulletin of the World Health Organization. 2023;**101**(11):743. DOI: 10.2471/BLT.23.289996

[8] Katz D. Staff burn-out. Journal of Social Issues. 1974;**30**(3):159–165. DOI: 10.1111/j.1540-4560.1974.tb00732.x

[9] Eisenstein L. To fight burnout, organize. New England Journal of Medicine. 2018;**379**(6):509–511. DOI: 10.1056/nejmp1803771

[10] Khammissa RAG, Nemutandani S, Feller G, Lemmer J, Feller L. Burnout phenomenon: Neurophysiological factors, clinical features, and aspects of management. Journal of International Medical Research. 2022;**50**(9):03000605221106428. DOI: 10.1177/03000605221106428

[11] Freudenberger HJ. Staff Burn-Out. Journal of Social Issues. 1974;**30**(1):159–165. DOI: 10.1111/j.1540-4560.1974.tb00706.x

[12] Maslach C, Jackson SE. The measurement of experienced burnout. Journal of Organizational Behavior. 1981;**2**(2):99–113. DOI: 10.1002/job.4030020205

[13] Adams RE, Boscarino JA, Figley CR. Compassion fatigue and psychological distress among social workers: A validation study. American Journal of Orthopsychiatry. 2006;**76**(1):103–108. DOI: 10.1037/0002-9432.76.1.103

[14] Yang J, Millman LSM, David AS, Hunter ECM. The Prevalence of Depersonalization-Derealization Disorder: A Systematic Review. Journal of Trauma and Dissociation. 2023;**24**(1):8–41. DOI: 10.1080/15299732.2022.2079796

[15] Bressi C, Porcellana M, Gambini O, Madia L, Muffatti R, Peirone A, et al. Burnout among psychiatrists in Milan: A multicenter survey. Psychiatric Services. 2009;**60**(7):985–988. DOI: 10.1176/ps.2009.60.7.985

[16] Salston MD, Figley CR. Secondary traumatic stress effects of working with survivors of criminal victimization. Journal of Traumatic Stress. 2003;**16**(2):167–174. DOI: 10.1023/A:1022899207206

[17] Palm KM, Polusny MA, Follette VM. Vicarious traumatization: Potential hazards and interventions for disaster and trauma workers. Prehospital and Disaster Medicine. 2004;**19**(1):73–78. DOI: 10.1017/S1049023X00001503. PubMed PMID: 2004165800

[18] Jin MJ, Kim JS, Lee HS, Kwon YJ, Shim SH, Choi BS, et al. The Impact of Emotional Exhaustion on Psychological Factors in Workers with Secondary Traumatic Experiences: A Multi-Group Path Analysis. Psychiatry Investigation. 2020;**17**(11):1064. DOI: 10.30773/pi.2019.0313

[19] Shorvon HJ. The Depersonalization Syndrome. Journal of the Royal Society of Medicine. 1946;**39**(12):779–792. DOI: 10.1177/003591574603901206

[20] Sierra M, Berrios GE. The Cambridge Depersonalisation Scale: A new instrument for the measurement of depersonalisation. Psychiatry Research. 2000;**93**(2):153–164. DOI: 10.1016/S0165-1781(00)00100-1

[21] Wilkhoo HS, Islam AW, Reji F, Sanghvi L, Potdar R, Solanki S. Depersonalization-Derealization Disorder: Etiological Mechanism. Diagnosis and Management. Discoveries. 2024;**12**(2):e190. DOI: 10.15190/d.2024.9

[22] Gascon S, Leiter MP, Andrés E, Santed MA, Pereira JP, Cunha MJ, et al. The role of aggressions suffered by healthcare workers as predictors of burnout. Journal of Clinical Nursing. 2013;**22**(21–22):3120–3129. DOI: 10.1111/j.1365-2702.2012.04255.x

[23] Toker S, Shirom A, Shapira I, Berliner S, Melamed S. The association between burnout, depression, anxiety, and inflammation biomarkers: C-reactive protein and fibrinogen in men and women. Journal of Occupational Health Psychology. 2005;**10**(4):344–362. DOI: 10.1037/1076-8998.10.4.344

[24] González-Morales MG, Peiró JM, Rodríguez I, Bliese PD. Perceived collective burnout: A multilevel explanation of burnout. Anxiety, Stress, & Coping. 2012;**25**(1):43–61. DOI: 10.1080/10615806.2010.542808

[25] Bakker AB, Le Blanc PM, Schaufeli WB. Burnout contagion among intensive care nurses. Journal of Advanced Nursing. 2005;**51**(3):276–287. DOI: 10.1111/j.1365-2648.2005.03494.x

[26] Spence Laschinger HK, Wong CA, Grau AL. The influence of authentic leadership on newly graduated nurses' experiences of workplace bullying, burnout and retention outcomes: A cross-sectional study. International Journal of Nursing Studies. 2012;**49**(10):1266–1276. DOI: 10.1016/j.ijnurstu.2012.05.012

[27] Maslach C, Schaufeli WB, Leiter MP. Job burnout. Annual Review of Psychology. 2001;**52**:397–422. DOI: 10.1146/annurev.psych.52.1.397

[28] Leiter MP, Maslach C. Nurse turnover: The mediating role of burnout. Journal of Nursing Management. 2009;**17**(3):331–339. DOI: 10.1111/j.1365-2834.2009.01004.x

[29] Kristensen TS, Borritz M, Villadsen E, Christensen KB. The Copenhagen Burnout Inventory: A new tool for the assessment of burnout. Work & Stress. 2005;**19**(3):192–207. DOI: 10.1080/02678370500297720

[30] Rosa I, Padula LP, Semeraro F, Marrangone C, Inserra A, De Risio L, et al. Endocannabinoids, depression, and treatment resistance: Perspectives on effective therapeutic interventions. Psychiatry Research. 2025:352. DOI: 10.1016/j.psychres.2025.116697

[31] Epstein EG, Haizlip J, Liaschenko J, Zhao D, Bennett R, Marshall MF. Moral distress, mattering, and secondary traumatic stress in provider burnout: A call for moral community. AACN Advanced Critical Care. 2020;**31**(2):146–157. DOI: 10.4037/aacnacc2020285

[32] Edú-valsania S, Laguía A, Moriano JA. Burnout: A Review of Theory and Measurement. International Journal of Environmental Research and Public Health. 2022;**19**(3):1780. DOI: 10.3390/ijerph19031780

[33] Lewig KA, Xanthopoulou D, Bakker AB, Dollard MF, Metzer JC. Burnout and connectedness among Australian volunteers: A test of the Job Demands-Resources model. Journal of Vocational Behavior. 2007;**71**(3):429–445. DOI: 10.1016/j.jvb.2007.07.003

[34] Salama W, Abdou AH, Mohamed SAK, Shehata HS. Impact of Work Stress and Job Burnout on Turnover Intentions among Hotel Employees. International Journal of Environmental Research and Public Health. 2022;**19**(15):9724. DOI: 10.3390/ijerph19159724

[35] Kavakli M, Ünal G. The effects of social comparison on the relationships among social media addiction, self-esteem, and general belongingness levels. Current Issues in Personality Psychology. 2021;**9**(2):114. DOI: 10.5114/cipp.2021.105349

[36] De Raeve L, Jansen NWH, van den Brandt PA, Vasse RM, Kant I. Risk factors for interpersonal conflicts at work. Scandinavian Journal of Work, Environment & Health. 2008;**34**(2):96–106. DOI: 10.5271/sjweh.1223

[37] Jiang F, Lu S, Zhu X, Song X. Social media impacts the relation between interpersonal conflict and job performance. Asia Pacific Journal of Human Resources. 2021;**59**(3):420–441. DOI: 10.1111/1744-7941.12250

[38] Sheng J, Zheng G, Wang H, Xu Z. Exploring the associations between work addiction, emotional intelligence, psychological detachment, and interpersonal conflicts in young employees. Frontiers in Public Health. 2025;**13**:1631122. DOI: 10.3389/fpubh.2025.1631122

[39] White T Burnout Among Special Education Teachers: A Transcendental Phenomenological Study. 2021

[40] Hine J, Schwell A, Kairys N. An Unlikely Cause of Hypokalemia. Journal of Emergency Medicine. 2017;**52**(5):e187–91. DOI: 10.1016/j.jemermed.2016.12.011

[41] Chu B, Marwaha K, Sanvictores T, Awosika AO, Ayers D. Physiology, Stress Reaction.. StatPearls [Internet]. Treasure Island (FL): StatPearls Publishing; 2026

[42] Hannibal KE, Bishop MD. Chronic Stress, Cortisol Dysfunction, and Pain: A Psychoneuroendocrine Rationale for Stress Management in Pain Rehabilitation. Physical Therapy. 2014;**94**(12):1816. DOI: 10.2522/ptj.20130597

[43] Han S, Shanafelt TD, Sinsky CA, Awad KM, Dyrbye LN, Fiscus LC, et al. Estimating the attributable cost of physician burnout in the United States. Annals of Internal Medicine. 2019;**170**(11):784–790. DOI: 10.7326/M18-1422

[44] Grow HM, McPhillips HA, Batra M. Understanding physician burnout. Current Problems in Pediatric and Adolescent Health Care. 2019;**49**(11). DOI: 10.1016/j.cppeds.2019.100656

[45] Carrasco GA, Van De Kar LD. Neuroendocrine pharmacology of stress. European Journal of Pharmacology. 2003;**463**(1–3):235–272. DOI: 10.1016/S0014-2999(03)01285-8

[46] Smith SM, Vale WW. The role of the hypothalamic-pituitary-adrenal axis in neuroendocrine responses to stress. Dialogues in Clinical Neuroscience. 2006;**8**(4):383. DOI: 10.31887/dcns.2006.8.4/ssmith

[47] Girotti M, Adler SM, Bulin SE, Fucich EA, Paredes D, Morilak DA. Prefrontal cortex executive processes affected by stress in health and disease. Progress in Neuropsychopharmacology & Biological Psychiatry. 2017;**85**:161. DOI: 10.1016/j.pnpbp.2017.07.004

[48] Liu S, Erkkinen MG, Healey ML, Xu Y, Swett KE, Chow HM, et al. Brain activity and connectivity during poetry composition: Toward a multidimensional model of the creative process. Human Brain Mapping. 2015;**36**(9):3351–3372. DOI: 10.1002/hbm.22849

[49] Barbey AK, Koenigs M, Grafman J. Dorsolateral prefrontal contributions to human working memory. Cortex. 2013;**49**(5):1195–1205. DOI: 10.1016/j.cortex.2012.05.022

[50] Kane MJ, Engle RW. The role of prefrontal cortex in working-memory capacity, executive attention, and general fluid intelligence: An individual-differences perspective. Psychonomic Bulletin & Review. 2002;**9**(4):637–671. DOI: 10.3758/BF03196323

[51] Nejati V, Majdi R, Salehinejad MA, Nitsche MA. The role of dorsolateral and ventromedial prefrontal cortex in the processing of emotional dimensions. Scientific Reports. 2021;**11**(1):1971. DOI: 10.1038/s41598-021-81454-7

[52] Davis LL, Hamner MB. Post-traumatic stress disorder: The role of the amygdala and potential therapeutic interventions – A review. Frontiers in Psychiatry. 2024;**15**:1356563. DOI: 10.3389/fpsyt.2024.1356563

[53] Zhang X, Ge TT, Yin G, Cui R, Zhao G, Yang W. Stress-Induced Functional Alterations in Amygdala: Implications for Neuropsychiatric Diseases. Frontiers in Neuroscience. 2018;**12**(5):367. DOI: 10.3389/fnins.2018.00367

[54] Ressler KJ. Amygdala Activity, Fear, and Anxiety: Modulation by Stress. Biological Psychiatry. 2010;**67**(12):1117. DOI: 10.1016/j.biopsych.2010.04.027

[55] Forghani N, Hosseinian S, Akhoond-Ali Z, Gholami AA, Assaran-

Darban R, Vafaee F. Effect of acute and chronic stress on memory impairment and hippocampal oxidative stress following global cerebral ischemia in adult male rats. Research in Pharmaceutical Sciences. 2024;**19**(4):436. DOI: 10.4103/RPS.RPS_24_23

[56] Kuhn HG, Toda T, Gage FH. Adult hippocampal neurogenesis: A coming-of-age story. Journal of Neuroscience. 2018;**38**(49):10401–10410. DOI: 10.1523/JNEUROSCI.2144-18.2018

[57] Leschik J, Lutz B, Gentile A. Stress-Related Dysfunction of Adult Hippocampal Neurogenesis—An Attempt for Understanding Resilience? International Journal of Molecular Sciences. 2021;**22**(14):7339. DOI: 10.3390/ijms22147339

[58] Libby P, Ridker PM, Hansson GK. Inflammation in Atherosclerosis. From Pathophysiology to Practice. Journal of the American College of Cardiology. 2009;**54**(23):2129–2138. DOI: 10.1016/j.jacc.2009.09.009

[59] Miller AH, Raison CL. The role of inflammation in depression: From evolutionary imperative to modern treatment target. Nature Reviews Immunology. 2016;**16**(1):22–34. DOI: 10.1038/nri.2015.5

[60] Balakin E, Yurku K, Ivanov M, Izotov A, Nakhod V, Pustovoyt V. Regulation of Stress-Induced Immunosuppression in the Context of Neuroendocrine, Cytokine, and Cellular Processes. Biology. 2025;**14**(1):76. DOI: 10.3390/biology14010076

[61] Obeagu EI. Stress, neutrophils, and immunity: A dynamic interplay. Annals of Medicine & Surgery. 2025;**87**(6):3573–3585. DOI: 10.1097/ms9.0000000000003304

[62] Rhie SJ, Jung EY, Shim I. The role of neuroinflammation on pathogenesis of affective disorders. Journal of Exercise Rehabilitation. 2020;**16**(1):2. DOI: 10.12965/jer.2040016.008

[63] van Dam A. A clinical perspective on burnout: Diagnosis, classification, and treatment of clinical burnout. European Journal of Work and Organizational Psychology. 2021;**30**(5):732–741. DOI: 10.1080/1359432X.2021.1948400

[64] Demerouti E. Burnout: A comprehensive review. Zeitschrift Für Arbeitswissenschaft. 2024;**78**(4):492–504. DOI: 10.1007/s41449-024-00452-3

[65] Khurshid K, Mushtaq R, Rauf U, Anwar N, Abbas Q, Aljhani S, et al. Cognitive behavior therapy for academic burnout, procrastination, self-handicapping behavior, and test anxiety among adolescents: A randomized control trial. BMC Psychology. 2025;**13**(1):94. DOI: 10.1186/s40359-025-02371-2

[66] Dou J, Lian Y, Lin L, Asmuri SNB, Wang P, Rajen Durai RA. Effectiveness of mindfulness-based interventions on burnout, resilience and sleep quality among nurses: A systematic review and meta-analysis of randomized controlled trials. BMC Nursing. 2025;**24**(1):739. DOI: 10.1186/s12912-025-03101-0

[67] Brown M, Glendenning A, Hoon AE, John A. Effectiveness of web-delivered acceptance and commitment therapy in relation to mental health and well-being: A systematic review and meta-analysis.

Journal of Medical Internet Research. 2016;**18**(8). DOI: 10.2196/jmir.6200

[68] Nakao M, Shirotsuki K, Sugaya N. Cognitive–behavioral therapy for management of mental health and stress-related disorders: Recent advances in techniques and technologies. BioPsychoSocial Medicine. 2021;**15**(1):16. DOI: 10.1186/s13030-021-00219-w

[69] Hofmann SG, Gómez AF. Mindfulness-Based Interventions for Anxiety and Depression. Psychiatric Clinics of North America. 2017;**40**(4):739. DOI: 10.1016/j.psc.2017.08.008

[70] Branstetter-Rost A, Cushing C, Douleh T. Personal Values and Pain Tolerance: Does a Values Intervention Add to Acceptance? Journal of Pain. 2009;**10**(8):887–892. DOI: 10.1016/j.jpain.2009.01.001

[71] Bai Z, Luo S, Zhang L, Wu S, Chi I. Acceptance and Commitment Therapy (ACT) to reduce depression: A systematic review and meta-analysis. Journal of Affective Disorders. 2020;**260**:728–737. DOI: 10.1016/j.jad.2019.09.040

[72] Arnold T, Haubrick KK, Klasko-Foster LB, Rogers BG, Barnett A, Ramirez-Sanchez NA, et al. Acceptance and Commitment Therapy Informed Behavioral Health Interventions Delivered by Non-Mental Health Professionals: A Systematic Review. Journal of Contextual Behavioral Science. 2022;**24**:185

[73] Membrive-Jiménez MJ, Gómez-Urquiza JL, Suleiman-Martos N, Velando-Soriano A, Ariza T, De la Fuente-solana EI, et al. Relation between Burnout and Sleep Problems in Nurses: A Systematic Review with Meta-Analysis. Healthcare. 2022;**10**(5):954. DOI: 10.3390/healthcare10050954

[74] Guan J, Sun Y, Fan Y, Liang J, Liu C, Yu H, et al. Effects and neural mechanisms of different physical activity on major depressive disorder based on cerebral multimodality monitoring: A narrative review. Frontiers in Human Neuroscience. 2024;**18**:1406670. DOI: 10.3389/fnhum.2024.1406670

[75] Ren J, Xiao H. Exercise for mental well-being: Exploring neurobiological advances and intervention effects in depression. Life. 2023;**13**(7):1505. DOI: 10.3390/life13071505

[76] Alkhawajah HA, Alshami AMY, Albarrati AM. The impact of autonomic nervous system modulation on heart rate variability and musculoskeletal manifestations in chronic neck pain: A double-blind randomized clinical trial. Journal of Clinical Medicine. 2024;**14**(1):153. DOI: 10.3390/jcm14010153

[77] Fournié C, Chouchou F, Dalleau G, Caderby T, Cabrera Q, Verkindt C. Heart rate variability biofeedback in chronic disease management: A systematic review. Complementary Therapies in Medicine. 2021;**60**(21):102750. DOI: 10.1016/j.ctim.2021.102750

[78] Consiglio C, Massa N, Sommovigo V, Fusco L. Techno-Stress Creators, Burnout and Psychological Health among Remote Workers during the Pandemic: The Moderating Role of E-Work Self-Efficacy. International Journal of Environmental Research and Public Health. 2023;**20**(22):7051. DOI: 10.3390/ijerph20227051

[79] Bondanini G, Giovanelli C, Mucci N, Giorgi G. The Dual Impact of

Digital Connectivity: Balancing Productivity and Well-Being in the Modern Workplace. International Journal of Environmental Research and Public Health. 2025;**22**(6):845. DOI: 10.3390/ijerph22060845

[80] Weiss S, Ortlieb R. Professional–personal boundary work: Individuals torn between integration and segmentation. German Journal of Human Resource Management. 2025;**39**(2):121–147. DOI: 10.1177/23970022241291503

[81] Marsh E, Vallejos EP, Spence A. The digital workplace and its dark side: An integrative review. Computers in Human Behavior. 2022;**128**(3):107118. DOI: 10.1016/j.chb.2021.107118

[82] Santiago-Torner C, González-Carrasco M, Miranda-Ayala R. Relationship Between Ethical Climate and Burnout: A New Approach Through Work Autonomy. Behavioral Sciences. 2025;**15**(2):121. DOI: 10.3390/bs15020121

[83] Grover S, Adarsh H, Naskar C, Varadharajan N. Physician burnout: A review. Journal of Mental Health and Human Behaviour. 2018;**23**(2):78. DOI: 10.4103/jmhhb.jmhhb_47_19

[84] Kossek EE. Managing worklife boundaries in the digital age. Organizational Dynamics. 2016;**45**(3):258–270. DOI: 10.1016/j.orgdyn.2016.07.010

[85] Steffens K, Sutter C, Sülzenbrück S. The concept of "Work-Life-Blending": A systematic review. Frontiers in Psychology. 2023;**14**:1150707. DOI: 10.3389/fpsyg.2023.1150707

[86] Ezawa ID, Hollon SD. Cognitive Restructuring and Psychotherapy Outcome: A Meta-Analytic Review. Psychotherapy (Chicago). 2023;**60**(3):396. DOI: 10.1037/pst0000474

[87] Kruger JM, De Klerk JJ. A pathway to greater meaning in life and well-being for senior executives beset by anti-meaning. Frontiers in Psychology. 2023;**14**:1187913. DOI: 10.3389/fpsyg.2023.1187913

[88] Duncan S, Pond R. Effective burnout prevention strategies for counsellors and other therapists: A systematic review and meta-synthesis of qualitative studies. Counselling Psychology Quarterly. 2025;**38**(3):526–555. DOI: 10.1080/09515070.2024.2394767

[89] Acoba EF. Social support and mental health: The mediating role of perceived stress. Frontiers in Psychology. 2024;**15**:1330720. DOI: 10.3389/fpsyg.2024.1330720

[90] Bhugra D. Burnout: Its meaning and how to deal with it? Journal of the Royal Society of Medicine. 2025;**118**(3):01410768251320167. DOI: 10.1177/01410768251320167

Chapter 2

The Heart of Resilience: Trauma-Informed Leadership in a Burnout Era

Clarine Jacobs

Abstract

Burnout syndrome is increasingly understood as a multifaceted phenomenon shaped by individual coping capacity and systemic organizational conditions. This chapter opens with a reflective narrative illustrating how prolonged occupational stress gradually erodes well-being, blurring the boundaries between professional demands and personal life. Emotional and psychological distress are reframed not as inevitable byproducts of demanding work but as signals of deeper organizational dysfunction. Grounded in organizational psychology, the chapter examines how persistent job demands, inadequate resources, and unsupportive leadership environments contribute to exhaustion, disengagement, and erosion of professional identity. The neurobiological foundations of burnout are explored, demonstrating how chronic stress disrupts neural functioning and hormonal balance, with cascading effects on cognition, emotional regulation, and physical health. Burnout is further situated within the context of trauma, highlighting how repeated or severe workplace adversity and unsupportive systems impair stress regulation, cognition, relationships, identity, and trust – leading to depletion and loss of purpose. In response, the chapter advocates trauma-informed leadership as a critical framework rooted in empathy, psychological safety, and relational intelligence to mitigate harm and rebuild connection within high-demand workplaces. Aligned with this book's holistic focus, the chapter argues that burnout is not a failure of personal endurance or resilience but a predictable outcome of environments failing to safeguard human well-being. In the post-pandemic landscape, where stress, moral injury, and compassion fatigue have intensified, trauma-informed leadership is no longer optional. By centering psychological safety and relational care, organizations can move beyond survival toward cultures in which individuals and teams recover, engage, and thrive.

Keywords: burnout, occupational stress, psychological safety, trauma, trauma-informed leadership

1. Introduction

For me, burnout is not theoretical; it is lived. It unfolded through years of ineffective leadership, chronic stress, and emotional exhaustion in environments that promised support yet delivered ambiguity. Compassion was often conditional, and in the post-pandemic push to "return to normal," longstanding dysfunction was exposed rather than resolved.

Burnout is not a failure of endurance, resilience, or a moral shortcoming. It is the predictable consequence of prolonged exposure to environments that are neurologically and psychologically unsafe. Over time, such conditions recalibrate the brain's stress systems, erode trust, and diminish the hope for a more connected, purposeful way forward.

Personal narrative and the emerging science of burnout are woven together – from the neurobiological imprint of chronic stress to the relational scaffolding required for healing. Beginning with lived experience, the chapter illustrates how occupational stress can quietly infiltrate daily life, reshaping identity and redefining what feels normal. These individual experiences mirror broader systemic patterns embedded within modern workplaces. I argue that to address burnout, especially in high-demand environments, we must move beyond policies and embrace leadership rooted in trauma sensitivity, relational trust, and neurobiological understanding.

Grounded in organizational psychology and neuroscience, the chapter frames burnout as a continuum of occupational stress rather than an individual failure. It examines how excessive demands, inadequate resources, and unsupportive leadership erode professional identity and well-being. The neurobiological mechanisms of burnout are explored, demonstrating how chronic stress disrupts neural pathways, hormonal balance, cognition, and emotional regulation.

The chapter further considers how sustained workplace adversity can become traumatic, leaving lasting marks on identity, health, and relationships. In response, it advances trauma-informed leadership as an essential framework for repair – one grounded in empathy, psychological safety, and relational intelligence. Ultimately, this chapter calls for a paradigm shift – from managing burnout as an individual concern to addressing it as an organizational responsibility, requiring courageous, human-centered leadership to foster healthier work environments.

2. Background

I remember vividly feeling trapped. I felt trapped at my desk, trapped by my computer, and trapped in a job I once loved but had come to dread. I had always been enthusiastic about my work. I pushed myself toward excellence, innovation, and growth. But slowly, that passion turned into chronic overwhelm. The excitement I once felt was replaced by frustration, anxiety, and the sensation that I could barely breathe. What had once been a desire to thrive shifted into something more primal: the need to survive each day.

Little by little, one after the other, employees were gone. Each day felt like bracing for the next announcement – the next cut, the next employee leaving, the next name removed from the directory. As employees disappeared, the workload only grew heavier. We were not compensated for the extra responsibilities; we absorbed them. With each new task added to our daily logs, our exhaustion deepened. We were all suspended in a state of uncertainty, waiting for something we could neither predict nor control.

A heavy, unspoken tension settled over the organization, with a mix of fear, helplessness, and quiet desperation. A sense of dissatisfaction and mistrust toward leadership grew by the minute. It felt as though a fight-or-flight culture had taken root. People withdrew themselves, became extremely guarded, or even turned on one another to cope with the experience or survive.

Despite meeting expectations and often exceeding them, employees were working harder than ever, yet most experienced a growing sense of being penalized rather than supported. Requests for clarity were routinely met with the same explanation – budget constraints – offered without transparency or meaningful dialog. Honest communication was absent, replaced by prolonged silence and uncertainty. Performance evaluations declined, not as a reflection of diminished effort or competence, but in ways that rationalized downsizing decisions rather than recognizing sustained contributions. Such practices eroded trust further and intensified occupational strain.

Based on my own experience as a professor, I observed a pattern that resonates not only in academia but across countless industries: employees often find themselves struggling to reconcile environments that prioritize familiarity and compliance rather than growth and innovation. I witnessed colleagues who taught the same courses year after year, remained in the same roles for decades, or consistently agreed with leadership, being favored and rewarded. In contrast, those who ventured into interdisciplinary work, embraced innovative teaching methods, or demonstrated an ongoing commitment to professional development were frequently marginalized.

This is not unique to higher education. Across organizations of all types, roles are not meant to be static or rooted solely in comfort and tradition. Instead, most professions demand continuous learning, adaptability, and intellectual curiosity – qualities that are increasingly vital in our complex, globalized world.

Institutions of higher education, like many organizations, rely on innovative individuals who are willing to move beyond their comfort zones, introduce new methodologies, contribute to broader conversations, challenge the status quo, drive progress, and adapt to rapidly changing demands – ensuring their teams remain resilient, competitive, and aligned with evolving industry standards. Most notably, to prepare others to thrive amid uncertainty. These educators and employees are essential to cultivating the next generation of ethical leaders and resilient teams. Yet, when such values go unrecognized or unsupported, a profound dissonance can arise. This disconnect can manifest as moral injury – a deep sense of distress that occurs when individuals are asked to act in ways that conflict with their own ethics and core values.

Observing leadership behaviors that contradicted the very principles we strive to teach – integrity, accountability, transparency, and care gave rise to very unsettling feelings. This experience is echoed by employees across sectors who are expected to model organizational values that are not upheld by those in authority. The resulting strain is not simply the product of heavy workloads or chronic stress; it is the ethical effect of being placed in systems where one's moral and professional commitments are routinely undermined. Burnout in these contexts is not just physical or emotional; it is deeply ethical, affecting one's sense of purpose and integrity, regardless of industry.

There were moments when I questioned myself – wondering if I was wrong to feel unsettled by what I witnessed. But, in truth, my concerns were rooted in genuine care for our institution and its people. It was difficult to watch leaders overlook the harm unfolding around them, and not wanting to be complicit in a culture of "do as I say, not as I do," further eroding my personal mission of modeling authenticity and integrity.

I do not believe any reasonable individual should question their feelings or their thoughts – in fact, these reflections are grounded in truth. Numerous resolute professionals feel disheartened when organizational values are presented as foundational principles yet are experienced only as words on a page, rather than as guiding practices. It is understandable to question why leaders fail to recognize or address harm, and why there is such a disconnect between stated values and actual behavior. A sense of morally injurious emotions is a valid response to this ethical conflict. Wanting to avoid hypocrisy demonstrates commitment to authenticity and ethical leadership.

This disconnect between stated values and daily reality was more than just disappointing; it became a source of chronic strain. The truth is that occupational stress began to seep into our lives long before the first layoffs were announced and at the sign of questionable leadership practices. My sleep was the first casualty. Daily routines grew harder; I became afraid to step away from my computer, terrified of missing something important. Leaving the house meant carrying my laptop like a life raft I dared not let out of sight. I scrutinized every word, every decision, every movement – haunted by the feeling that I was being watched.

Like countless other workplaces, monitoring systems were implemented to track employee productivity during one of my experiences. If the keyboard remained idle for too long, the status light would turn red. Even pausing to think, make notes, or talk through an idea with a colleague – a process I have always found most productive on paper – triggered a jolt of panic. The constant fear of appearing unproductive turned every break into a source of anxiety, as even brief pauses felt like risky acts under watchful eyes.

This hypervigilance bled into my personal life. The line between work and home faded so completely that it felt as if I never truly stepped away from the office. My body could not relax; sleep deprivation became constant fatigue. Headaches escalated into migraines, muscles clenched, and my heart raced for no reason. I became irritable, anxious, and emotionally numb all at once. Concentration slipped; I forgot names, dates, even tasks I had just finished. Joy vanished from activities I once loved. Over time, I became increasingly isolated, lacking the energy to see friends or engage in hobbies that once brought me happiness. All I could manage was work and the hope for a few hours of restless sleep, as my sense of normalcy, relationships, and interests slipped further away. Even the smallest request felt overwhelming.

These were not isolated symptoms but the manifestations of chronic occupational stress and encroaching burnout.

This was the environment employees inhabited: fear-ridden, exhausting, and relentlessly monitored. Every decision felt scrutinized, every pause suspect. Hypervigilance became a survival instinct, not a mere response to a crisis. Over time, my nervous system stayed on high alert, my body tense, my mind unable to rest – even after the workday ended. Well-being did not collapse suddenly; it eroded quietly, predictably, and thoroughly deteriorated.

This was burnout rather than weakness or lack of resilience. It was the cumulative result of relentless occupational stress. Even before the term was widely recognized, burnout was transforming lives from within: disrupting sleep, impairing cognition, destabilizing emotions, and eroding professional identity. It was never just my story, nor confined to one role or institution.

Surviving burnout once did not make me immune. On the contrary, each recurrence struck with greater intensity, compounded by memories of previous experiences and the anxiety of knowing just how devastating the descent could be. Research confirms what lived experience makes painfully clear: repeated, unresolved stress increases vulnerability to more severe burnout, deeper emotional exhaustion, and growing disengagement over time [1]. The question we must ask is: why do organizations allow such cycles to persist, and why are so many employees left vulnerable to the consequences of ineffective leadership?

Burnout does not discriminate by profession or geography. Across every sector and culture, burnout flourishes where demands are relentless, resources are scarce, autonomy is constrained, and psychological safety is absent [2].

From the outside, the answer seems simple: why not just find another job? The question is deceptively simple and profoundly disconnected from reality. Leaving is rarely just a professional decision. It is tangled with seniority, health insurance, financial stability, retirement, caregiving, and identity. At its worst, burnout makes even imagining change feel impossible. The application process itself – rewriting résumés, interviewing, proving worth – becomes an insurmountable hurdle when exhaustion has drained every reserve.

As burnout deepens, self-efficacy evaporates. Confidence is replaced by doubt. Skilled professionals begin to question their abilities, their value, and their place in the world. Inadequacy sets in, not because skills are gone, but because chronic stress has rewired perception and motivation. What remains is not laziness or apathy, but a nervous system stuck in survival mode, too depleted to find a way forward.

This chapter begins in that fraught space between endurance and collapse. It examines burnout not as a personal failing but as a predictable, preventable outcome of how work is designed, managed, and experienced. By weaving lived experience with empirical research, it calls for a deeper understanding of burnout as a neurobiological, psychological, and organizational phenomenon, demanding more than resilience training. It calls for systemic change, compassionate leadership, and a reimagining of what it means to protect the whole person at work. To fully understand the scope of this challenge, it is critical to explore how occupational stress and burnout intersect with mental health, influencing not only how individuals perform at work but also how they experience life.

3. Mental health

As workplace stress intensifies, its effects extend well beyond productivity and job performance, reverberating through our mental and emotional well-being. As such, the connection between occupational stress and mental health is explored as a relationship that shapes not only how we work but also how we live.

Mental health plays a fundamental role in shaping our thoughts, feelings, and behaviors. It has a direct influence on how we manage stress, make choices, and nurture our relationships. The World Health Organization (WHO) describes health as a holistic state of complete physical, mental, and social well-being, not simply the absence of illness [3:100]. Expanding on this, the WHO defines mental health as a state in which individuals recognize their abilities, manage normal life stresses, work productively, and contribute to their communities. This perspective positions mental health as a foundational component of overall well-being, enabling individuals to make sound decisions, form meaningful connections, and contribute effectively to the world around them. These definitions make an important distinction between feeling happy or satisfied (hedonic well-being) and functioning effectively and meaningfully (eudaimonic well-being) [3, 4].

According to the American Psychological Association [5], mental health involves emotional stability, adaptive behaviors, minimal anxiety or disabling symptoms, and the capacity to form positive relationships and cope with everyday challenges. Good mental health helps maintain emotional balance, while poor mental health can result in persistent stress, social isolation, or increased reliance on substances. If ignored, these issues may progress into more serious conditions such as anxiety disorders, depression, or substance use disorders. Galderisi et al. described mental health as a dynamic state of internal balance that empowers individuals to use their abilities in alignment with societal values [6]. This includes cognitive and social skills, emotional awareness and regulation, empathy, flexibility, resilience in the face of adversity, effective social functioning, and a harmonious connection between mind and body, which contribute to this internal equilibrium.

Mental health affects individuals of all ages and backgrounds. Mental health is deteriorating quickly and significantly globally [7]. In 2025, the mental health landscape was shaped by persistent challenges and evolving trends, influenced by factors such as the psychological aftermath of the COVID-19 pandemic and shifting societal demands, highlighting the need for targeted mental health support. Despite increased public awareness and education, stigma remains a significant barrier. Research from the American Psychological Association reported that 84% of U.S. adults believe "mental illness" still carries stigma, and 35% would view someone differently if they knew that person had a mental health condition [8]. Nonetheless, a considerable proportion of adults who disclose their struggles do so because they feel emotionally safe (55%) or experience relief (54%). While greater visibility and advocacy have encouraged more open conversations, discrimination and judgment continue to hinder progress, especially in workplaces, social circles, and broader society [9].

However, despite increased awareness, public dissatisfaction with the mental health care system remains high. Over half (57%) report an unfavorable view of the system, with most believing policymakers are falling short. Nearly two-thirds (64%) believe Congress is not providing adequate support, while 58% say the same of the president. At the state level, 46% are dissatisfied with their governor's efforts, and 50% with their state legislature. Similarly, 64% believe the U.S. invests too little in mental health resources. A large share of Americans wants Congress to prioritize mental health care (63%), affordable housing (60%), suicide prevention (55%), and the 988-crisis line (55%) [10].

In addition to these systemic concerns, mental health conditions are highly prevalent in the United States. Nearly half of U.S. adults experience disorders such as anxiety and depression, and over half of these individuals also contend with co-occurring conditions. According to the Centers for Disease Control and Prevention, 12.5% of adults regularly experience feelings of worry, nervousness, or anxiety, and

5% report frequent depression – indicating that anxiety is more than twice as common as depression among American adults [11].

The economic effect is substantial, with an estimated $1 trillion lost annually in U.S. productivity due to depression and anxiety among employees [12]. Globally, over one billion people live with a mental disorder, yet only 9% receive adequate treatment [12]. In the United States, the National Alliance on Mental Illness (2025) reports that 1 in 6 Americans (17%) currently rate their mental health as poor. Contributing factors include uncertainty about the future (80%), rising cost of living (78%), financial worries (71%), health concerns (64%), the political environment (63%), current events (62%), social isolation (56%), and the federal government shutdown in late 2024 (55%) [10].

Emerging trends are helping address gaps in mental health care and promote a more inclusive approach to mental wellness. Although progress has been made, overcoming mental health stigma remains an ongoing challenge. Continued education, expanded access to services, and open conversations are vital to building a more supportive environment for everyone affected by mental health issues.

At the heart of these challenges lies occupational stress – an ever-present force that, when left unaddressed, can quietly fuel the progression from everyday strain to full-blown burnout. Exploring this continuum reveals patterns that are as universal as they are urgent.

4. Occupational stress and burnout

A stressful day at work may not be uncommon. However, when long hours, relentless demands, and persistent fatigue become the norm rather than the exception, the consequences for well-being – particularly cognitive and psychological health – can be profound. According to the National Institute for Occupational Safety and Health (NIOSH), occupational stress arises when the demands of a job exceed a worker's abilities, resources, or needs, resulting in negative physical and emotional reactions. This type of stress can contribute to health problems and may even cause injury [13]. Occupational stress is a global phenomenon arising when job demands exceed an individual's skills or capacity to cope, resulting in significant economic, social, and health consequences.

Occupational stress often emerges when workloads consistently exceed what an individual can reasonably manage, or when workplace pressures become chronic and unavoidable. While a degree of stress is inherent to most jobs, prolonged exposure to excessive demands can erode mental and physical health over time, impair cognitive functioning, and diminish overall quality of life. When such stress remains unresolved, it may evolve into burnout and/or depression [14–19].

4.1 Burnout is a consequence of chronic occupational stress

Burnout syndrome is a widespread psychological condition that develops from sustained occupational stress. A comprehensive review of 45 studies published between 2010 and 2025 identifies early warning signs of burnout and proposes a three-domain model for initiative-taking recognition [20]. The first domain encompasses intrapersonal symptoms, including chronic exhaustion, impaired concentration, sleep disturbances, and somatic complaints. The second domain highlights interpersonal indicators, such as emotional detachment, irritability, diminished empathy, and expressed dissatisfaction. The third domain captures occupational manifestations, including absenteeism, lateness, declining performance, and excessive work involvement despite diminishing productivity [20].

The WHO formally recognizes burnout as an occupational phenomenon, rather than a medical diagnosis, in the eleventh revision of the International Classification of Diseases (ICD-11) [2, 21]. According to the WHO, burnout is characterized by three core dimensions: (1) emotional exhaustion, (2) depersonalization or increased mental distance from one's work, and (3) reduced professional efficacy [2, 22]. This framework aligns with the Maslach Burnout Inventory (MBI), one of the most widely used assessment tools for burnout, which conceptualizes the condition as arising from overwhelming job-related stress and evaluates exhaustion, depersonalization, and diminished personal accomplishment [23].

4.2 The role of workplace stress in emotional burnout

Workplace stress is a significant contributor to emotional burnout, especially in demanding roles or environments that lack support [24]. Chronic job pressure, strict deadlines, and deficient control or recognition can exhaust employees emotionally. Limited support from colleagues or supervisors intensifies feelings of isolation, increasing the risk of burnout. This not only reduces productivity and job satisfaction but also leads to increased absenteeism and long-term health complications, underscoring the importance of workplace interventions [25].

4.3 Relationship between burnout and depression

Burnout frequently overlaps with symptoms of depression, including impaired memory and concentration, persistent fatigue, sleep disturbances, physical discomfort, irritability, anxiety, and emotional depletion [26]. Depression itself is understood as existing along a continuum, with only the most severe manifestations meeting formal diagnostic criteria [27]. The Diagnostic and Statistical Manual of Mental Disorders specifies that depressive disorders must involve symptoms causing clinically significant distress or impairment in social, occupational, or other critical areas of functioning. Although burnout and depression are distinct constructs, research consistently demonstrates that they often coexist and mutually reinforce one another, with higher levels of burnout associated with increased depressive symptoms [26].

4.4 Organizational drivers of occupational stress

A key driver of occupational stress is the mismatch between job demands and the support, structure, and resources provided by the organization. Unrealistic expectations inevitably lead to stress. Because individuals vary in background, skills, coping abilities, and resources, excessive demand is not the same for everyone; therefore, "fit" is a dynamic organizational issue rather than simply a personal one. When employees experience this misalignment, morale, turnover, performance, and overall well-being are affected. Burnout arises not from a lack of individual resilience but from systemic failure to balance workloads with adequate support. Although often viewed as a personal weakness, burnout is primarily rooted in organizational factors, especially when job demands exceed available skills, resources, autonomy, or support.

Common organizational stressors include:

- Excessive or insufficient workloads
- Limited job control or autonomy
- Poor work–life balance
- Intense time pressures
- Unsafe or inadequate working conditions
- Tasks lacking meaning or personal value
- Interpersonal conflict
- Job insecurity and organizational change

Stress is further intensified by role ambiguity, conflicting responsibilities, and disproportionate workloads, all of which erode predictability and control [28, 29]. Career-related stressors – such as limited advancement opportunities, insufficient training, or career stagnation – can foster feelings of inefficacy and anxiety about the future [30]. Negative interpersonal dynamics, including poor supervisory relationships, workplace bullying, discrimination, and lack of social support, undermine psychological safety and well-being [31–33]. Organizational cultures characterized by rigid hierarchies, inefficient systems, limited autonomy, and unclear values further amplify occupational stress, particularly when employees feel undervalued or powerless [34].

4.5 Measuring occupational stress and burnout: Objective and subjective approaches

Workplace stress is assessed through both objective and subjective approaches. Objective measures evaluate external stressors such as workload, role demands, and organizational change, while subjective measures capture individual perceptions of stress and coping capacity [35]. Because individuals differ in skills, backgrounds, resilience, and available resources, subjective assessment is essential. Employees exposed to similar stressors may experience vastly different psychological and physical outcomes [36].

4.6 Burnout as a systemic and economic problem

Burnout is not a personal weakness; it disproportionately affects highly dedicated and high-performing employees who are deeply invested in their work and organizational mission. Burnout is far more complex than simple exhaustion. It often affects the most resolute and high-performing employees; those who consistently go beyond expectations and deeply value their work, colleagues, and organizational mission.

The global scope of burnout is substantial. The WHO estimates that depression and anxiety account for the loss of approximately 12 billion workdays each year, costing the global economy nearly $1 trillion annually [37]. The situation continues to intensify: Society for Human Resource Management (SHRM) reported that half of workers feel depleted (51%), emotionally drained (45%), or burned out (44%). Employees experiencing burnout are three times more likely to resign than their engaged counterparts. Globally, more than 30% of workers report feeling burned out, with even higher rates among early-career professionals [38].

The economic consequences of disengagement are substantial: Gallup's 2025 State of the Global Workplace report estimates that disengaged employees cost the global economy $438 billion in 2024, while indicating that up to $9.6 trillion in productivity could be recovered through full workforce engagement [39]. Globally, 58% of employees report struggling, and 9% report suffering; 50% are seeking or actively seeking a new job, and 51% believe now is a suitable time to do so – a trend occurring alongside significant stress reported by 40% of employees worldwide. Engagement levels remain critically low, with 62% of employees not engaged and 17% actively disengaged [39].

Consistent with these findings, a SHRM study reports that 30% of U.S. workers would accept a pay cut in exchange for stronger mental health support at work; the leading contributors to workplace stress include excessive workloads (47%), inadequate compensation (42%), and poor leadership (40%). Only 25% of organizations focus more on preventing mental health issues, while 38% focus more on reacting to issues [40]. The Great Resignation further illustrated the consequences, as employees left toxic workplaces in search of environments that prioritized mental health and well-being [41]. These findings reinforce that burnout is fundamentally a structural and operational issue – not a personal failure.

4.7 Person-environment fit theory

The concept of person–environment (PE) fit, introduced by French and colleagues in 1974 [42], builds on Lewin's idea that behavior results from the interaction between individuals and their surroundings [43]. Grounded in interactional psychology, PE fit theory draws from Gestalt principles, emphasizing that the whole is different from the sum of its parts. This framework bridges two perspectives: one focused on environmental characteristics and the other on individuals' traits, abilities, and needs. Organizational settings are seen as particularly influential contexts where alignment – or misalignment – between people and their work environments can occur.

Stress arises when there is a mismatch between a person and their environment, shaped by both objective conditions and subjective experiences. In the workplace, this misalignment often occurs when job demands exceed or conflict with an individual's abilities or resources. The foundational premise of PE fit theory is that individuals are naturally better suited to certain environments, and when alignment is lacking, strain and stress are likely to result [44].

A mismatch may develop even when a worker can perform their duties; if additional tasks or pressures accumulate beyond what they can manage, the fit worsens. Because individuals differ in their responses to stressors and in their coping capacities and thresholds, the point at which a mismatch becomes harmful is not universal. Still, the consequences are well recognized: alignment between a person and their environment supports healthy functioning, motivation, and performance, whereas misalignment can lead to psychological and physical stress for the individual (the "P" side) and organizational strain, such as absenteeism or reduced effectiveness, on the environment side (the "E" side) of the PE fit equation [44].

Building on the idea that alignment between individuals and their environments is crucial for well-being, the Job Demands-Resources (JD–R) framework offers a similar perspective on understanding how workplace factors influence stress and motivation. According to the JD–R framework, job demands, such as physical, social, or organizational requirements, require sustained effort and can lead to physical and psychological strain [45]. In contrast, job resources are aspects of work that help employees achieve their goals, reduce the impact of job demands, and promote personal growth. The theory suggests that high job demands can lead to stress and health problems, whereas ample job resources are associated with increased motivation, productivity, and overall well-being [46]. This theoretical approach aligns with PE fit theory, emphasizing the importance of balancing job demands, resources, and individual needs for optimal well-being.

But burnout is not merely an emotional or psychological experience; it is rooted in tangible, biological changes within the brain and body. Unpacking the neurobiology of burnout uncovers why its effects are so pervasive and why recovery requires more than willpower alone.

5. Neurobiology of burnout

If you have noticed that burnout has genuinely changed how your brain works, your intuition is correct. Persistent stress does more than cause exhaustion; it can reshape neural pathways, trigger inflammation, and disrupt hormonal balance, resulting in lasting changes to brain function. In the workplace, the neurobiological effects of leadership stressors are significant. Negative or toxic leadership behaviors can impact both the brain and body of employees, often leading to long-term psychological and physiological consequences.

The neurobiology underlying mental health is complex, involving intricate networks of neurons, neurotransmitters, hormones, and various brain regions. Neurotransmitters are chemical messengers that facilitate communication between brain cells. When a message travels along a neuron, it triggers the release of neurotransmitters, which cross the synaptic gap and bind to receptors on the next neuron, propagating the signal. This process, known as neurotransmission, regulates a wide range of bodily and mental functions, such as emotions, mood, sleep, learning, memory, pain, pleasure, and even vital processes such as breathing and heartbeat [47].

5.1 Why emotional burnout manifests physically

The mind and body are intricately linked, particularly during periods of stress. Emotional burnout triggers the body's stress response systems, such as the autonomic nervous system and the hypothalamic-pituitary-adrenal (HPA) axis, due to ongoing psychological strain. This results in physical symptoms: muscle tension, headaches, digestive disturbances, and persistent fatigue. Over time, these symptoms can reinforce emotional distress, creating a cycle where physical discomfort worsens mental exhaustion [2].

Burnout affects both mental and physical health, influencing mood, cognition, and physiological functioning. Individuals may experience persistent headaches, muscle tension, chronic fatigue, sleep disruption, and changes in appetite, all of which further compromise health and resilience [25]. Emotionally, burnout is often characterized by cynicism, irritability, and detachment – symptoms frequently intertwined with physical discomfort. Early identification is critical, as unaddressed burnout can escalate into more serious health conditions and may require professional intervention [25].

5.2 Recognizing emotional exhaustion before it becomes physical

Spotting emotional exhaustion early can help prevent physical symptoms. Warnings include ongoing fatigue despite adequate sleep, trouble focusing, reduced motivation, and increased sensitivity to feedback. Reflective questions such as "Do I feel emotionally numb or disconnected from my work?" or "Is it hard to find the energy for daily tasks?" can be helpful. Recognizing these early indicators enables timely action to stop emotional exhaustion from developing into more serious physical health problems [25].

5.3 Neurobiological consequences of burnout

Chronic occupational stress is correlated with a noticeable decrease in both emotional and cognitive functioning. Research into neural mechanisms reveals significant alterations in brain activity and modified patterns of event-related potentials in individuals experiencing burnout [48]. Workplace burnout can change neural pathways in the brain. In a troubling cycle, prolonged stress reduces individuals' neurological resilience in recovering from adverse situations, leading to even greater stress [49].

Chmiel and Malinowska (2025) argued that burnout demonstrates a consistent neurophysiological profile that is comparable in severity to recognized psychiatric disorders, challenging its current designation as a non-disease. Objective EEG markers can enhance symptom assessment for earlier diagnosis, treatment tracking, and public health monitoring. Acknowledging burnout as a clinical disorder and allocating funding for its prevention and management is not only medically warranted but also economically essential [50].

5.4 Activation of the stress response system (HPA axis)

Research has demonstrated that chronic stress, such as that experienced during burnout, can induce structural and functional changes in the brain through neuroplasticity, increase neuroinflammation, and dysregulate hormonal systems like the hypothalamic-pituitary-adrenal (HPA) axis [50, 51]. These mechanisms can contribute to cognitive difficulties and emotional disturbances often reported by individuals with burnout.

When exposed to poor leadership, such as authoritarian control, lack of psychological safety, unpredictability, or emotional invalidation, the hypothalamic-pituitary-adrenal (HPA) axis is activated. This triggers the release of cortisol and adrenaline, which prepare the body for a "fight, flight, or freeze" response. Chronic activation leads to:

- Emotional dysregulation
- Impaired memory and concentration (hippocampal disruption)
- Fatigue and burnout
- Increased risk of anxiety, depression, and cardiovascular disease.

5.5 Impaired prefrontal cortex functioning

Burnout has a profound effect on other key brain regions. The prefrontal cortex (PFC), responsible for executive functions such as decision-making, attention, self-regulation, and social behavior, is notably affected. Chronic stress associated with burnout can lead to reductions in PFC volume, impairing essential cognitive processes and resulting in difficulties with concentration, memory, and decision-making [50]. Under chronic stress from toxic leadership, PFC activity is reduced, resulting in:

- Decreased problem-solving ability
- Poor emotional regulation
- Increased reactivity and impulsivity
- Lower motivation and creativity

All of which can drastically affect an employee's ability to adapt, perform, and interact within teams.

5.6 Amygdala and emotional processing

The amygdala, a brain region critical for processing emotions such as fear and stress, is also notably affected by burnout. Ongoing exposure to chronic stress can increase amygdala activity, leading to heightened anxiety and greater emotional reactivity. This overactivation can establish a reinforcing cycle that amplifies stress responses, making it increasingly difficult to break free from burnout [48, 49]. Under persistent negative leadership (e.g., micromanagement, public shaming, emotional invalidation), this hyperactivity leads to:

- Heightened emotional reactivity (e.g., fear, anger, withdrawal)
- Hypervigilance and anticipation of criticism or punishment
- Amplification of trauma-related symptoms in vulnerable individuals

At the neurobiological level, persistent stress has been shown to affect the hippocampus, a brain region essential for memory formation and emotional regulation. Prolonged exposure to stress hormones, such as cortisol, is associated with hippocampal volume reduction, impaired memory, and diminished emotional self-regulation – changes that contribute to the helplessness and reduced efficacy commonly reported in burnout [49, 50].

5.7 Social and attachment neurobiology

Human brains are wired for connection. Human neurobiology is fundamentally organized around connection, safety, and relational attunement [52–54]. From an attachment and social neuroscience perspective, leadership behaviors that lack empathy, fairness, or emotional presence disrupt core relational needs, activating neurobiological stress responses rather than engagement and trust [55, 56]. When individuals perceive social threats, such as exclusion, unpredictability, or inequitable treatment, the brain responds as if physical danger is present, prioritizing survival over learning, collaboration, and creativity [57–59].

Polyvagal theory offers a valuable framework for understanding the body's responses to perceived safety and threat. Environments that are perceived as unsafe suppress ventral vagal activity, the neural pathway responsible for social connection, emotional regulation, and prosocial behavior [52, 60]. When ventral vagal activity is inhibited, individuals may shift into sympathetic activation (manifesting as anxiety, hypervigilance, or anger) or into dorsal vagal shutdown (resulting in withdrawal, disengagement, or emotional numbing). In organizational contexts, chronically unsafe or unsupportive leadership climates can, therefore, foster relational trauma, diminish cognitive flexibility, and erode psychological safety at both individual and collective levels [52, 60].

Leaders play a crucial role as social regulators within organizations. Attuned leadership – marked by transparency, consistency, and compassion – promotes healthy vagal regulation and fosters neural states that support trust, resilience, and higher-order functioning. In contrast, leadership that dismisses, marginalizes, or destabilizes employees does more than lower morale; it also disrupts neurobiological functioning, embedding stress responses that can persist long after the immediate interaction has ended [60, 61].

5.8 Neurotransmitters and stress regulation

Table 1 summarizes key neurotransmitters and stress-related hormones involved in emotional regulation, motivation, arousal, and physiological stress responses. Dysregulation of these systems under chronic occupational stress contributes to burnout, cognitive fatigue, emotional exhaustion, and impaired functioning.

Serotonin and GABA exert inhibitory effects that promote emotional stability, while glutamate and norepinephrine support alertness and a threat response. Dopamine modulates motivation and reward processing. Cortisol functions as an adaptive stress hormone in the short term but is associated with exhaustion and physiological dysregulation when chronically elevated.

Neurotransmitter/ Hormone	Primary function	Core effects relevant to stress, cognition, and behavior
Adrenaline (Epinephrine)	*Acute stress activation (fight-or-flight)*	*Rapidly mobilizes physiological and cognitive resources during a perceived threat by increasing heart rate, blood flow, and alertness, enabling immediate action and heightened awareness.*
Noradrenaline (Norepinephrine)	*Vigilance and attention (concentration)*	*Sustains alertness, focus, and readiness to respond; prolonged activation is associated with chronic stress, hypervigilance, and difficulty disengaging from threat-related cues.*
Cortisol	*Stress regulation and energy mobilization*	*Supports short-term adaptation to stress by regulating energy availability and inflammatory responses; chronic elevation is linked to exhaustion, immune suppression, cognitive impairment, and burnout.*
Dopamine	*Motivation and reward processing*	*Drives goal-directed behavior, reinforcement learning, and movement; dysregulation is associated with diminished motivation, fatigue, burnout, or compulsive reward-seeking behaviors.*
Serotonin	*Mood regulation and emotional stability*	*Contributes to emotional balance, psychological well-being, sleep–wake regulation, and digestive functioning; reduced levels are associated with mood disturbances and heightened stress sensitivity.*
GABA (Gamma-aminobutyric acid)	*Neural inhibition and calming*	*Dampens excessive neural activity, promoting relaxation, emotional regulation, and cognitive clarity; insufficient activity is linked to anxiety, irritability, and heightened tension.*
Glutamate	*Learning, memory, and neural plasticity*	*Primary excitatory neurotransmitter involved in cognition and learning; excessive activation under chronic stress may contribute to cognitive overload and neurotoxicity.*
Acetylcholine	*Attention, learning, and arousal*	*Supports memory formation, attentional control, and neuromuscular activation; plays a key role in sustained focus, alertness, and cognitive engagement.*
Endorphins	*Pain modulation and emotional relief*	*Released during physical activity and positive experiences, reducing pain perception and promoting feelings of relief, resilience, and emotional uplift.*

Table 1.
Key neurotransmitters, hormones, and their roles in stress, cognition, and behavior. Created by the author; Adapted from guy-evans, 2025. Nuerotransmitters: types, function and examples [62].

5.9 Long-Term effects: Neuroplasticity and health outcomes

Repeated exposure to harmful or ineffective leadership may induce changes to neural pathways, a phenomenon known as negative neuroplasticity. This maladaptive rewiring, over time, increases vulnerability to chronic mental health conditions, including post-traumatic stress disorder (PTSD) and complex trauma [50, 63]. The relationship between serotonin and mental health is clear but complex; lower serotonin levels are linked to depression and anxiety, and the notion that simply increasing serotonin will produce greater happiness is an oversimplification. Prolonged stress in toxic workplace environments is also associated with a higher incidence of autoimmune disorders, systemic inflammation, and sleep disturbances [48, 64]. Moreover, continued exposure to such environments can erode trust, foster disengagement, and undermine both individual and organizational well-being [63, 65].

In certain cases, the relentless pressure of work, ineffective leadership, or hostile working environments does not just induce stress or exhaustion; it can rise to the level of trauma, leaving lasting imprints on identity and well-being. Examining how trauma emerges in the workplace and how it differs from stress and burnout is critical for a holistic understanding.

6. Trauma

The word "trauma" has its roots in the Greek language, where it means "wound" or "hurt." The DSM-5 defines traumatic events as those that involve exposure to death, threatened death, severe injury, or sexual violence, either through direct experience, witnessing, or learning about the event indirectly. These experiences are typically marked by intense emotions such as shock, helplessness, or a sense of losing control [66, 67].

6.1 Trauma in the workplace: An overlooked yet widespread influence

Despite being common, trauma often goes unrecognized in professional environments [68, 69]. Employees may be unaware of how past trauma shapes their work lives, having developed unconscious coping mechanisms over time [70]. In the corporate context, trauma can manifest in various behaviors. For example, individuals with trauma histories may interpret constructive feedback as personal criticism, resulting in defensiveness, withdrawal, or heightened stress [71]. Others may overcompensate for past instability or neglect through perfectionism and excessive work efforts [72]. Negative experiences with authority figures can lead to avoidance of supervisors or difficulty asserting boundaries [73]. Emotional detachment or a lack of motivation can also emerge when suppressed emotions from significant distress remain unresolved [74]. Additionally, unresolved trauma can result in trust issues and challenges in team collaboration [75].

Trauma is not limited to individual experiences; it can also be embedded in organizational culture. Workplaces characterized by high pressure, competition, micromanagement, or a lack of psychological safety can inadvertently contribute to chronic stress and trauma-like responses [69, 70]. Research indicates that ongoing exposure to such environments increases burnout, decreases job satisfaction, and raises turnover [1]. Leaders who are not trauma-informed may misinterpret missed deadlines as inefficiency rather than recognizing potential executive dysfunction related to stress [76].

Similarly, an employee who avoids social interaction may not be unfriendly but could be demonstrating self-protective withdrawal due to psychological distress [77]. Recognizing these patterns should prompt a shift from punitive management to supportive leadership strategies. Furthermore, multinational organizations must consider cultural differences in how trauma is experienced and addressed; a uniform approach to employee well-being risks missing culturally specific responses to trauma [75].

The most self-aware leaders understand that trauma can originate within the workplace environment, not just be brought in from outside [78]. Workplace trauma encompasses psychological, physical, and emotional responses to negative incidents or chronic stressors that affect employee well-being. This trauma may arise from a single event or develop cumulatively through prolonged stress, anxiety, or relational harm, such as betrayal or neglect. Workplace trauma is prevalent across all professions and is increasingly recognized as a significant but under-addressed epidemic. Workplace trauma is not specifically defined in the DSM-5, but it is acknowledged as an important contributor to trauma-related conditions, including PTSD. According to the DSM-5, traumatic experiences can occur in the workplace and may include incidents like bullying or exposure to a toxic or hostile work environment. Although the DSM-5 does not use the term "workplace trauma," it highlights the need to recognize and address trauma responses within the workplace to foster a supportive environment for employees [79].

Trauma within organizational systems undermines trust and connection, particularly when inconsistent leadership or chaotic environments perpetuate re-traumatization. Rebuilding relational trust requires transparency, humility, and shared accountability. Humble leaders prioritize the well-being of their team members over organizational interests, enabling progress and growth. Humility in leadership involves modesty, leading by example, and maintaining calm and composure regardless of circumstances [80]. Fostering psychological safety by encouraging participation and learning from failure further supports recovery and resilience.

Trauma-informed workplaces intentionally create safe, supportive environments where individuals are empowered to bring their whole selves to work and feel genuinely valued [81]. Trauma-informed leadership offers a path forward, emphasizing empathy, safety, and systemic support. By embracing these principles, organizations can foster resilience, restoration, and genuine engagement.

7. Trauma-Informed leadership

As leadership scholarship has advanced, it has become increasingly evident that context fundamentally shapes how leadership is perceived and enacted. Culture, generational differences, neurodiversity, and individual histories of trauma or burnout all filter leadership behaviors, producing diverse responses to the same style of leadership. As Kuhlmann and Kadgien posited, "if we know anything about the functions of the human brain and our interpersonal behaviors, it is that they are exquisitely complex and context dependent" [82:103].

At the biological level, emotions are shaped by brain regions such as the amygdala, insula, and periaqueductal gray, which influence responses to fear, disgust, pain, and social behavior – all significant workplace dynamics. Understanding these neurobiological mechanisms is key to fostering resilience within organizations. Unlike automatic reflexes, emotions have evolved to help individuals adapt to changing environments and are organized according to the brain's general information-processing principles [82, 83].

While Western traditions once separated reason from emotion, contemporary neuroscience reveals that cognition and emotion are deeply interconnected. These neural circuits constantly interact, influencing attention, perception, decision-making, and reasoning in a reciprocal, adaptive process [84–88].

Resilience is best understood as a dynamic process shaped by the interaction of individuals and their environments, as described by the ecological systems approach [89]. It is neither static nor universal; the balance of risk, protective, and promotive factors shifts with changing circumstances [90–92]. What fosters resilience in one context may not in another, and these influences can emerge or diminish over time. This variability is especially evident for neurodivergent individuals, whose resilience depends on a broad range of personal and environmental factors [92]. For instance, a directive leadership style might motivate some employees but alienate others, particularly in organizations with a history of exclusion or harm.

Structural dysfunction, such as limited resources, poor communication, or excessive workloads, can undermine even the most capable leaders. Recognizing and responding to these shifting dynamics is essential for effective leadership development, as leaders must adapt to the evolving resilience and support needs of their teams.

Traditional performance metrics that focus solely on productivity and profit can obscure deeper organizational harm. High-profile cases – such as Elon Musk's leadership at Twitter (now X), characterized by rapid workforce reductions and changing cultural norms [93], and Howard Schultz's return to Starbucks during unionization efforts and employee activism [94] – demonstrate that leadership effectiveness is not fixed. Instead, it evolves in response to context, culture, and employee well-being [95, 96]. Therefore, even when companies meet financial goals, neglecting organizational health and employee experience can result in instability and reputational risk.

To deepen understanding of the factors that contribute to leadership ineffectiveness – particularly when accounting for contextual influences – recent research has increasingly drawn on the fields of neuroleadership and social cognitive neuroscience. Neuroleadership is commonly conceptualized as an applied branch of social cognitive neuroscience that seeks to analyze and explain leadership behavior [97, 98]. From this perspective, leadership is shaped by the interaction of cognitive, emotional, and neurobiological processes that influence decision-making, stress responses, and relational outcomes [96, 99, 100].

Social cognitive neuroscience demonstrates that leadership and followership are profoundly complex and context-dependent [101]. Emotions regulated within the amygdala and prefrontal cortex further influence decision-making, impulse control, and stress responsiveness, directly shaping leadership behavior and relational outcomes in the workplace [102]. Chronic stress or emotional dysregulation can undermine executive functioning, leading to habitual patterns of ineffective leadership – such as avoidance, rigidity, or emotional reactivity – even when leaders are aware of contextual expectations [103, 104].

Advances in neuroscience also reveal the brain's capacity for neuroplasticity, where repeated leadership behaviors, whether adaptive or maladaptive, become default responses [96]. This helps explain why leaders may struggle to change ineffective patterns, even within supportive environments. Neuroleadership thus provides a valuable framework for developing the hidden skills required for effective leadership, such as emotional regulation, resilience, and self-awareness [105, 106].

Recent studies further indicate that changes in leadership styles can significantly impact employee well-being and job satisfaction, reinforcing the value of integrating emotional and cognitive neuroscience into leadership development [107, 108]. Social cognitive neuroscience helps explain both what leaders do and why they do it by linking neurological variables to observable behaviors [99, 109]. Advocating for a neuroscientific approach to ineffective leadership enriches both theory and practice.

Trauma-informed leadership is an emerging, evidence-based approach that acknowledges the widespread effects of trauma and chronic stress on employee well-being, engagement, and organizational health. Trauma-informed leaders lead with empathy and compassion, recognizing that employee well-being and organizational health are inseparable [81, 110]. Leaders who embrace these principles intentionally create environments rooted in psychological safety, trust, empathy, and transparency – key factors in preventing and addressing employee burnout [31, 34].

Fostering high-performing employees starts with resilient, mentally healthy leaders who model trust and support rather than fear. Such leadership promotes collaboration, creativity, and long-term organizational success [31, 111]. Building a culture of trust requires inclusivity, open and honest communication, reducing stigma, supporting psychological safety, continuous learning, transparent decision-making, authentic advocacy, and nurturing connection and belonging [31, 34].

Transformational leaders are attuned to the needs and motivations of their teams and adapt their approach to inspire engagement and growth [111]. Trauma is one of the most underrecognized challenges in the work environment. Integrating trauma-informed leadership is essential for combating burnout and supporting resilience.

Importantly, trauma-informed leadership extends beyond supporting those with known trauma histories; it cultivates a workplace culture where all employees feel safe, valued, and empowered [112, 113]. This approach acknowledges how adversity and stress can manifest in the workplace, leading to disengagement, diminished productivity, or heightened stress responses, and aims to create an environment characterized by support, predictability, and flexibility.

Research identified six key domains that influence burnout: workload, control, reward, community, fairness, and values [34].

- **Workload:** Chronic overload depletes energy and prevents recovery, raising burnout risk. Sustainable workloads promote growth and skill development.

- **Control:** Limited autonomy and influence over work decisions contribute to burnout, while greater control enhances engagement.

- **Reward:** Insufficient recognition – whether financial, institutional, or social – undermines motivation. Consistent, meaningful rewards support well-being.

- **Community:** Poor workplace relationships and unresolved conflicts increase burnout, whereas strong social support and collaboration foster engagement.

- **Fairness:** Perceived inequity or disrespect in workplace decisions breeds cynicism and resentment. Fair and respectful treatment reduces burnout risk.

- **Values:** Alignment between personal and organizational values motivates employees, while value conflicts can force difficult trade-offs and increase burnout.

7.1 Why leaders must understand trauma

In the workplace, unrecognized trauma can manifest as absenteeism, reduced concentration, interpersonal conflict, and declining performance, often affecting not only individuals but entire teams. These reactions are not signs of weakness; they are normal physiological and psychological responses to abnormal experiences.

Trauma responses commonly appear as fight, flight, freeze, or fawn behaviors, each reflecting an automatic survival mechanism [114]. Without proper training, leaders may misinterpret these responses as disengagement, resistance, or poor attitude, inadvertently exacerbating stress and burnout. Trauma-informed leadership equips managers to respond with empathy, set appropriate boundaries, and provide support that promotes psychological safety. Successful approaches for recognizing burnout include regularly observing shifts in behavior, using reliable assessment instruments, applying predictive analytics, conducting workplace surveys, and monitoring physiological indicators of stress. Key organizational measures involve supportive leadership, training in resilience and emotional intelligence, effective workload management, and cultivating a positive organizational culture [20].

7.2 Trauma-informed leaders implement practices such as:

- Prioritizing psychological safety and open communication
- Recognizing and addressing early signs of stress and exhaustion
- Establishing predictable routines and transparent decision-making
- Providing opportunities for autonomy, professional growth, and employee voice
- Encouraging self-care and flexible work arrangements

7.3 Addressing trauma responses through a culture of care

Leaders play a critical role in determining whether trauma-related behaviors are met with empathy, structure, and support – or misinterpreted and punished. By recognizing employees as whole individuals and responding skillfully to stress-related behaviors, organizations can reduce burnout, strengthen engagement, and cultivate healthier, more productive workplaces.

Fight (agitation, defensiveness, confrontation):

Respond with calm presence and empathy while setting clear behavioral boundaries. Leaders should acknowledge emotions without validating harmful conduct, redirect conversations respectfully, and reinforce psychological safety by addressing concerns privately and constructively.

Flight (avoidance, withdrawal, overworking, disengagement):

Cultivate care by checking in individually, expressing concern rather than suspicion, and offering flexibility or practical support. Leaders should normalize help-seeking and collaboratively identify manageable expectations to reduce stress-driven avoidance.

Freeze (silence, indecision, dissociation):

Address freeze responses through patience and gentle inclusion. Leaders can provide structure, allow additional processing time, and create low-pressure opportunities for participation, ensuring individuals feel safe rather than rushed or exposed.

Fawn (over-accommodation, people-pleasing, boundary erosion):

Demonstrate care by restoring choice and reinforcing boundaries. Leaders should clarify what is voluntary rather than required, discourage self-sacrifice as a measure of commitment, and model healthy limits and self-care.

By responding to trauma-related behaviors with awareness and care, leaders reduce misinterpretation, prevent escalation, and protect employee well-being. A culture of care does not lower standards; it creates the conditions under which individuals and teams can function effectively, recover from stress, and sustain performance. Trauma-informed leadership "meets people where they are," responding with compassion and clarity, which has been shown to reduce absenteeism, lower burnout, improve morale, increase engagement, and boost retention [112, 113].

8. Conclusion

8.1 Reimagining workplaces as engines of well-being

The journey through stress, burnout, and trauma leads to a pivotal question: How can we reimagine our workplaces to sustain – not diminish – the people within them? The answer lies in collective action, courageous leadership, and a renewed commitment to human well-being.

8.2 Toward cultures of healing and sustainable engagement

Burnout must be understood as both an organizational and public health issue, not merely an individual failing. A growing body of evidence demonstrates that chronic workplace stress is driven primarily by systemic factors, including excessive demands, lack of control, value incongruence, and relational breakdowns [1, 2]. As such, meaningful solutions demand a reconfiguration of organizational landscapes – one in which leaders assume responsibility for driving structural, cultural, and relational change that prioritizes human sustainability alongside performance [2, 34, 115]. When interventions operate at multiple levels – individual, team, and systemic – they can create environments of engagement and resilience.

8.3 Innovative pathways for organizational healing and development

To move beyond traditional wellness initiatives, organizations must adopt neurobiologically informed and trauma-aware strategies that address how chronic stress alters cognition, emotional regulation, and social engagement. Sustained exposure to workplace stressors reshapes neural functioning, narrowing attention, impairing executive control, and heightening threat sensitivity. Neurobiologically informed interventions, grounded in science and empathy, support recovery by restoring cognitive flexibility and adaptive capacity.

When organizations provide predictability, role clarity, and growth opportunities, they create the conditions necessary for resilience, learning, and innovation to re-emerge [50, 52]. Predictability in workflows, transparency in decision-making, and clearly defined role expectations reduce unnecessary threat activation within the nervous system. These conditions allow employees to shift from survival-oriented responses to engagement-oriented states, enabling collaboration, creativity, and meaning-making to emerge.

8.4 Traum-informed leadership and relational repair

Trauma-informed leadership remains foundational to sustainable organizational health. Leaders who consistently demonstrate empathy, fairness, and commitment to psychological safety play a critical role in repairing relational ruptures that often perpetuate burnout, disengagement, and moral injury. By modeling accountability, openness, and care, trauma-informed leaders address not only the symptoms of burnout but also its relational and systemic roots, fostering trust and a sense of belonging across the organization [31, 81].

Relational practices, such as trust-building rituals, open communication, and meaningful feedback, form the connective tissue that unites teams and empowers individuals. These practices enhance belonging, buffer physiological stress responses, and build collective resilience, especially in high-demand environments [116]. Leaders must consistently observe, maintain an employee-centered mindset, and provide appropriate resources.

It's important to recognize that genuine connection, validation, and support are universally valued. Employees must feel seen and heard. Trust cannot be expected, assumed, or demanded from individuals who have repeatedly felt dismissed or harmed. Psychological safety is built through consistent, authentic action, not episodic initiatives.

8.5 Advancing recovery through organizational innovation

Beyond foundational support, several innovation-oriented practices can promote collective recovery, participation, and healing:

8.6 Establishing psychological safety

A psychologically safe workplace enables employees to reflect openly on stressors, ethical tensions, and organizational change without fear of judgment or retaliation. Psychological safety rests on four essential elements: a willingness to help, inclusive norms that value diversity, acceptance of learning through failure, and open, candid dialog.

Leaders should initiate explicit conversations about psychological safety, clarify its purpose, and dispel misconceptions that equate it with comfort or a lack of accountability. Practices such as promoting accountability without blame, addressing bias, modeling vulnerability, and encouraging constructive risk-taking reduce impression management and foster authentic engagement.

Validated tools, such as Edmondson's Psychological Safety Scale or structured dialogic methods (e.g., "jazz dialogues"), can strengthen team dynamics by prioritizing listening, building on collective input, and valuing diverse perspectives. Emphasis should be placed on listening before responding, contributing meaningfully to shared dialog, and allowing insights to emerge organically rather than adhering to predetermined scripts [117].

Ongoing reassessment and anonymous feedback mechanisms, ideally managed by a designated, neutral role, support transparency and continuous improvement, ensuring psychological safety remains an active organizational priority.

Collective forums can further support recovery by providing psychologically safe spaces for employees to reflect on organizational stressors, ethical dilemmas, and change fatigue. By externalizing shared stressors and fostering collective sensemaking, these forums reduce burnout risk and enhance shared meaning [118].

8.7 Recovery-centered work design

Recovery-centered work design acknowledges that sustained performance carries a measurable neurophysiological cost and that recovery is not optional but essential to cognitive functioning, emotional regulation, and long-term well-being. Embedding intentional recovery cycles, such as cognitive reset days, predictable pauses, and protected non-work time, helps prevent cumulative exhaustion from becoming normalized.

This approach aligns closely with the stressor–detachment model, which conceptualizes recovery as a process of temporary psychological and physiological disengagement from work-related stressors. Effective recovery depends not simply on time away from work but on psychological detachment that allows stress-activated systems to return to baseline. Without such detachment, stressors remain cognitively active, prolonging strain responses and increasing vulnerability to burnout, sleep disruption, and impaired self-regulation [119].

Work designs that normalize constant availability, urgency, and boundary erosion undermine recovery, even when formal leave policies exist. Integrating recovery-oriented and trauma-informed principles into work design reframes recovery as an organizational responsibility, not an individual burden. These practices emphasize predictability, choice, safety, and empowerment – conditions that restore agency and support psychological detachment under chronic stress [120].

8.8 Psychological load audits

Psychological load audits represent an essential yet underutilized strategy for burnout prevention. Traditional workload assessments often overlook emotional labor, ambiguity, and cognitive overload – stressors strongly associated with burnout and disengagement. Mental workload has been widely studied; however, no universally accepted framework exists, in part due to inconsistent definitions and reliance on isolated measurement approaches.

A more robust assessment requires integrating self-report measures, task performance indicators, and physiological data to capture the full scope of psychological load and its effects on well-being and performance [121]. Such comprehensive audits enable organizations to identify hidden stressors and intervene before harm becomes systemic.

8.9 Empathy, leadership transition, and moral repair

Organizations that fail to demonstrate empathy face significant consequences. Unempathetic workplaces experience markedly higher rates of attrition, absenteeism, disengagement, and toxicity, resulting in economic losses estimated to reach billions of dollars each year. Employees in these environments are much more likely to suffer from mental health challenges and disengagement. Furthermore, both toxicity and mental health issues tend to escalate in organizations where empathy is lacking [122].

In some cases, meaningful recovery may require re-evaluating leadership structures. Employees are unlikely to feel safe under the same leadership that contributed to their distress, regardless of intent. Trauma-informed and empathetic leadership requires more than training – it demands emotional competence, contextual awareness, and moral courage. Leaders must understand frontline realities to calibrate empathy accurately and reduce the disconnect between policy decisions and lived experience.

Practicing wise empathy involves discerning not only how others feel but also how to respond effectively within context. Practical strategies include pausing to observe, tuning into situational cues, clarifying needs, balancing care with boundaries, and engaging in continuous reflection and learning [123].

8.10 Well-being stewardship

Well-being stewardship represents a decisive shift from reactive, compliance-driven responses to occupational stress toward proactive, ethically grounded systems of care. Rather than locating well-being solely within Human Resources, which are often constrained by power dynamics, organizations can establish a designated, credentialed stewardship role responsible for monitoring psychological safety, identifying early warning signs of distress, and facilitating appropriate support. Crucially, this role should operate independently of disciplinary authority to reduce fear-based silence and promote openness [31].

Embedding well-being support into daily operations, rather than limiting it to surveys or crisis interventions, creates the conditions necessary for recovery. Psychological safety, trust, and transparency are prerequisites for healing from chronic organizational stress and cannot emerge where fear of reprisal persists [1].

Stewardship, as conceptualized here, is not merely a role but an outcome of leadership behavior. Drawing from stewardship theory, leaders who foster identification with organizational purpose, intrinsic motivation, and shared responsibility position themselves as caretakers of collective well-being rather than controllers of performance. Through moral courage, accountability, and relational care, leaders cultivate trust and enable sustainable organizational functioning [124].

Well-being stewardship also requires recognizing and redistributing invisible labor – the emotional, relational, and cognitive work that sustains organizations but often goes unacknowledged. Making this labor visible and equitably supported is essential to recovery. When organizations account for emotional and relational demands, they affirm employees' humanity and strengthen cultures of fairness, trust, and sustainability.

As a recovery-oriented strategy, well-being stewardship aligns ethical leadership with human sustainability. By embedding psychological safety, recognizing invisible labor, and fostering stewardship through relationally grounded leadership practices, organizations create environments where healing is possible – not only for individuals, but for the organizational system.

8.11 Measuring, sustaining, and advancing well-being

Cultures of organizational healing cannot be sustained without deliberate measurement, accountability, and continuous refinement. Progress toward psychological safety, recovery, and well-being must be systematically assessed, actively maintained, and iteratively improved. Regular evaluation of psychological safety, burnout risk, and moral distress – paired with real-time, psychologically safe feedback mechanisms – enables organizations to intervene proactively rather than reactively. These practices are not ancillary; they are central to organizational effectiveness, ethical leadership, and long-term performance [31, 34].

Analytic tools, including predictive modeling of burnout risk, offer promising avenues for early intervention when paired with ethical oversight and human-centered implementation. Tools such as the NIOSH Worker Well-Being Questionnaire (WellBQ) provide a comprehensive assessment of employees' quality of working life, integrating physical and mental health, workplace climate, supervisory relationships, benefits, policies, and non-work determinants of well-being [125]. When used thoughtfully, such tools move organizations beyond narrow engagement metrics toward a more holistic understanding of human sustainability at work.

Sustained progress also requires ongoing research that examines the dynamic relationships among leadership practices, employee well-being, and organizational performance. By examining contextual factors, power dynamics, and lived experiences, organizations can develop leadership approaches that are both adaptive and humane, capable of supporting employee well-being while navigating complexity in an evolving global environment [126].

8.12 A necessary reckoning for the future of work

As artificial intelligence continues to reshape the nature of work, superficial niceness is no longer sufficient. The future of work demands something far more substantive: genuine kindness, moral responsibility, and authentic human connection embedded within organizational systems and leadership practices. Empathy, when enacted consistently and skillfully, becomes a strategic and ethical imperative rather than a soft skill or aspirational value [127].

Leaders and organizations must move beyond surface-level pleasantries and symbolic wellness initiatives, and intentionally cultivate environments in which employees feel valued, heard, and protected. This is not merely a recommendation; it is essential to organizational health, engagement, and long-term viability in the age of AI.

As both a scholar and a sufferer of occupational stress and burnout, I urge organizations to confront a difficult but necessary truth: the way some work is currently designed is harming people and, by extension, harming organizations themselves. The age-old adage, "treat your employees well and they will treat your business well," is not antiquated wisdom; it is a foundational principle that must re-emerge with urgency and intention.

8.13 Leadership, accountability, and the limits of trust

Meaningful transformation cannot be led by those who have repeatedly eroded trust without reckoning or accountability. In many organizations, cumulative harm, unresolved relational ruptures, and unaddressed moral injury have left employees feeling exposed and unsupported. When leadership remains disengaged, dismissive, or defensive, calls for resilience lose credibility and moral force.

The leadership practices that contributed to chronic stress and burnout are unlikely to produce recovery unless accompanied by genuine listening, learning, behavioral change, and accountability. Even then, organizations must acknowledge a difficult reality: employees may be unwilling (or unable) to extend trust to those associated with prior harm. Healing cannot be mandated, and trust cannot be demanded.

Reluctance to invest in meaningful change due to perceived short-term costs is both shortsighted and dangerous. The true cost of inaction manifests in turnover, absenteeism, presenteeism, disability claims, disengagement, and declining performance. With 76% of employees reporting at least one mental health symptom [114], this is not a peripheral concern – it is a systemic crisis. When fear, silence, and emotional withdrawal become normalized, they signal organizational deterioration, not resilience.

8.14 From endurance to sustainability

Organizations cannot continue to demand more from fewer people while offering diminishing resources and expect different outcomes. What may appear to be short-term efficiency is ultimately unsustainable. Systems pushed beyond capacity do not strengthen; they fracture. Over time, employees reach levels of exhaustion from which recovery becomes increasingly difficult, if not impossible.

Sustainable change requires investment: in people, in leadership development, in ethical systems of care, and in work designs that recognize human limits. Temporary fixes, rebranded programs, and symbolic gestures are insufficient substitutes for structural change.

Now is the time for decisive, accountable action for employee well-being and organizational survival. Employees must be given genuine opportunities to speak without fear of retaliation, bias, or dismissal. Psychological safety cannot exist where truth is punished or ignored. Just as organizations establish accountability mechanisms for employee performance, they must also confront ineffective or harmful leadership. Leadership is not a protected status; it is a responsibility with measurable consequences for human lives.

Organizations must be willing to ask – and answer – difficult questions:

How can employees trust leadership that has repeatedly failed to protect them?

How can healing occur where harm has gone unacknowledged?

How can transformation emerge without accountability?

8.15 Final note: Re-engagement after harm: When safety precedes voice

Employees who have experienced dismissal, retaliation, or prolonged invalidation often respond not with resistance but with adaptive self-protection shaped by prior harm. Heightened vigilance, cautious communication, emotional withdrawal, and strategic silence reflect a nervous system that has learned that visibility carries risk. Effective recovery from organizational stress, therefore, requires more than encouragement to "speak up" or demonstrate resilience; it demands structural and relational safeguards that make participation genuinely safe.

Beyond psychological safety, recovery-oriented work design, stewardship, and workload audits, organizations must implement predictability practices (clear standards, timelines, and decision criteria), procedural justice mechanisms (transparent review and appeal pathways), voice insulation (intermediaries and protected escalation channels), choice-preserving accommodations (flexibility without career penalty), and intentional trust-repair protocols following harm. These approaches recognize that healing is not an individual mindset shift but a systemic recalibration of power, accountability, and care. Only when organizations consistently demonstrate fairness, clarity, and restraint does re-engagement become reasonable – and only then can workplaces function as engines of well-being rather than sources of ongoing injury.

Critically, success must also be redefined. Voice is not valuable only when it produces institutional change. Success may instead be found in self-alignment, boundary setting, and health protection. Strategic silence is not avoidance; it is an ethical, self-protective response when trust has been breached. Healing does not require forcing trust where it has been violated; it requires organizations to demonstrate – through consistent, accountable action – that trust is warranted.

Ultimately, meaningful organizational change requires more than new initiatives, revised titles, or rebranded wellness strategies. It demands moral courage, transparent reckoning with past failures, and a sustained commitment to redesigning work that prioritizes psychological safety, dignity, and human sustainability. Only through this level of honesty and investment can organizations evolve from sources of harm into environments where people, and the systems they sustain, can genuinely heal, participate, and thrive.

As U.S. Surgeon General Murthy reminds us, workplaces have the potential to become engines of mental health and well-being – but only if organizations fundamentally rethink their practices. By prioritizing safety, connection, authenticity, and long-term growth, organizations can rise to meet this moment. The journey may be challenging, but the rewards – a thriving workforce and a healthier community – are well worth the effort.

9. Dedications

To every employee who has suffered trauma in the workplace and whose pain has gone unheard or unseen by leadership; to those who have borne the burden of burnout without support or assistance – may you find your voice, and may your experiences be acknowledged, honored, and addressed.

To the leaders who have chosen to listen, learn, and grow – who have embraced the principles of trauma-informed leadership with authenticity, genuineness, and unwavering integrity – your transformation lights the way toward a more compassionate and resilient workplace.

To the leaders who have not yet embarked on the journey of trauma-informed leadership, remaining in their comfort zones and resisting change, may you one day recognize the transformative power of human-centered leadership in a world defined by uncertainty. The call to lead with empathy and compassion is more urgent than ever.

In these times, human-centered leadership is not just an aspiration but a critical necessity. It is the path forward to healing, resilience, and collective growth. It is the foundation for healing, trust, and progress in today's ever-changing landscape.

To Joseph, whom I love with all that I am. Your remarkable leadership, compassion, and hopefulness inspire me every day, renewing my faith in a future shaped by those who lead with heart, humility, and integrity. I am endlessly proud of your achievements and aspirations, but even more grateful for your golden smile and genuine presence. Your unwavering sincerity and strength remind me that true leadership is measured not just by deeds but by character. Thank you for loving me and for showing, through your actions and spirit, the extraordinary influence of authentic leadership. You truly light up my world!

And to my husband, whose quiet sacrifices have given me the space – both literal and emotional – to heal, reflect, and create. Thank you for giving up your office so I could find sanctuary in my writing. You have witnessed and endured the effects of prolonged stress alongside me, and our shared resilience through every challenge fills me with pride. Ours is a partnership built on faith and strength, and for that, I am grateful.

To my beloved Mother, who has passed on – the heart of kindness, a beacon of insight, the most self-aware leader, and the voice of comfort in every storm. Your unwavering love, faith, authenticity, and gentle spirit have illuminated the way with kindness and care. You have been a guiding light through challenges for all who crossed your path. Thank you for showing me the true strength found in compassion and for teaching me that healing begins with kindness. As you always said, there is nothing more gentle than love and nothing more loving than gentleness. This chapter is dedicated to you, with all my love and gratitude.

This work has been both professionally meaningful and personally restorative, and I am deeply grateful to share life with friends and professionals who understand that well-being is foundational, not optional. It is a priority, not a privilege, and essential not just for surviving but for truly thriving.

Acknowledgement

The author acknowledges the use of Grammarly for language polishing of the manuscript.

DOI: http://dx.doi.org/10.5772/intechopen.1014797

Author details

Clarine Jacobs
Independent Researcher, Osage Beach, USA

*Address all correspondence to: clarinejacobs@gmail.com

References

[1] Maslach C, Leiter MP. Burnout: A brief history and how to prevent it. Harvard Business Review. 2016. Available from: https://hbr.org/2022/02/burnout-a-brief-history-and-how-to-prevent-it [Accessed: 2025-November-08]

[2] World Health Organization (WHO). Burn-out an "occupational phenomenon": International Classification of Diseases [Internet]. 2019. Available from: https://www.who.int/mental_health/evidence/burn-out/en/ [Accessed: 2025-November-10]

[3] World Health Organization. Summary Reports on Proceedings Minutes and Final Acts of the International Health Conference held in New York from 19 June to 22 July 1946 [Internet]. Geneva: World Health Organization; 1948. Available from: https://apps.who.int/iris/handle/10665/85573 [Accessed: 2025-November-22]

[4] World Health Organization, Regional Office for the Eastern Mediterranean. Mental Health: Introduction [Internet]. Cairo: WHO EMRO; 2024. Available from: https://www.emro.who.int/health-topics/mental-health/introduction.html [Accessed: 2025-November-10]

[5] American Psychological Association. Mental health. Adapted from the APA Dictionary of Psychology [Internet]. 2025. Available from: https://www.apa.org/topics/mental-health [Accessed: 2025-November-11]

[6] Galderisi S, Heinz A, Kastrup M, Beezhold J, Sartorius N. Toward a new definition of mental health. World Psychiatry. 2015;**14**:231–233. DOI: 10.1002/wps.20231

[7] Su Z, Bentley BL, McDonnell D, Cheshmehzangi A, Šegalo S, da Veiga CP, Xiang YT. Post-COVID mental health crises: Globally minded for solutions and solidarity. Disaster Medicine and Public Health Preparedness. 2024;**18**:e295. DOI: 10.1017/dmp.2024.165

[8] De Angelis T. Beliefs about mental health have evolved, but stigma remains. American Psychological Association [Internet]. 2025. Available from: https://www.apa.org/monitor/2025/09/mental-health-stigma [Accessed: 2025-November-08]

[9] Resilience Behavioral Health Centers. Mental Health Stigma and Awareness [Internet]. 2024. Available from: https://resiliencebehavioralhealthcenters.com [Accessed: 2025-November-08]

[10] National Alliance on Mental Illness (NAMI). Poll of public perspectives on the U.S. mental health care system [Internet]. 2025. Available from: https://www.nami.org/support-education/publications-reports/survey-reports/poll-of-public-perspectives-on-the-u-s-mental-health-care-system-2025/ [Accessed: 2025-November-08]

[11] The Global Statistics. United States mental health statistics [Internet]. 2024. Available from: https://www.theglobalstatistics.com/united-states-mental-health-statistics/ [Accessed: 2025-November-09]

[12] World Health Organization. World mental health today [Internet]. 2025. Available from: https://iris.who.int/server/api/core/bitstreams/31714489-1345-4439-8b37-6cbdc52e15ca/content [Accessed: 2025-November-14]

[13] National Institute for Occupational Safety and Health (NIOSH). About workplace stress. Centers for Disease Control and Prevention [Internet]. n d. Available from: https://www.cdc.gov/niosh/stress/about/index.html [Accessed: 2025-November-21]

[14] Maslach C. Job burnout in professional and economic contexts. In: Arivanto, et al. editors. Diversity in Unity: Perspectives from Psychology and Behavioral Sciences. Routledge: Taylor & Francis; 2018. p. 11–15. DOI: 10.1201/9781315225302-2

[15] Hammen C. Stress and depression. Annual Review of Clinical Psychology. 2005;**1**(1):293–319. DOI: 10.1146/annurev.clinpsy.1.102803.143938

[16] Hammen CL. Stress and depression: Old questions, new approaches. Current Opinion in Psychology. 2015;**4**:80–85. DOI: 10.1016/j.copsyc.2014.12.024

[17] Schaufeli WB, Leiter MP, Maslach C. Burnout: 35 years of research and practice. Career Development International. 2009;**14**(3):204–220. DOI: 10.1108/13620430910966406

[18] Bakker AB, Demerouti E. The job demands-resources model: State of the art. Journal of Management Psychology. 2007;**22**(3):309–328. DOI: 10.1108/02683940710733115

[19] Maslach C, Leiter MP. Understanding the burnout experience: Recent research and its implications for psychiatry. World Psychiatry. 2016;**15**(2):103–111. DOI: 10.1002/wps.20311

[20] Karakolias S. Seeing burnout coming: Early signs and recognition strategies in health professionals. Frontiers in Public Health. 2025;**13**:1721220. DOI: 10.3389/fpubh.2025.1721220

[21] World Health Organization. Burn-out an "occupational phenomenon": International Classification of Diseases [Internet]. 2019. Available from: https://www.who.int/news/item/28-05-2019-burn-out-an-occupational-phenomenon-international-classification-of-diseases [Accessed: 2025–November–08]

[22] Tang YL, Raffone A, Wong SYS. Burnout and stress: New insights and interventions. Scientific Reports. 2025;**15**(1):8335. DOI: 10.1038/s41598-025-92909-6

[23] Kinman G. Maslach Burnout Inventory. Occupational Medicine. 2024;**74**(9):630–631. DOI: 10.1093/occmed/kqae116

[24] Centers for Disease Control and Prevention. Providing support for worker mental health. 2025 June 9. Available from: https://www.cdc.gov/mental-health/caring/providing-support-for-workers-and-professionals.html [Accessed: 2025-November-10]

[25] Soliman R. Burnout symptoms explained: Why emotional exhaustion and workplace stress cause real physical pain. Medical Daily. 2026. Available from: https://www.medicaldaily.com/burnout-symptoms-explained-why-emotional-exhaustion- [Accessed: 2025-November-10]

[26] Schonfeld IS, Bianchi R. From burnout to occupational depression: Recent developments in research on job-related distress and occupational health. Frontiers in Public Health. 2021;**9**:796401. https://www.ncbi.nlm.nih.gov/pmc/articles/PMC8702721/

[27] Truschel J. Depression definition and DSM-5 diagnostic criteria: Depression, otherwise known as major depressive disorder or clinical depression, is a common and serious mood disorder. Health Central. 2022. Available from: https://www.healthcentral.com/condition/depression/dsm-5-depression-criteria [Accessed: 2025-December-10]

[28] Kahn RL, Wolfe DM, Quinn RP, Snoek JD, Rosenthal RA. Organizational Stress: Studies in Role Conflict and Ambiguity. New York: John Wiley; 1964

[29] Shinde S. Role ambiguity and employee well-being: The critical need for clear job descriptions. Kaav International Journal of Arts Humanities & Social Science. 2025;**12** (2):6–12. DOI: 10.52458/23484349.2025.v12.iss2.kp.a2

[30] Kreiner GE, Hollensbe EC, Sheep ML, Smith BR, Kataria N. The future of work–life flexibility: Key themes and directions for research. Academy of Management Annals. 2023;**17**(1):174–211

[31] Edmondson A. The Fearless Organization: Creating Psychological Safety in the Workplace for Learning, Innovation, and Growth. Hoboken: Wiley; 2019

[32] Einarsen S, Hoel H, Zapf D, Cooper CL. Bullying and Harassment in the Workplace: Theory, Research, and Practice. 3rd ed. Boca Raton: CRC Press; 2020

[33] Berglund D, Toropova A, Björklund C. Workplace bullying, stress, burnout, and the role of perceived social support: Findings from a Swedish national prevalence study in higher education. European Journal of Higher Education. 2025;**15**(2):185–205. DOI: 10.1080/21568235.2023.2301588

[34] Maslach C, Leiter MP. The Burnout Challenge: Managing People's Relationships with Their Jobs. Cambridge: Harvard University Press; 2022

[35] Lazarus RS, Folkman S. Stress, Appraisal, and Coping. New York: Springer; 1984

[36] Jacobs CM. Occupational stress and burnout. In: Burnout syndrome - characteristics and interventions [Internet]. IntechOpen; 2024 February. Available from: https://www.intechopen.com/online-first/1153211 [Accessed: 2025–December–22]

[37] World Health Organization. Mental health at work. 2024. Available from: https://www.who.int/news-room/fact-sheets/detail/mental-health-at-work [Accessed: 2025–November–22]

[38] Society for Human Resource Management (SHRM). Here's how bad burnout has become at work. 2024Available from: https://www.shrm.org/topics-tools/news/inclusion-diversity/burnout-shrm-research-2024 [Accessed: 2025 November 22]

[39] Gallup. Global data summary – State of the global workplace 2025. 2025. Available from: https://www.gallup.com/workplace/697904/state-of-the-global-workplace-global-data.aspx [Accessed: 2025–November–22]

[40] Society for Human Resource Management (SHRM). Poor Leadership, Heavy Workloads Top Contributors for Workplace Burnout, New SHRM Research Finds. 2025. Available from: https://www.shrm.org/about/press-roo

m/poor-leadership–heavy-workloads-top-contributors-for-workplace- [Accessed: 2025–November–22]

[41] Moore J. The silent struggles of the workforce: How mental health is shaping America's labor landscape [Internet]. Psychology Today. 2025. Available from: https://www.psychologytoday.com/us/blog/putting-america-to-work/202501/the-silent-struggles-of-the-workforce?msockid=35c2e725fb8d6cc238fff18ffaf36d81 [Accessed: 2025–November–22]

[42] French J, Rodgers W, Cobb S. Adjustment as person–environment fit. In Coelho G, Hamburg D, Adams J, editors. Coping and Adaptation. New York: Basic Books; 1974. p. 316–333d

[43] Lewin K. Field Theory in Social Science. New York: Harper; 1951

[44] De Cooman R, Vleugels W. Person–Environment Fit: Theoretical Perspectives, Conceptualizations, and Outcomes. Oxford Research Encyclopedia of Business and Management. 2022. DOI: 10.1093/acrefore/9780190224851.013.377

[45] Demerouti E, Bakker AB, Nachreiner F, Schaufeli WB. The job demands-resources model of burnout. Journal of Applied Psychology. 2001; **86**(3):499–512

[46] Schaufeli WB, Taris TW. A critical review of the job demands-resources model: Implications for improving work and health. In: Bauer GF, Hämmig O, editors. Bridging Occupational, Organizational and Public Health: A Transdisciplinary Approach. Dordrecht: Springer Science + Business Media; 2014. p. 43–68. DOI: 10.1007/978-94-007-5640-3_4

[47] Gautam S, Jain A, Chaudhary J, Gautam M, Gaur M, Grover S. Concept of mental health and mental well-being, it's determinants and coping strategies. Indian Journal of Psychiatry. 2024;**66**(Suppl 2):S231–S244. DOI: 10.4103/indianjpsychiatry.indianjpsychiatry_707_23

[48] Afek N, Harmatiuk D, Gawłowska M, Ferreira JMA, Golonka K, Tukaiev S, Popov A, Marek T. Functional connectivity in burnout syndrome: A resting-state EEG study. Frontiers in Human Neuroscience. 2025;**19**:1481760. DOI: 10.3389/fnhum.2025.1481760

[49] Association for Psychological Science. Helping others dampens effects of everyday stress [Internet]. Science Daily. 2015. Available from: https://www.sciencedaily.com/releases/2015/12/151214084744.htm [Accessed: 2025-November-29]

[50] Chmiel J, Malinowska A. Neural Correlates of Burnout Syndrome Based on Electroencephalography (EEG)—A Mechanistic Review and Discussion of Burnout Syndrome Cognitive Bias Theory. Journal of Clinical Medicine. 2025;**14**(15):5357. DOI: 10.3390/jcm14155357

[51] Liston C, McEwen BS, Casey BJ. Psychosocial stress reversibly disrupts prefrontal processing and attentional control. Proceedings of the National Academy of Sciences of the United States of America. 2009;**106**(3):912–917. DOI: 10.1073/pnas.0807041106

[52] Porges SW. The Polyvagal Theory: Neurophysiological Foundations of Emotions, Attachment, Communication, and Self-regulation. New York: NY: W. W. Norton & Company; 2011

[53] Siegel DJ. The Developing Mind: How Relationships and the Brain Interact to Shape Who We are. 2nd ed. New York: Guilford Press; 2012

[54] Cozolino L. The Neuroscience of Human Relationships: Attachment and the Developing Social Brain. 2nd ed. New York: W. W. Norton & Company; 2014

[55] Schore AN. The Science of the Art of Psychotherapy. New York: W. W. Norton & Company; 2012

[56] Boyatzis RE, McKee A. Resonant Leadership: Renewing Yourself and Connecting with Others through Mindfulness, Hope, and Compassion. Boston: Harvard Business School Press; 2005

[57] Rock D. SCARF: A brain-based model for collaborating with and influencing others. NeuroLeadership Journal. 2008;**1**:1–9

[58] Eisenberger NI, Lieberman MD. Why it hurts to be left out: The neurocognitive overlap between physical and social pain. Trends in Cognitive Sciences. 2004;**8**(7):294–300. DOI: 10.1016/j.tics.2004.05.010

[59] Lieberman MD. Social: Why Our Brains are Wired to Connect. New York: Crown; 2013

[60] Porges SW. Polyvagal Safety: Attachment, Communication, Self-regulation. New York: W. W. Norton & Company; 2022

[61] Coan JA, Sbarra DA. Social baseline theory: The social regulation of risk and effort. Current Opinion in Psychology. 2015;**1**:87–91. DOI: 10.1016/j.copsyc.2014.12.021

[62] Guy-Evans O. Neurotransmitters: Types, function and examples [Internet]. Simply Psychology. 2025. Available from: https://www.simplypsychology.org/neurotransmitter.html [Accessed: 2025-July-26]

[63] Koutsimani P, Montgomery A, Georganta K. The relationship between burnout, depression, and anxiety: A systematic review and meta-analysis. Frontiers in Psychology. 2019;**10**:284. DOI: 10.3389/fpsyg.2019.00284

[64] Slavich GM. Social Safety Theory: A biologically based evolutionary perspective on life stress, health, and behavior. Annual Review of Clinical Psychology. 2020;**16**:265–295. DOI: 10.1146/annurev-clinpsy-032816-045159

[65] Harms PD, Credé M, Tynan M, Leon M, Jeung W. Leadership and stress: A meta-analytic review. The Leadership Quarterly. 2018;**29**(1):104–117. DOI: 10.1016/j.leaqua.2016.10.006

[66] Kleber RJ. Trauma and public mental health: A focused review. Frontiers in Psychiatry. 2019;**10**:451. DOI: 10.3389/fpsyt.2019.00451

[67] Friedberg JP, Malefakis DE. Resilience, Trauma, and Coping. Psychodyn Psychiatry. 2018;**46**(1): 81–113 DOI: 10.1521/pdps.2018.46.1.81

[68] Sutton L, Rowe S, Hammerton G, Billings J. The contribution of organisational factors to vicarious trauma in mental health professionals: A systematic review and narrative synthesis. European Journal of Psychotraumatology. 2022;**13**(1):2022278

[69] Wyatt Z. Trauma-Informed Leadership: Recognising, responding, and rebuilding organizational resilience.

2025. https://www.researchgate.net/publication/391693793_Trauma-Informed_Leadership_Recognising_Responding_and_Rebuilding_Organisational_Resilience [Accessed: 2025-June-22]

[70] van der Kolk BA. The Body Keeps the Score: Brain, Mind, and Body in the Healing of Trauma. New York: Viking; 2014

[71] Kim J Understanding the relationship between traumatic experience and employee organizational commitment using a posttraumatic cognitive model and self-determination theory [dissertation]. Madison: University of Wisconsin-Madison; 2023

[72] Verrastro V, Cuzzocrea F, Calaresi D, Saladino V. Childhood emotional abuse, neuroticism, perfectionism, and workaholism in an Italian sample of young workers. Behavioral Sciences. 2024;**14**(4):298

[73] Hansen BD Disclosure of abuse to empowerment: Exploring psychological safety as a leadership tool to support women struggling with workplace performance [doctoral dissertation]. Los Angeles: University of Southern California; 2024

[74] Jonker C, Botma N. Chapter 1. The emotion experiences of employees in a work setting. In: Research on Emotion in Organizations: Experiencing and Managing Emotions in the Workplace. Vol. **8**. Bingley: Emerald Group Publishing Limited; 2012. p. 3–24

[75] Tehrani N, editor. Managing Trauma in the Workplace. London: Routledge; 2010

[76] Choitz V, Wagner S. A Trauma-informed Approach to Workforce. 2021. Available from: https://nationalfund.org/wp-content/uploads/2021/04/A-Trauma-Informed-Approach-to-Workforce.pdf [Accessed: 2025-December-28]

[77] Benenson JF, Webb CE, Wrangham RW. Self-protection as an adaptive female strategy. Behavioral and Brain Sciences. 2022;**45**:e128

[78] Peterson SH. Why trauma-informed leadership matters: A new standard for leadership. 2024. https://www.thecenterforconsciousleadership.com/learn/why-trauma-informed-leadership-matters [Accessed: 2025-June-15]

[79] Powers A. The debate over trauma in the new DSM revision. Why definitions matter for clinical care [Internet]. Psychology Today. 2024. Available from: https://www.psychologytoday.com/us/blog/science-therapy-and-whole-body-health/202405/the-debate-over-trauma-in-the-new-dsm-revision?msockid=35c2e725fb8d6cc238fff18ffaf36d81 [Accessed: 2025 July 22]

[80] Huizinga RB. Emerging Leadership Journeys. 2016. Available from: https://www.regent.edu/acad/global/publications/elj/vol9iss1/2ELJ-Huizinga.pdf [Accessed: 2025-November-30]

[81] Bloom SL, Farragher B. Restoring sanctuary: A new operating system for trauma-informed systems of care [Internet]. Oxford: Oxford University Press; 2013, Available from: 10.1093/acprof:oso/9780199796366.001.0001 [Accessed: 2026-January-10]

[82] Pessoa L. The emotional brain. In: Conn P, editor. Conn's Translational Neuroscience. New York: 2nd. Academic Press; 2017. p. 635–656. DOI: 10.1016/B978-0-12-802381-5.00046-4

[83] Gračanin A, Kardum I. Primary emotions as modular mechanisms of the human mind. In Žebec MS, Sabol G, Šakić M, Topić MK, editors. Brain and Mind: A Lasting Challenge. Zagreb, Croatia: Institute of Social Sciences "Ivo Pilar"; 2006. p. 89–103

[84] Šimić G, Tkalčić M, Vukić V, Mulc D, Španić E, Šagud M, Olucha-Bordonau FE, Vukšić M, Hof PR. Understanding emotions: Origins and roles of the amygdala. Biomolecules. 2021;**11**(6):823. DOI: 10.3390/biom11060823

[85] Ochsner KN, Phelps E. Emerging perspectives on emotion–cognition interactions. Trends in Cognitive Sciences. 2007;**11**:317–318. DOI: 10.1016/j.tics.2007.06.008

[86] Storbeck J, Clore GL. On the interdependence of cognition and emotion. Cognition and Emotion. 2007;**21**:1212–1237. DOI: 10.1080/02699930701438020

[87] Phelps EA. Emotion and cognition: Insights from studies of the human amygdala. Annual Review of Psychology. 2006;**57**:27–53. DOI: 10.1146/annurev.psych.56.091103.070234

[88] Okon-Singer H, Hendler T, Pessoa L, Shackman J. The neurobiology of emotion–cognition interactions: Fundamental questions and strategies for future research. Frontiers in Human Neuroscience. 2015;**9**:58. DOI: 10.3389/fnhum.2015.00058

[89] Ungar M, Theron L. Resilience and mental health: How multisystemic processes contribute to positive outcomes. The Lancet Psychiatry. 2020;**7**(5):441–448

[90] Luthar SS, Cicchetti D, Becker B. The construct of resilience: A critical evaluation and guidelines for future work. Child Development. 2000;**71**(3):543–562

[91] Rutter M. Resilience as a dynamic concept. Development and Psychopathology. 2012;**24**(2):335–344

[92] Black MH, Helander J, Segers J, Ingard C, Bervoets J, Grimaldi de Puget V, Bölte S. Resilience in the face of neurodivergence: A scoping review of resilience and factors promoting positive outcomes. Clinical Psychology Review. 2024;**113**:102487. DOI: 10.1016/j.cpr.2024.102487

[93] Kantor J, Isaac M. Elon Musk's Twitter takeover. The New York Times. 2023 Nov 3

[94] Greenhouse S. Howard Schultz returns to Starbucks facing a labor crisis. The New York Times. 2022 Mar 18

[95] Avolio BJ, Walumbwa FO, Weber TJ. Leadership: Current theories, research, and future directions. Annual Review of Psychology. 2009;**60**:421–449

[96] Goleman D, Boyatzis R. What makes a leader? Harvard Business Review [Internet]. 2020. Available from: https://hbr.org/2020/05/what-makes-a-leader [Accessed 2025-June-05]

[97] Badenhorst C Identifying and managing the impact of neuroleadership during organisational change [master's thesis]. New Zealand: Unitec; 2015

[98] Liu YZ, Jing YD, Gao M. Transformational leadership: From the

perspective of neurological leadership. Open Journal of Business and Management. 2015;**4**:143–152. DOI: 10.4236/ojl.2015.44013

[99] Waldman DA, Balthazard PA, Peterson SJ. Social cognitive neuroscience and leadership. The Leadership Quarterly. 2011;**22**(6): 1092–1106

[100] Boyatzis RE, Rochford K, Taylor SN. The role of the positive emotional attractor in vision and shared vision: Toward effective leadership, relationships, and engagement. Frontiers in Psychology. 2012;**3**:623

[101] Kuhlmann N, Kadgien CA. Neuroleadership: Themes and limitations of an emerging interdisciplinary field. In: Sage. 2018;**31** (3). DOI: 10.1177/0840470417747004

[102] Porter J. The neuroscience of leadership. Harvard Business Review. 2024;**102**(1):34–41

[103] Hannah ST, et al. The psychological and neurological bases of leader self-complexity and effects on adaptive decision-making. The Leadership Quarterly. 2021;**32**:101441

[104] Ruiz-Rodríguez M, et al Neuroscience and leadership: A review. Frontiers in Psychology. 2023;**14**:1178562

[105] Goldsmith M. What Got You Here Won't Get You There. London: Profile Books; 2010

[106] Buckingham M, Coffman C. First, Break All the Rules. New York: Simon & Schuster; 1999

[107] Ahmadiyan Z, Zareiyan A, Azizi M, Jahandari P, Jame SZB, Ganjizadeh H. Mediating role of happiness in the relationship between quantum leadership and organizational health at AJA University of Medical Sciences. Journal of Military Medicine. 2022;**23**(10):802–811. DOI: 10.30491/JMM.23.10.802

[108] Salas-Vallina A, Alegre J. Uncovering the link between leadership and happiness: A study of the mediating role of positive affect. Leadership & Organization Development Journal. 2018;**39**(7):917–929

[109] Ochsner KN, Lieberman MD. The emergence of social cognitive neuroscience. American Psychologist. 2001;**56**(9):717–734

[110] Substance Abuse and Mental Health Services Administration (SAMHSA). SAMHSA's concept of trauma and guidance for a trauma-informed approach [Internet]. 2014. Available from: https://ncsacw.samhsa.gov/userfiles/files/SAMHSA_Trauma.pdf [Accessed: 2025-December-05]

[111] Northouse PG. Leadership: Theory and Practice. 9th ed. Thousand Oaks: Sage; 2022

[112] Forbes Coaches Council. Understanding trauma-informed leadership [Internet]. Forbes. 2025 Apr 18. Available from: https://www.forbes.com/councils/forbescoachescouncil/2025/04/18/understanding-trauma-informed-leadership/ [Accessed 2025-December-27]

[113] The Center for Conscious Leadership. Why trauma-informed leadership matters. 2024. Available from: https://www.thecenterforconsciousleadership.com/learn/why-trauma-informed-leadership-matters [Accessed 2025-December-27]

[114] Guy-Evans O. Fight, flight, freeze, or fawn: How we respond to threats [Internet]. Simply Psychology. 2025. Available from: https://www.simplypsychology.org/fight-flight-freeze-fawn.html [Accessed 2025-December-28]

[115] U.S. Department of Health and Human Services. Workplace mental health and well-being: Report from the U.S. Surgeon General. 2022. Available from: https://www.hhs.gov/sites/default/files/workplace-mental-health-well-being.pdf [Accessed: 2025-December-13]

[116] Deci EL, Ryan RM. The "What" and "Why" of goal pursuits: Human needs and the self-determination of behavior. Psychological Inquiry. 2000;**11**(4):227–268. https://www.jstor.org/stable/1449618

[117] Cote C. How to Build Psychological Safety in the Workplace. Harvard Business School Online. 2025 May 20. Available from: https://online.hbs.edu/blog/post/psychological-safety-in-the-workplace [Accessed 2025-December-28]

[118] Weick KE, et al. Organizing and the Process of Sensemaking. Organization Science. 2005;**16**(4):409–421. https://www.jstor.org/stable/25145979

[119] Sonnentag S, Fritz C. Recovery from job stress: The stressor-detachment model as an integrative framework. Journal of Organizational Behavior. 2015;**36**(Suppl 1):S72–S103. DOI: 10.1002/job.1924

[120] Melillo A, Sansone N, Allan J, Gill N, Herrman H, Cano GM, Rodrigues M, Savage M, Galderisi S. Recovery-oriented and trauma-informed care for people with mental disorders to promote human rights and quality of mental health care: A scoping review. BMC Psychiatry. 2025;**25**(1):125. DOI: 10.1186/s12888-025-06473-4

[121] Longo L, Wickens CD, Hancock G, Hancock PA. Human Mental Workload: A Survey and a Novel Inclusive Definition. Frontiers in Psychology. 2022;**13**:883321. DOI: 10.3389/fpsyg.2022.883321

[122] Business Solver. State of Workplace Empathy [Internet]. 2025. Available from: https://378546.fs1.hubspotusercontent-na1.net/hubfs/378546/2025%20State%20of%20Workplace%20Empathy/Executive%20Report/businessolver-2025-state-of-workplace-empathy-report.pdf

[123] Hobson N, Depow GJ. How leaders can practice wise empathy. Harvard Business Review. 2026 Jan 14. Available from: https://hbr.org/2026/01/five-steps-to-identify-the-right-emotional-response-for-each-moment [Accessed 2026-January-15]

[124] Hernandez M. Promoting stewardship behavior in organizations: A leadership model. Journal of Business Ethics. 2008;**80**(1):121–128. https://www.jstor.org/stable/41219197

[125] Chari R, Chang -C-C, Sauter SL, Petrun Sayers EL, Huang W, Fisher GG. NIOSH Worker Well-being Questionnaire (Wellbq). Cincinnati, OH: U.S. Department of Health and Human Services, Centers for Disease Control and Prevention, National Institute for Occupational Safety and Health, DHHS (NIOSH) Publication No. 2021-110, (revised 05/2024); 2024. DOI: 10.26616/NIOSHPUB2021110revised052024

[126] Burger M, Coun MJH, Stoffers J, Van Den Heuvel S, Vanderstukken A, Van Waeyenberg T. Editorial: Positive leadership and worker well-being in dynamic regional contexts. Frontiers in Psychology. 2024;**14**:1349522. DOI: 10.3389/fpsyg.2023.1349522

[127] Jacobs C. Compassion in Leadership: Do You Lead with Heart? American Journal of Biomedical Science and Research. 2025;**26**(1):003404. DOI: 10.34297/AJBSR.2025.26.003404

Chapter 3

Burnout and Psychological Resilience in Healthcare Professionals: A Protective Psychosocial Resource

Nilgün Ulutaşdemir and Nevin Günaydın

Abstract

Burnout is a prevalent and multidimensional occupational syndrome that arises from unmanaged, chronic, work-related stress and is characterized by emotional exhaustion, depersonalization, and a reduced sense of personal accomplishment. Beyond its detrimental effects on individual mental health, burnout poses substantial risks to workforce sustainability, quality of care, patient safety, and the overall resilience of health systems. Due to persistent time pressure, chronic workload, ethical stress, emotional labor, and enduring organizational constraints, health professionals are among the occupational groups at the highest risk for burnout. This book chapter aims to provide a comprehensive perspective on burnout among health professionals by addressing the phenomenon within specific subsections focusing on nurses, physicians, and mental health professionals. The chapter emphasizes the necessity of conceptualizing burnout not merely as an individual-level problem, but as a phenomenon emerging from the dynamic interaction of organizational, individual, and systemic factors. Within this framework, psychological resilience is examined as a key protective psychosocial resource that buffers the development and consequences of burnout and regulates the adverse effects of work-related stress. Rather than being conceptualized as a fixed personality trait, psychological resilience is framed as a dynamic construct shaped by individual resources, organizational conditions, and systemic determinants. To explicate this multidimensional structure, a conceptual model is proposed. The chapter underscores that strategies aimed at reducing and preventing burnout among health professionals should not be confined to individual-level interventions alone, but must be supported by comprehensive approaches at the organizational and systemic levels.

Keywords: burnout, health professionals, psychological resilience, work-related stress, protective psychosocial resources, nursing, physicians, mental health professionals

1. Introduction

Burnout, characterized by depersonalization (cynicism), emotional exhaustion, and a diminished sense of personal accomplishment, is an occupational syndrome that develops as a result of prolonged and unmanaged work-related stress [1]. The consequences of burnout are wide-ranging, extending from adverse effects on individual mental health (including depression and anxiety disorders) to increased turnover intention, deterioration in the quality of patient care, and a higher incidence of medical errors and occupational injuries [2].

In recent years, growing attention has been directed toward the association between burnout and insufficient protective psychosocial resources. Accordingly, there is an increasing need to examine psychological resilience as a fundamental regulatory resource that enables health professionals to maintain functional capacity in the face of intense job demands [3, 4]. Evidence further suggests that the presence of psychological resilience can significantly mitigate the severity and persistence of burnout's adverse effects; however, it does not completely eliminate them.

In this chapter, burnout among health professionals will be examined through its systemic, individual, and organizational determinants. In addition, psychological resilience will be discussed as a protective psychosocial resource that regulates both the development and the impact of burnout.

2. Burnout among health professionals

Burnout, a syndrome frequently observed among health professionals, emerges as a consequence of chronic stress inherent to working life. According to the recent international consensus among experts, burnout is defined as *"a state of physical and emotional exhaustion experienced by an employee as a result of prolonged struggle with work-related problems"* [5, 6]. Due to continuous exposure to human suffering, time pressure, emotional labor, and high workload, health professionals constitute one of the occupational groups at the highest risk for burnout. In other words, unresolved and persistent stressors in the work environment precipitate the development of burnout. However, it has been reported that burnout levels vary among health professionals who are exposed to similar working conditions, indicating the influence of both organizational and individual factors. Within this context, psychological resilience is conceptualized as a key mediating variable that delays or prevents the transformation of chronic work-related stress into burnout [3, 7].

Burnout syndrome manifests across three core dimensions: emotional exhaustion, reduced personal accomplishment, and depersonalization [8–10]. Particularly among health professionals, factors such as long working hours, excessive workload, lack of organizational support, and challenging patient interactions play a decisive role in the development of burnout [9, 11, 12]. Studies conducted during epidemic periods, especially the COVID-19 pandemic, have identified clinical levels of burnout symptoms in a substantial proportion of health professionals – approximately half of the workforce [13, 14]. Burnout prevalence has been reported to be particularly high among those working in emergency departments and intensive care units [15].

Accordingly, the pandemic has demonstrated that psychological resilience among health professionals is not merely an individual attribute but also a capacity shaped by systemic conditions. Evidence suggests that health professionals with higher levels of psychological resilience report better psychological well-being and lower levels of burnout despite exposure to similar traumatic circumstances; however, in environments lacking organizational support, individual resilience alone has been shown to be insufficient [4, 13].

Burnout, which adversely affects the physical and mental well-being of health professionals, also leads to serious consequences for the quality of care, patient safety, and the sustainability of health systems [8, 16, 17]. Research indicates that burnout among health professionals is associated with increased medical errors, higher turnover intentions, and elevated risks to patient safety [12, 18, 19]. Consequently, the prevention and early identification of burnout have become priority issues in health policy at both institutional and individual levels [5, 9, 16].

The etiology of burnout is multifactorial. Excessive workload, long working hours, low professional recognition, inadequate social and organizational support, work–life imbalance, and ineffective leadership are among the primary risk factors [1, 7]. During the pandemic period, additional stressors, such as infection risk, uncertainty, resource shortages, and heightened societal expectations, further exacerbated these risks [2, 13, 14].

2.1 Profession-specific dynamics of burnout

Although the etiology of burnout shares common features across health professions, profession-specific role expectations, organizational positioning, and the inherent nature of the work give rise to distinct risk profiles across occupational groups (see **Table 1**).

2.1.1 Burnout among physicians

Physician burnout is a structurally embedded workplace syndrome with a global prevalence exceeding 50% in many settings [20–22]. Excessive workload, a heavy bureaucratic and clinical documentation burden, inefficient work processes, work–home conflict, limited professional autonomy, and weak institutional leadership have consistently been identified as the primary determinants of physician burnout [21–23]. Accordingly, physician burnout represents a widespread and chronic condition fueled by the convergence of high job demands, increasing administrative

Profession	Dominant risk factors	Factors strengthening psychological resilience
Physicians	High workload, administrative burden, limited autonomy	Supportive leadership, sense of meaning, and purpose
Nurses	Shift work, ethical stress, workplace violence	Team support and collegial collaboration
Mental health professionals	Emotional labor, countertransference	Clinical supervision

Table 1.
Risk and protective factors for burnout across health professions.

and electronic health record requirements, work–life imbalance, inadequate organizational leadership, and constrained autonomy. Across numerous countries, burnout symptoms have been reported in one-third or more of practicing physicians [11, 21, 23].

Extended working hours, time pressure, on-call duties, and the cognitive and emotional demands of clinical decision-making contribute substantially to emotional exhaustion. Simultaneously, insufficient resources, lack of organizational support, and effort–reward imbalance negatively affect both physicians' personal well-being and the quality of patient care [11, 24]. Higher burnout rates have been reported among younger and female physicians, particularly those working in high-intensity settings such as intensive care units, emergency departments, and other high-risk clinical environments. These elevated burnout levels have been associated with increased risks of depression, turnover intention, suicidal ideation, and medical errors [25–28]. Beyond its impact on individual physicians, burnout has detrimental consequences for the quality of care, patient safety, and healthcare system costs [21–23, 28].

Recent studies indicate that psychological resilience in physicians is positively associated not only with lower burnout levels but also with a greater intention to remain in the profession, higher-quality clinical decision-making, and improved perceptions of patient safety. Psychological resilience appears to function as a particularly important buffer against physician burnout when considered in conjunction with a sense of meaningful work, supportive leadership, and professional autonomy [22, 23].

2.1.2 Burnout among nurses

Burnout among nurses is defined as a structurally determined risk domain that is strongly associated with adverse working conditions, including long shifts (often exceeding 12 hours), high workloads, inadequate nurse-to-patient ratios, limited professional autonomy, and weak team or institutional climates [16, 29–32]. These conditions, sustained by chronic work-related stress, create a fertile ground for the development of a pervasive and persistent syndrome characterized by emotional exhaustion and a diminished sense of personal accomplishment among nurses [33–36].

Evidence from meta-analyses, systematic reviews, and umbrella reviews consistently demonstrates that the prevalence of emotional exhaustion and low personal accomplishment among nurses is high on a global scale. These patterns appear to be particularly pronounced among nurses working in mental health settings, intensive care units, and oncology departments [27, 32, 35, 37].

Burnout has been robustly linked to absenteeism, reduced job satisfaction, and increased staff turnover. Moreover, it has been consistently shown to compromise patient safety and quality of care, leading to higher rates of adverse events such as medication errors, healthcare-associated infections, and patient falls [16, 27, 29, 32–35].

From a psychosocial and organizational perspective, work–family conflict, lack of managerial support, work–life imbalance, effort–reward imbalance, role conflict, exposure to aggression and violence, and moral or ethical stress – such as providing care under resource constraints and value-based conflicts – constitute central determinants of nurse burnout [16, 23, 24, 27, 29, 36–38]. These organizational stressors are repeatedly identified as core risk factors contributing to burnout among nurses [23, 27, 33, 35, 36].

Against this background, psychological resilience emerges as a critical psychosocial resource that buffers the adverse effects of occupational risks, such as high workload and moral or ethical stress. Nurses with higher levels of self-compassion, perceived social support, and team cohesion have been reported to exhibit significantly lower levels of burnout symptoms compared with their counterparts working under similar conditions [4, 39].

2.1.3 Burnout among other mental health professionals

Burnout among other mental health professionals represents a multidimensional phenomenon arising from the convergence of continuous exposure to traumatic material, work practices requiring intensive emotional labor, complex and demanding caseloads, difficulties in managing countertransference processes, and frequently limited organizational resources [23, 37–39]. These psychosocial and structural factors contribute to sustained work-related stress, thereby creating conditions conducive to the development of burnout among professionals working in mental health settings.

Meta-analyses and systematic reviews indicate that psychologists and other mental health professionals experience relatively high levels of emotional exhaustion, moderate levels of depersonalization, and comparatively preserved levels of personal accomplishment [37, 39, 40]. The relative preservation of personal accomplishment has been interpreted as being associated with profession-inherent resources, such as perceived professional competence, motivation to help others, and a strong sense of meaning derived from therapeutic work [39].

From an organizational perspective, interpersonal difficulties, high workload, role ambiguity, role conflict, limited autonomy, ethical or moral distress, and perceptions of organizational injustice are identified as primary risk factors contributing to burnout among mental health professionals [23, 37–40]. In contrast, professional autonomy and role clarity, fair treatment, a supportive and ethically grounded institutional climate, regular clinical supervision, and work environments that foster professional identity emerge as key protective factors against burnout in this occupational group [23, 37–40].

Among psychotherapists, burnout constitutes a particularly critical and bidirectional risk domain, as it adversely affects not only clinicians' psychological well-being but also the quality of the therapeutic relationship and client outcomes [37, 39].

In mental health professionals, psychological resilience plays a central role in regulating emotional labor, secondary traumatization, and countertransference processes. Psychological resilience, nurtured by a sense of professional meaning and robust ethical support mechanisms, is therefore considered a critical protective factor against burnout in this population [39].

3. Psychological resilience as a protective factor

Psychological resilience is conceptualized as a regulatory mechanism that modulates the duration, severity, and consequences of burnout when the

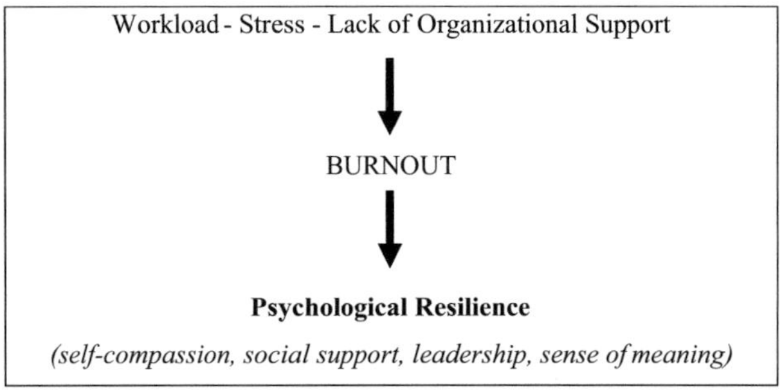

Figure 1.
A relational model of burnout and psychological resilience among health professionals.

balance between individual and organizational resources and job demands is disrupted. Psychological resilience is defined as an individual's capacity to maintain functioning and to adapt to, withstand, and recover from stressful, challenging, and traumatic life events (see **Figure 1**) [3, 41]. Among health professionals, psychological resilience is positively associated with professional commitment, job satisfaction, and psychological well-being, and is regarded as a key protective factor against burnout [42–44]. In the design of interventions targeting health professionals, the contemporary shift toward conceptualizing psychological resilience not as a static personality trait but as a developable and time-sensitive process represents a paradigmatic transformation in the field [3, 7].

Health professionals with higher levels of resilience have been shown to exhibit stronger emotional regulation skills, more effective coping with stress, and a greater ability to preserve a sense of professional meaning. Social support, self-compassion, a positive workplace climate, self-care behaviors, and supportive leadership are among the core factors that strengthen psychological resilience [45, 46].

4. Structural and individual determinants of psychological resilience

Psychological resilience is conceptualized not as an outcome confined to specific intervention programs, but as a dynamic psychosocial resource shaped by individuals' personal characteristics in continuous interaction with their work context and sense of professional meaning. Recent systematic reviews indicate that psychological resilience is inversely associated with burnout and depressive symptoms through core components such as cognitive flexibility, emotional regulation, and a sense of professional meaning [3, 47].

Rather than constituting an individual attribute in isolation, psychological resilience emerges from the interaction of factors operating at the individual, organizational, and systemic levels. This multilevel structure is summarized in the conceptual model presented in **Figure 2**.

Self-care orientation, self-compassion, and perceived social support are among the core individual-level components of psychological resilience [45, 46]. At the organizational level, work–life balance, perceptions of supportive leadership, and

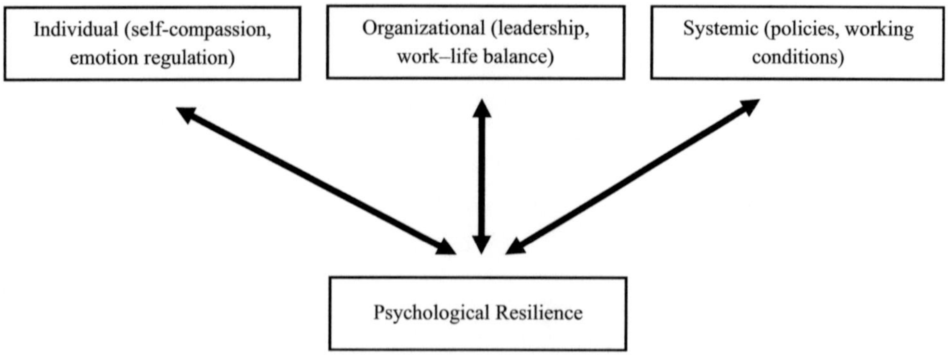

Figure 2.
Individual and structural components of psychological resilience (a buffering mechanism against burnout).

team-based social support are identified as key determinants shaping psychological resilience within the workplace context [4, 7].

5. Conclusion

Burnout among health professionals is a prevalent and multidimensional problem that directly affects the functioning of health systems. The existing literature indicates that burnout levels vary across professional groups; in particular, physicians and nurses have been reported to exhibit higher levels of burnout and lower levels of psychological resilience compared with other health professionals.

Strengthening psychological resilience has, therefore, emerged as a core strategy for the prevention and reduction of burnout at both individual and organizational levels. Future research should conceptualize psychological resilience not merely as an individual skill but as a protective resource that is shaped through continuous interaction with the organizational context.

From this perspective, psychological resilience should be regarded not as the outcome of standardized interventions, but as a psychosocial state that health professionals develop dynamically throughout their professional lives. Accordingly, initiatives aimed at enhancing psychological resilience should not be limited to individual-level training programs; rather, they should be implemented as multilevel interventions encompassing organizational culture, leadership practices, and working conditions. In parallel, health policies should support these efforts through structural reforms that target working conditions, organizational climate, and leadership practices.

AI use disclosure

The author acknowledges the use of AI for language polishing and refinement of the book chapter. The tables and figures used in the chapter were created by the authors.

Author details

Nilgün Ulutaşdemir[1*] and Nevin Günaydın[2]

1 Department of Public Health, Faculty of Medicine, Ordu University, Ordu, Turkey

2 Department of Psychiatric Nursing, Faculty of Health Sciences, Ordu University, Ordu, Turkey

*Address all correspondence to: nulutasdemir@yahoo.com

References

[1] Bridgeman PJ, Bridgeman MB, Barone J. Burnout syndrome among healthcare professionals. The Bulletin of the American Society of Hospital Pharmacists. 2018;**75**(3):147–152. DOI: 10.2146/ajhp170460

[2] Leo CG, Sabina S, Tumolo MR, Bodini A, Ponzini G, Sabato E, Mincarone P. Burnout among healthcare workers in the COVID 19 era: A review of the existing literature. Frontiers in Public Health. 2021;**9**:750529. DOI: 10.3389/fpubh.2021.750529

[3] Kunzler AM, Helmreich I, Chmitorz A, Koenig J, Binder H, Wessa M, Lieb K. Psychological interventions to foster resilience in healthcare professionals. Cochrane Database of Systematic Reviews. 2020;**2020**(7). DOI: 10.1002/14651858.CD012527.pub2

[4] Labrague LJ. Psychological resilience, coping behaviours and social support among health care workers during the COVID-19 pandemic: A systematic review of quantitative studies. Journal of Nursing Management. 2021;**29**(7):1893–1905. DOI: 10.1111/jonm.13336

[5] Canu IG, Marca SC, Dell'Oro F, Balázs Á, Bergamaschi E, Besse C, . . . Wahlen A. Harmonized definition of occupational burnout: A systematic review, semantic analysis, and Delphi consensus in 29 countries. Scandinavian Journal of Work, Environment & Health. 2021;**47**(2):95–107. DOI: 10.5271/sjweh.3935

[6] Schaufeli W. The burnout enigma solved? Scandinavian Journal of Work, Environment & Health. 2021;**47**(3):169–170. DOI: 10.5271/sjweh.3950

[7] Meredith LS, Bouskill K, Chang J, Larkin J, Motala A, Hempel S. Predictors of burnout among US healthcare providers: A systematic review. BMJ Open. 2022;**12**(8):e054243. DOI: 10.1136/bmjopen-2021-054243

[8] Chemali Z, Ezzeddine FL, Gelaye B, Dossett ML, Salameh J, Bizri M, . . . Fricchione G. Burnout among healthcare providers in the complex environment of the Middle East: A systematic review. BMC Public Health. 2019;**19**(1):1337. DOI: 10.1186/s12889-019-7713-1

[9] Tang YL, Raffone A, Wong SYS. Burnout and stress: New insights and interventions. Scientific Reports. 2025;**15**(1):8335. DOI: 10.1038/s41598-025-92909-6

[10] Yang Y, Hayes JA. Causes and consequences of burnout among mental health professionals: A practice-oriented review of recent empirical literature. Psychotherapy. 2020;**57**(3):426–436

[11] De Hert S. Burnout in healthcare workers: Prevalence, impact and preventative strategies. Local and Regional Anesthesia. 2020;**13**:171–183. DOI: 10.2147/LRA.S240564

[12] Gasciauskaite G, Lunkiewicz J, Braun J, Kolbe M, Seelandt J, Spahn DR, . . . Tscholl DW. Burnout and its determinants among anaesthesia care providers in Switzerland: A multicentre cross-sectional study. Anaesthesia. 2024;**79**(2):168–177. DOI: 10.1111/anae.16171

[13] Ghahramani S, Lankarani KB, Yousefi M, Heydari K, Shahabi S, Azmand S. A systematic review and meta-analysis of burnout among healthcare workers during COVID-19. Frontiers in Psychiatry. 2021;**12**:758849. DOI: 10.3389/fpsyt.2021.758849

[14] Jalili M, Niroomand M, Hadavand F, Zeinali K, Fotouhi A. Burnout among healthcare professionals during COVID-19 pandemic: A cross-sectional study. International Archives of Occupational and Environmental Health. 2021;**94**(6):1345–1352. DOI: 10.1007/s00420-021-01695-x

[15] Krishna GG, Harbli NMA, Krishnan N, Ghundul LB, Aldhahri R, Aldossary AB, … AlAhmari AD. Burnout among ICU and non-ICU healthcare professionals in Saudi Arabia: A comparative cross-sectional analysis. Journal of Multidisciplinary Healthcare. 2025;**18**:995–1005. DOI: 10.2147/JMDH.S503896

[16] Cohen C, Pignata S, Bezak E, Tie M, Childs J. Workplace interventions to improve well-being and reduce burnout for nurses, physicians and allied healthcare professionals: A systematic review. BMJ Open. 2023;**13**(6):e071203. DOI: 10.1136/bmjopen-2022-071203

[17] Nagarajan R, Ramachandran P, Dilipkumar R, Kaur P. Global estimate of burnout among the public health workforce: A systematic review and meta-analysis. Human Resources for Health. 2024;**22**(1):30. DOI: 10.1186/s12960-024-00917-w

[18] de Godoy CCF, Lima AR, Hino P, Taminato M, Okuno MFP, Fernandes H. Burnout syndrome and accidents in primary healthcare nursing workers: A scoping review. BMC Nursing. 2025;**24**(1):410. DOI: 10.1186/s12912-025-03004-0

[19] Jachmann A, Loser A, Mettler A, Exadaktylos A, Müller M, Klingberg K. Burnout, depression, and stress in emergency department nurses and physicians and the impact on private and work life: A systematic review. JACEP Open. 2025;**6**(2):100046. DOI: 10.1016/j.acepjo.2025.100046

[20] Chandawarkar A, Chaparro JD. Burnout in clinicians. Current Problems in Pediatric and Adolescent Health Care. 2021;**51**(11):101104. DOI: 10.1016/j.cppeds.2021.101104

[21] Macaron MM, Segun-Omosehin OA, Matar RH, Beran A, Nakanishi H, Than CA, Abulseoud OA. A systematic review and meta analysis on burnout in physicians during the COVID-19 pandemic: A hidden healthcare crisis. Frontiers in Psychiatry. 2023;**13**:1071397. DOI: 10.3389/fpsyt.2022.1071397

[22] West CP, Dyrbye LN, Shanafelt TD. Physician burnout: Contributors, consequences and solutions. Journal of Internal Medicine. 2018;**283**(6):516–529. DOI: 10.1111/joim.12752

[23] Amiri 3S, Mahmood N, Mustafa H, Javaid SF, Khan MA. Occupational risk factors for burnout syndrome among healthcare professionals: A global systematic review and meta-analysis. International Journal of Environmental Research and Public Health. 2024;**21**(12):1583. DOI: 10.3390/ijerph21121583

[24] Hämmig O. Explaining burnout and the intention to leave the profession among health professionals-a cross-sectional study in a hospital setting in Switzerland. BMC Health Services Research. 2018;**18**(1):785. DOI: 10.1186/s12913-018-3556-1

[25] Cotobal Rodeles S, Martín Sánchez FJ, Martínez-Sellés M. Physician and medical student burnout, a narrative literature review: Challenges, strategies, and a call to action. Journal of Clinical Medicine. 2025;**14**(7):2263. DOI: 10.3390/jcm14072263

[26] Kansoun Z, Boyer L, Hodgkinson M, Villes V, Lançon C, Fond G. Burnout in French physicians: A systematic review and meta-analysis. Journal of Affective Disorders. 2019;**246**:132–147. DOI: 10.1016/j.jad.2018.12.056

[27] Papazian L, Hraiech S, Loundou A, Herrid4ge MS, Boyer L. High-level burnout in physicians and nurses working in adult ICUs: A systematic review and meta-analysis. Intensive Care Medicine. 2023;**49**(4):387–400. DOI: 10.1007/s00134-023-07025-8

[28] Williams ES, Rathert C, Buttigieg SC. The personal and professional consequences of physician burnout: A systematic review of the literature. Medical Care Research and Review. 2020;**77**(5):371–386. DOI: 10.1177/1077558719856787

[29] Aiken LH, Lasater KB, Sloane DM, Pogue CA, Rosenbaum KEF, Muir KJ; US Clinician Wellbeing Study Consortium. Physician and nurse well-being and preferred interventions to address burnout in hospital practice: Factors associated with turnover, outcomes, and patient safety. JAMA Health Forum. 2023;**4**(7):e231809. DOI: 10.1001/jamahealthforum.2023.1809

[30] Dall'Ora C, Ball J, Reinius M, Griffiths P. Burnout in nursing: A theoretical review. Human Resources for Health. 2020;**18**(1):41. DOI: 10.1186/s12960-020-00469-9

[31] Jaber MJ, Bindahmsh AA, Baker OG, Alaqlan A, Almotairi SM, Elmohandis ZE, . . . Abuzir BM. Burnout combating strategies, triggers, implications, and self-coping mechanisms among nurses working in Saudi Arabia: A multicenter, mixed methods study. BMC Nursing. 2025;**24**(1):590. DOI: 10.1186/s12912-025-03191-w

[32] Quesada-Puga C, Izquierdo-Espin FJ, Membrive-Jimenez MJ, Aguayo-Estremera R, Cañadas-De La Fuente GA, Romero-Bejar JL, Gomez-Urquiza JL. Job satisfaction and burnout syndrome among intensive-care unit nurses: A systematic review and meta-analysis. Intensive and Critical Care Nursing. 2024;**82**:103660. DOI: 10.1016/j.iccn.2024.103660

[33] Batista TC, Nappi I, Xavier MVM, Fiuza IO, de Vasconcelos CBM, Enohi RT. Burnout in nursing: Causal factors and impacts on health and professional performance-a systematic review. Revista Brasileira de Medicina Do Trabalho. 2025;**23**(3):e20251432. DOI: 10.47626/1679-4435-2025-1432

[34] Cao Y, Dong Y, Shi L, Chappell K, Jia Z, Yan T, Gao Y. Occupational burnout in nurses is due to long-term work stress rather than COVID-19 pandemic event. Journal of Advanced Nursing. 2025. DOI: 10.1111/jan.17085

[35] Getie A, Ayenew T, Amlak BT, Gedfew M, Edmealem A, Kebede WM. Global prevalence and contributing factors of nurse burnout: An umbrella review of systematic review and meta-analysis. BMC Nursing. 2025;**24**(1):596. DOI: 10.1186/s12912-025-03266-8

[36] Nogueira LDS, Sousa RMCD, Guedes EDS, Santos MAD, Turrini RNT, Cruz DDALMD. Burnout and nursing work environment in public health institutions. Revista Brasileira de Enfermagem. 2018;**71**(2):336–342. DOI: 10.1590/0034-7167-2016-0524

[37] López-López IM, Gómez-Urquiza JL, Cañadas GR, De la Fuente EI, Albendín-García L, Cañadas-de la Fuente GA. Prevalence of burnout in mental health nurses and related factors: A systematic review and meta-analysis. International Journal of Mental Health Nursing. 2019;**28**(5):1035–1044. DOI: 10.1111/inm.12606

[38] Kjos AL, Gnacinski SL, Wahl CA. An exploratory model of how ethical indicators predict health professional burnout. Research in Nursing & Health. 2025;**48**(3):310–323. DOI: 10.1002/nur.22453

[39] O'Connor K, Neff DM, Pitman S. Burnout in mental health professionals: A systematic review and meta-analysis of prevalence and determinants. European Psychiatry. 2018;**53**:74–99. DOI: 10.1016/j.eurpsy.2018.06.003

[40] Claponea RM, Iorga M. Burnout, organizational justice, workload, and emotional regulation among medical and non-medical personnel working in Romanian healthcare units. Behavioral Sciences. 2023;**13**(3):225. DOI: 10.3390/bs13030225

[41] Bozdağ F, Ergün N. Psychological resilience of healthcare professionals during Covid-19 Pandemic. Psychological Reports. 2021;**124**(6):2567–2586. DOI: 10.1177/0033294120965477

[42] Alonazi O, Alshowkan A, Shdaifat E. The relationship between psychological resilience and professional quality of life among mental health nurses: A cross-sectional study. BMC Nursing. 2023;**22**(1):184. DOI: 10.1186/s12912-023-01346-1

[43] Dhillon PK, Das S. Psychological resilience of frontline healthcare workers in India: A mixed-methods exploratory study during COVID-19 pandemic in India. Preventive Medicine: Research & Reviews. 2024;**1**(3):121–124. DOI: 10.4103/PMRR.PMRR_56_23

[44] Mcizana T, Adams S, Khan S, Ntatamala I. Sociodemographic and work-related factors associated with psychological resilience in South African healthcare workers: A cross-sectional study. BMC Health Services Research. 2024;**24**(1):979. DOI: 10.1186/s12913-024-11430-0

[45] Pank C, von Boros L, Lieb K, Dalkner N, Egger-Lampl S, Lehr D, ... Wessa M. The role of self-care and self-compassion in networks of resilience and stress among healthcare professionals. Scientific Reports. 2025;**15**(1):18545. DOI: 10.1038/s41598-025-01111-1

[46] Hashem Z, Zeinoun P. Self-compassion explains less burnout among healthcare professionals. Mindfulness. 2020;**11**(11):2542–2551. DOI: 10.1007/s12671-020-01469-5

[47] Heath C, Sommerfield A, von Ungern-sternberg BS. Resilience strategies to manage psychological distress among healthcare workers during the COVID-19 pandemic: A narrative review. Anaesthesia. 2020;**75**(10):1364–1371. DOI: 10.1111/anae.15180

Chapter 4

Burnout Syndrome in Neurosurgeons: Prevalence, Determinants and Prevention Strategies

Ram Prasad Subedi, Aashish Baniya, Bikram Bhandari, Suraj Thulung, Suresh Bishokarma and Sagun Ghimire

Abstract

The neurosurgical profession, while hugely rewarding, poses a unique kind of stressor that predisposes its practitioners to burnout at increasing rates. This syndrome, characterized by emotional exhaustion, depersonalization, and a reduced sense of personal accomplishment, has significant implications for clinician well-being, patient safety, and healthcare system stability. This chapter provides an overview of the current global scenario of burnout in neurosurgery. The aetiology of burnout is analysed through an ecological framework, examining macro-level healthcare system failures, meso-level departmental cultural factors, and micro-level individual vulnerabilities. A central focus of this chapter is that effective mitigation requires a move beyond individual-focused resilience training toward mandated systemic and organizational reforms. Evidence-based interventions are evaluated across these levels, proposing a cohesive strategy that includes optimizing bureaucratic workflows, cultivating empathetic leadership, and fostering a culture that normalizes well-being. The conclusion asserts that the sustainability of the neurosurgical workforce depends on a fundamental re-evaluation of professional structures and norms to prioritize the human capital within the specialty.

Keywords: burnout, neurosurgical burnout, physician well-being, occupational stress, healthcare systems, organizational interventions

1. Introduction

Burnout syndrome (BS) is defined as a condition of emotional exhaustion (EE), feelings of depersonalization (DP), and a lack of personal accomplishment (PA), specifically related to stress at work [1]. Although the medical community has shown increasing interest in this topic in recent years, BS has been recognized for decades, ever since Freudenberger first described it in 1974. The term 'burnout'was first defined by him to describe the EE experienced by civil servants [2].

Burnout has been associated with reduced job satisfaction and a higher likelihood of medical errors. It is also linked to greater alcohol and substance misuse, as well as difficulties in maintaining healthy interpersonal relationships. Considering its potential effects on the quality of patient care, burnout could carry medico-legal and financial consequences for surgeons and their healthcare institutions [3–6].

Burnout also serves as a contributing factor to depression and substance abuse among healthcare professionals [7–12]. It is one of the most prevalent mental health challenges encountered by medical and surgical residents – junior doctors with Bachelor of Medicine and Bachelor of Surgery or undergraduate Doctor of Medicine degrees – who are completing supervised specialty training [13]. Moreover, burnout leads to decreased job satisfaction and adversely affects both the mental and physical well-being of these trainees [14–16].

Neurosurgical residency presents an intense and demanding path characterized by steep learning curves, rigorous experiences, and high expectations [17]. Residents must balance a complex mix of cognitive sharpness, technical skill, emotional strength, and sustained wellness [18]. These aspects of neurosurgical training are deeply interconnected – each influencing and being influenced by the others – creating a dynamic relationship that profoundly affects both the residents' personal well-being and their professional development [10, 11].

A surgeon's ability to perform with precision and accuracy is closely linked to their overall health [19]. However, many surgeons tend to push themselves beyond their physical and mental limits, often neglecting their own well-being, ultimately compromising the quality of care they deliver to patients [20, 21]. Healthy sleep is defined by subjective satisfaction, sufficient duration, high efficiency, proper timing, and sustained alertness during the day [22]. Burnout, resulting from demanding work conditions and emotional strain, poses a serious threat to surgeons' health. Chronic sleep deprivation among doctors can lead to frequent nighttime awakenings, insomnia, excessive daytime sleepiness, irritability, and a higher likelihood of making errors [23–25]. Research by St-Onge et al. [26] revealed that individuals with shorter sleep durations tend to consume more calories, primarily from snacks and fatty foods. Persistent lack of sleep also significantly increases the risk of developing cardiovascular diseases, hypertension, and diabetes mellitus [27].

This chapter aims to provide a contemporary and exhaustive review of burnout in neurosurgery. We will briefly talk about its global prevalence, deconstruct its multifactorial aetiology with a specific focus on systemic drivers, and critically appraise a hierarchy of interventions, arguing that sustainable change is contingent upon foundational reforms to the structure and culture of neurosurgical practice.

2. Global prevalence

Extensive research over the past decade consistently confirms that burnout is not an isolated issue but an endemic challenge within neurosurgery worldwide, affecting a significant majority of its workforce at various career stages [28, 29]. Burnout results from prolonged professional and emotional strain that develops when workplace dissatisfaction goes unaddressed [30]. However, burnout should not be seen as an inevitable outcome of routine job stress or personal dedication. Instead, it arises when emotional strain is not adequately balanced by the internal satisfaction gained from practicing medicine or by restorative activities, such as hobbies and physical exercise [31].

2.1 The burden on practicing neurosurgeons

A landmark national survey of American neurosurgeons by Attenello et al. [13] revealed that about 67% of respondents reported symptoms consistent with burnout, with particularly high scores in the domains of EE and DP. This study identified the mid-career stage as a period of heightened vulnerability, likely due to the convergence of peak clinical, administrative, and academic duties. Contemporary reports indicate this crisis persists. Recent industry surveys, such as the Medscape [19] report, continue to find that approximately half of all neurosurgeons experience burnout, consistently citing excessive bureaucratic tasks and long working hours as primary reasons.

This phenomenon goes beyond national borders. Research by Zaed et al. [23], involving neurosurgeons across multiple continents, found remarkably consistent burnout rates of 48%, while that of neurosurgeons was a bit higher, that is, 51.1%, suggesting that the core stressors of the specialty are universal. While local healthcare policies may modulate certain pressures, the fundamental challenges of the work appear to generate a shared experience of psychological strain among neurosurgeons globally.

2.2 The vulnerable population of trainees

Neurosurgical residency represents a period of extreme occupational hazard for burnout. The confluence of extended duty hours, immense academic pressure, and the transition to managing high-stakes cases creates a perfect storm [32–36]. A systematic review and meta-analysis by Zaed et al. [23] consolidated data from numerous studies and found a pooled burnout prevalence of 51.56% among neurosurgery residents, a figure that starkly exceeds rates in many other medical specialties, as shown in **Table 1**.

3. Determinants of burnout

3.1 Multi-systems analysis

The aetiology of burnout is best understood not as a result of a single stressor, but as the outcome of a complex interaction between factors at different ecological levels [37]. These factors can be categorized into three sub-headings: Macro-system, Meso-system, and Micro-system, as shown in **Figure 1**.

Study	Country/Region	Population (n)	Key finding
Attenello et al. [13]	United States of America (USA)	Attending neurosurgeons (1,023)	67% reported burnout; the mid-career stage was a key risk factor.
Medscape [19]	USA	Practicing neurosurgeons	53% reported burnout; bureaucracy (61%) was the top cause.
Zaed et al. [23]	Multi-national	Physicians (3310)	51.1% overall burnout rate among neurosurgeons, consistent across continents.

Table 1.
Summary of studies on burnout prevalence in neurosurgery.

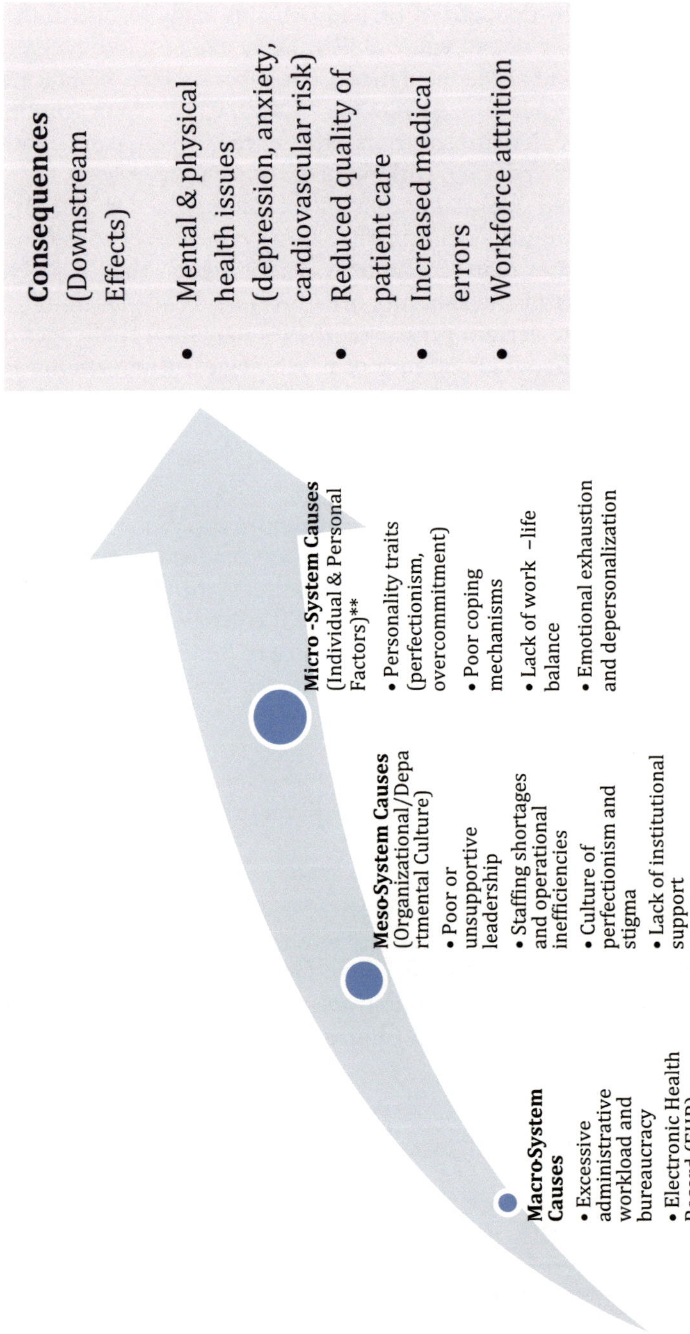

Figure 1.
Burnout in neurosurgeons: Causes and consequences.

3.2 Macro-system: The broader healthcare environment

This level encompasses the large-scale, often rigid structures that define modern medical practice.

- **Administrative and documentation burden:** The most frequently cited contemporary stressor is the overwhelming burden of electronic health records (EHRs) and regulatory paperwork. Neurosurgeons now expend significant portions of their workday on data entry and clerical tasks, often during personal time, which decreases clinical engagement and directly contributes to exhaustion [12].

- **Productivity-focused economic models:** The prevailing emphasis on relative value units (RVUs) and clinical throughput creates tension between financial viability and patient-centred care. This pressure can force surgeons to prioritize volume over the time required for complex decision-making and empathetic communication.

- **The litigious environment:** Operating under the constant shadow of high malpractice risk fosters a deep sense of vulnerability. This environment encourages the practice of defensive medicine, where clinical decisions are influenced more by mitigating legal risk than by purely medical rationale [18].

3.3 Meso-system: The departmental and organizational culture

The immediate work environment, shaped by local leadership and institutional norms, plays a critical role in modulating stress.

- **The impact of leadership:** The style and quality of departmental leadership are powerfully correlated with burnout rates. Unsupportive leadership exacerbates distress, whereas leaders who demonstrate empathy, transparency, and foster psychological safety – where team members can voice concerns without fear – can significantly buffer against burnout [20, 38].

- **Operational inefficiencies:** Inadequate access to operating rooms, staffing shortages, and lack of support from advanced practice providers create a daily struggle and impede workflow, preventing neurosurgeons from practicing efficiently and effectively [37].

- **A culture of perfectionism and stigma:** The traditional surgical culture has historically valued invulnerability and relentless endurance. Within this framework, acknowledging psychological distress is often misconstrued as weakness, creating a powerful barrier to seeking help and perpetuating a cycle of silent suffering [17].

3.4 Micro-system: Individual factors and vulnerabilities

While systemic factors are paramount, individual characteristics influence susceptibility.

- **Personality and disposition:** The self-selection into neurosurgery often attracts individuals with high levels of diligence, perfectionism, and drive. While these traits are assets for mastering a complex field, they can become risk factors when they manifest as an inability to delegate, unrealistic self-criticism, or a lack of self-compassion in the face of adverse events [39].

- **Coping:** The strategies an individual employs to manage stress are pivotal. Adaptive mechanisms, such as mindfulness practice, physical activity, and maintaining social connections, build resilience [40]. In contrast, maladaptive strategies, like social isolation or substance use, accelerate the progression of burnout [24].

- **Work–life integration:** The all-encompassing nature of neurosurgical practice frequently leads to the neglect of personal health, family relationships, and restorative leisure activities. This imbalance fosters a life perceived as dominated by obligation, fuelling cynicism and emotional depletion.

4. Consequences of burnout

The impact of burnout creates a destructive cascade that extends from the individual surgeon to the patient and the broader healthcare ecosystem.

4.1 Impact on the neurosurgeon

- **Psychological and physical health:** Burnout is a significant risk factor for the development of major depressive disorder, anxiety disorders, and substance misuse. It is also associated with an increased incidence of cardiovascular disease and is a key contributor to the disproportionately high rate of suicide within the medical profession [20].

4.2 Impact on patient care and safety

- **Patient safety and medical errors:** A direct correlation exists between physician burnout and self-reported medical errors [41]. Cognitive depletion and emotional disengagement impair the vigilance and clinical judgment necessary for safe practice [22]. People who felt that they had too many patients to care for were more likely to express a sense of emotional distance and negative attitudes toward their patients [28].

- **The patient–physician relationship:** DP directly impairs communication, reduces expressed empathy, and leads to lower levels of patient satisfaction and trust.

- **Quality of clinical outcomes:** The cognitive deficits associated with chronic burnout can result in diagnostic delays, less optimal surgical planning, and, ultimately, poorer overall patient outcomes.

4.3 Impact on the healthcare system

- **Workforce sustainability:** Burnout is a primary driver behind neurosurgeons reducing their clinical hours, leaving academic practice, or opting for early retirement. The financial cost of recruiting and on boarding a replacement subspecialist surgeon is monumental, representing a severe economic loss to healthcare institutions [16].

- **Cultural degradation:** Widespread burnout fosters a toxic, self-perpetuating work environment, making it difficult to attract new talent and creating a culture characterized by disengagement, irritability, and low morale.

5. Multi-level framework for intervention and prevention

Addressing this multifactorial crisis requires an integrated, multi-level approach. Isolated, individual-focused wellness initiatives are insufficient; the solution must be as comprehensive and integrated as the problem.

5.1 Tier 1: Macro-system and institutional reforms

These high-level interventions target the root causes of burnout. To effectively and safely meet the needs of a growing patient population, it is crucial to establish institutional programs aimed at reducing potential stressors that contribute to excessive stress and burnout within the neurosurgical community [40, 41].

- **EHR optimization and team-based documentation:** Healthcare organizations must invest in user-centred design for EHR systems. A highly effective strategy is the deployment of medical scribes, which has been demonstrated in controlled studies to significantly reduce physician documentation burden, improve job satisfaction, and lower burnout rates without sacrificing the quality of medical records [15].

- **Rationalizing compensation and incentives:** Changing from purely productivity-based models to blended systems that also reward quality, patient experience, teaching, and teamwork can help realign financial incentives with professional values and fulfilment.

- **Advocating for policy-level guardrails:** Following the precedent set by resident duty-hour limits, there is a growing imperative to establish similar protective policies for attending physicians, such as mandated time off between consecutive night-call shifts and reasonable limits on clinical work hours.

5.2 Tier 2: Meso-system and departmental initiatives

By creating policies that ensure employees can fully disconnect from work during their time off, organizations can better support mental recovery. Since two-thirds of neurosurgeons cited sleep deprivation as a major factor in burnout, tackling this issue is also essential. Modifying call schedules and providing on-site sleep facilities could help lessen fatigue, improving rest and readiness to meet professional demands. Moreover, initiatives that strengthen neurosurgeons' sense of PA – such as mentorship, career development, and recognition programs – may help prevent burnout. Institutions should aim not only to reduce EE and DP but also to build workplaces that value and celebrate achievement, thereby improving job satisfaction and long-term well-being [29].

Departmental leadership possesses the agency to cultivate a local culture of well-being.

- **Investing in leadership development:** Training programs for department chairs and division chiefs, focused on empathetic leadership, change management, and the early recognition of burnout in team members, are essential. Leader evaluations should incorporate metrics related to faculty well-being and engagement [21].

- **Promoting autonomy and flexibility:** Granting neurosurgeons greater control over their schedules, clinic structures, and administrative duties can restore a crucial sense of agency and self-determination.

- **Establishing robust support infrastructures:** This includes creating formal, confidential peer support programs for clinicians involved in adverse events, ensuring access to mental health professionals skilled in treating physicians, and forming departmental well-being committees with the authority and resources to implement meaningful change.

5.3 Tier 3: Micro-system and individual empowerment strategies

While secondary to systemic change, individual strategies are vital for building personal resilience. For neurosurgical residents, factors such as age, marital status, and participation in sports or leisure activities have minimal impact on the likelihood of experiencing burnout [32].

- **Mindfulness-based stress reduction (MBSR):** This empirically validated, structured program is the most well-supported individual intervention for reducing symptoms of burnout, enhancing emotional regulation, and improving cognitive focus [24]. Another intervention that provided an educational program on mindfulness meditation, self-awareness, and meaningful clinical narratives demonstrated improvements in mindfulness, burnout reduction, decreased DP, an enhanced sense of PA, and greater empathy [39].

- **Professional coaching:** Distinct from therapy, professional coaching focuses on skill-building, goal achievement, and personal development. Evidence indicates that executive coaching for physicians can lead to significant improvements in well-being, leadership efficacy, and career satisfaction [14]. Establishing support groups is essential for neurosurgeons and residents, as these provide a space to share experiences, gain expert guidance on recognizing the signs and symptoms of burnout, learn effective coping strategies for managing severe burnout, and promote the development of wellness programs [33–36].

- **Intentional cultivation of meaning and community:** Proactively reconnecting with the fundamental purpose of neurosurgery, through mentoring, teaching, or engaging in quality improvement, can rekindle professional fulfilments. Nurturing strong, supportive collegial relationships provides an indispensable buffer against the inherent stresses of the profession. Furthermore, the implementation of frequent interviews and psychological assessments can also be used as a good tool for screening and prevention of burnout among neurosurgeons and residents in neurosurgery [37]. An intervention that incorporates facilitated physician discussion groups focused on mindfulness, reflection, shared experiences, and small-group learning has been shown to enhance empowerment and workplace engagement while reducing DP and overall burnout among participating physicians [38].

6. Conclusion

The nature of burnout in neurosurgery is an absolute indicator of a professional ecosystem in distress. It is a systemic failure, not an individual one. The evidence is clear, the causative factors are well-documented, and the human and financial costs are unsustainable. The era of imploring neurosurgeons to simply become more resilient without concurrently fixing the broken systems in which they work must conclude. The path forward demands a huge shift in how the well-being of healthcare professionals is valued. It requires healthcare systems, regulatory bodies, and professional societies to acknowledge their responsibility and act boldly. This includes fundamentally redesigning bureaucratic processes, creating rational and humane economic models, and cultivating leadership that prioritizes its people. Alongside, the cultural narrative within neurosurgery must evolve from one of silent endurance to one of collective support, psychological safety, and shared purpose. For the individual neurosurgeon, the motto is to maintain their own well-being with the same determination they apply to their craft and to advocate unwaveringly for the systemic changes that are their right. The future vitality, integrity, and clinical excellence of neurosurgery depend on this transformation. By confronting the burnout crisis with the same resolve and ingenuity applied to the most complex surgical challenges, the profession can cross from its current state of crisis to a future of sustainable practice and renewed purpose.

7. Recommendations

It is becoming more widely acknowledged that burnout among neurosurgeons is a result of organizational and structural issues rather than a sign of personal weakness or insufficient coping mechanisms. Neurosurgeons are under constant strain from a variety of factors, including an overwhelming clinical workload, lengthy and erratic work hours, administrative obligations, medico-legal stress, limited professional autonomy, and inadequate institutional support.

Evidence from large multicentre studies and meta-analyses consistently indicates that structural elements – including the work environment, staffing adequacy, and institutional culture – play a dominant role in driving burnout across neurosurgery and other surgical specialties.

In the current era, burnout is emerging as a system-level issue, and we recommend some strong strategies for its mitigation. Reducing non-clinical administrative duties, ensuring sufficient staffing and resource distribution, rationalizing duty hours and on-call schedules, and bolstering supportive leadership and mentorship structures are some of these tactics. Developing a culture of psychological safety and offering easily accessible, institutionally sponsored mental health and wellness activities are also prioritized. Without active participation from healthcare leadership and the execution of policy-level initiatives, a significant and long-lasting decrease in burnout is improbable. The systemic perspective and the suggested interventions have been supported by appropriate references.

Acronyms and abbreviations

BS	Burnout syndrome
EE	Emotional exhaustion
PA	Personal accomplishment
USA	United States of America
EHR	Electronic health records
RVU	Relative value unit
MBSR	Mindfulness-based stress reduction

Acknowledgments

An artificial intelligence-based academic research assistant (ScholarGPT) was used as a supportive tool during the research process to facilitate literature identification, organization, and preliminary synthesis; it helped retrieve recent publications, summarize key findings, compare outcomes across studies, prepare initial structural outlines, and polish language. All AI-assisted content was critically reviewed, cross-checked with original sources, and revised to maintain factual accuracy, originality, and academic integrity. This chapter was developed using a systematic scientific methodology to examine burnout among neurosurgeons.

Conflict of Interest

The authors declare no conflict of interest.

Author details

Ram Prasad Subedi[1*], Aashish Baniya[1], Bikram Bhandari[2], Suraj Thulung[1], Suresh Bishokarma[1] and Sagun Ghimire[3]

1 Upendra Devkota Memorial National Institute of Neurological and Allied Sciences, Kathmandu, Nepal

2 BP Koirala Institute of Health Sciences, Dharan, Nepal

3 B and B Hospital, Lalitpur, Nepal

*Address all correspondence to: dr.ramprasadsubedi@gmail.com

IntechOpen

References

[1] IsHak WW, et al. Burnout during residency training: A literature review. Journal of Graduate Medical Education 2009;**1**:236–242

[2] Freudenberger HJ. Staff burnout. Journal of Social Issues. 1974;**30**:159–165

[3] West CP, Huschka MM, Novotny PJ, et al. Association of perceived medical errors with resident distress and empathy: A prospective longitudinal study. JAMA. 2006;**296**:1071–1078

[4] Shanafelt TD, Bradley KA, Wipf JE, Back AL. Burnout and self-reported patient care in an internal medicine residency program. Annals of Internal Medicine. 2002;**136**:358–367

[5] Shanafelt TD, Balch CM, Bechamps G, et al. Burnout and medical errors among American surgeons. Annals of Surgery. 2010;**251**:995–1000

[6] Kahill S. Relationship of burnout among professional psychologists to professional expectations and social support. Psychological Reports. 1986;**59**:1043–1051

[7] Wurm W, Vogel K, Holl A, Ebner C, Bayer D, Morkl S, Szilagyi IS, Hotter E, Kapfhammer HP, Hofmann P. Depression–burnout overlap in physicians. PLoS ONE. 2016;**11**:e0149913

[8] Rosenstein AH, O'Daniel M. Impact and implications of disruptive behavior in the perioperative arena. Journal of the American College of Surgeons. 2006;**203**:96–105

[9] Ledikwe JH, Kleinman NJ, Mpho M, Mothibedi H, Mawandia S, Semo BW, O'Malley G. Associations between healthcare worker participation in workplace wellness activities and job satisfaction, occupational stress, and burnout: A cross-sectional study in Botswana. BMJ Open. 2018;**8**:e018492

[10] Bourne SK, Walcott BP, Sheth SA, Coumans J-VCE. Neurological surgery: The influence of physical and mental demands on humans performing complex operations. Journal of Clinical Neuroscience. 2013;**20**(3):342–348

[11] Whitfield PC, Van Loon J, Peul W. European training requirements in neurological surgery: A new outcomes-based 3-stage UEMS curriculum. Brain and Spine. 2023;**3**:101744

[12] Arndt BG, Beasley JW, Watkinson MD, Temte JL, Tuan WJ, Sinsky CA, Gilchrist VJ. Tethered to the EHR: Primary care physician workload assessment using EHR event log data and time-motion observations. Annals of Family Medicine. 2017;**15**(5): 419–426. DOI: 10.1370/afm.2121

[13] Attenello FJ, Buchanan IA, Wen T, Donoho DA, McCartney S, Cen SY, Khalafallah AM, Mukherjee D, Chang DC, Cohen-Gadol AA, Mack WJ. Factors associated with burnout among US neurosurgery residents: A nationwide survey. Journal of Neurosurgery. 2018;**129**(5):1349–1363. DOI: 10.3171/2017.9.JNS17996

[14] Dyrbye LN, Shanafelt TD, Gill PR, Satele DV, West CP. Effect of a professional coaching intervention on the well-being and distress of physicians: A pilot randomized clinical trial. JAMA Internal Medicine. 2019;**179**

(10):1406–1414. DOI: 10.1001/jamainternmed.2019.2425

[15] Gidwani R, Nguyen C, Kofoed A, Carragee C, Rydel T, Nelligan I, Sattler A, Mahoney M. Impact of scribes on physician satisfaction, patient satisfaction, and charting efficiency: A randomized controlled trial. Annals of Family Medicine. 2017;**15**(5):427–433. DOI: 10.1370/afm.2122

[16] Han S, Shanafelt TD, Sinsky CA, Awad KM, Dyrbye LN, Fiscus LC, Goh J, Trockel M. Estimating the attributable cost of physician burnout in the United States. Annals of Internal Medicine. 2019;**170**(11):784–790. DOI: 10.7326/M18-1422

[17] Hu YY, Ellis RJ, Hewitt DB, Yang AD, Cheung EO, Moskowitz JT, Potts JR, Buyske J, Hoyt DB, Nasca TJ, Bilimoria KY. Discrimination, abuse, harassment, and burnout in surgical residency training. New England Journal of Medicine. 2019;**381**(18):1741–1752. DOI: 10.1056/NEJMsa1903759

[18] Jena AB, Seabury S, Lakdawalla D, Chandra A. Malpractice risk according to physician specialty. New England Journal of Medicine. 2011;**365**(7):629–636. DOI: 10.1056/NEJMsa1012370

[19] Medscape. Neurosurgeon burnout & depression report 2023. Medscape. 2023. Available from: https://www.medscape.com/slideshow/2023-lifestyle-burnout-6016058 [Accessed: 2025-November-28]

[20] Shanafelt TD, Gorringe G, Menaker R, Storz KA, Reeves D, Buskirk SJ, Sloan JA, Swensen SJ. Impact of organizational leadership on physician burnout and satisfaction. Mayo Clinic Proceedings. 2015;**90**(4):432–440. DOI: 10.1016/j.mayocp.2015.01.012

[21] Shanafelt TD, Noseworthy JH. Executive leadership and physician well-being: Nine organizational strategies to promote engagement and reduce burnout. Mayo Clinic Proceedings. 2017;**92**(1):129–146. DOI: 10.1016/j.mayocp.2016.10.004

[22] Tawfik DS, Scheid A, Profit J, Shanafelt T, Trockel M, Adair KC, Sexton JB, Ioannidis JPA. Evidence relating health care provider burnout and quality of care: A systematic review and meta-analysis. Annals of Internal Medicine. 2019;**171**(8):555–567. DOI: 10.7326/M19-1152

[23] Zaed I, Jaaiddane Y, Chibbaro S, Tinterri B. Burnout among neurosurgeons and residents in neurosurgery: A systematic review and meta-analysis of the literature. World Neurosurgery. 2020;**143**:e529–e534. DOI: 10.1016/j.wneu.2020.08.005

[24] West CP, Dyrbye LN, Erwin PJ, Shanafelt TD. Interventions to prevent and reduce physician burnout: A systematic review and meta-analysis. The Lancet. 2016;**388**(10057):2272–2281. DOI: 10.1016/S0140-6736(16)31279-X

[25] World Health Organization. Burn-out an "Occupational Phenomenon": International Classification of Diseases. Geneva: WHO; 2019. https://www.who.int/news/item/28-05-2019-burn-out-an-occupational-phenomenon-international-classification-of-diseases

[26] St-Onge MP, Mikic A, Pietrolungo CE. Effects of diet on sleep quality. Advances in Nutrition. 2016;7(5):938–949

[27] Dhivakar S, Rai A, Sandhu H, Das A, Subedi RP, Reddy KMR. Occupational stress and burnout among young surgeons: A review. International Journal of Research in Medical Sciences. 2023;**11**:1050–1055

[28] Boontoterm P, Urasyanandana K, Fuengfoo P. Impact of Burnout Syndrome among Thai Neurosurgeons: Prevalence, contributing factors, and consequences. Indian Journal of Neurosurgery. 2025;**14**(02):156–164. DOI: 10.1055/s-0045-1806927

[29] Schneider D, Mishra A, Shao M, Larry Lo S-F, Sciubba DM. Burnout in Neurosurgery in the Postpandemic Era. World Neurosurgery. 2025;**194**:123369. DOI: 10.1016/j.wneu.2024.10.098

[30] Klimo Jr P, DeCuypere M, Ragel BT, McCartney S, Couldwell WT, Boop FA. Career satisfaction and burnout among U.S. neurosurgeons: A feasibility and pilot study. World Neurosurgery. 2013;**80**:e59–e68

[31] Eddleman CS, Aoun SG, Batjer HH. How to identify the edge of a cliff in the dark: Burnout and neurosurgery. World Neurosurgery. 2013;**80**:e111–e113

[32] Attenello FJ, Buchanan IA, Wen T, Donoho DA, McCartney S, Cen SY, Khalessi AA, Cohen-Gadol AA, Cheng JS, Mack WJ, Schirmer CM, Swartz KR, Prall JA, Stroink AR, Giannotta SL, Klimo P. Factors associated with burnout among US neurosurgery residents: A nationwide survey. Journal of Neurosurgery. 2018;**129**(5):1349–1363. DOI: 10.3171/2017.9.jns17996

[33] Fargen KM, Spiotta AM, Turner RD, Patel S. Operation La Sierra: A novel wellness initiative for neurological surgery residents. Journal of Graduate Medical Education. 2016;**8**(3):457–458

[34] Hamade YJ, Aoun RJ, Zimmerman RS, Bendok BR. The modern neurosurgical leader as a cure for team burnout. Neurosurgery. 2015;**77**(2):N13

[35] Buchholz AL, Henderson JF, Lowe S, Alshareef M, Wolgamott L, Patel S, Spiotta AM. Perspectives from a residency training program following the implementation of a wellness initiative. World Neurosurgery. 2018;**119**:e947

[36] Spiotta AM, Fargen KM, Patel S, Larrew T, Turner RD. Impact of a residency-integrated wellness program on resident mental health, sleepiness, and quality of life. Neurosurgery. 2019;**84**(2):341–346

[37] Wolfe SQ, West JL, Hunt MA, Murad GJ, Fox WC, Dow J, Morone PJ, Wellons III JC, Podet A, Wilson J, Wu JK. A comparison of the existing wellness programs in neurosurgery and institution champion's perspectives. Neurosurgery. 2019;**84**(5):1149–1155

[38] Zaed I, Menna G, Caccavella VM, Stumpo V, Giordano M, Caimmi E, Wheeler DR, Tinterri B. Italian neurosurgical residents' experience with research activities: A national survey. World Neurosurgery. 2020;**142**:e101

[39] West CP, Dyrbye LN, Rabatin JT, Call TG, Davidson JH, Multari A, Romanski SA, Hellyer JM, Sloan JA, Shanafelt TD. Intervention to promote physician well-being, job satisfaction, and professionalism: A randomized clinical trial. JAMA Internal Medicine. 2014;**174**(4):527–533

[40] Bianchi R, Schonfeld IS, Laurent E. Burnout–depression overlap: A review. Clinical Psychology Review. 2015;**36**:28–41

[41] Krasner MS, Epstein RM, Beckman H, Suchman AL, Chapman B, Mooney CJ, Quill TE. Association of an educational program in mindful communication with burnout, empathy, and attitudes among primary care physicians. Jama. 2009;**302**(12): 1284–1293

Chapter 5

Burnout Syndrome in Family Medicine Practice

Nesli̧sah Gürel Köksal

Abstract

This chapter, "Burnout Syndrome in Family Medicine Practice," synthesizes evidence on burnout in primary care. It reviews definitions, dimensions, and measurement tools, noting challenges in interpretation in practice. Risk factors are examined at individual, organizational, and system levels, with attention to workload, time pressure, and structural constraints in family medicine. The chapter highlights that burnout affects not only physicians' well-being but also professional satisfaction, sense of meaning at work, and mental health, including associations with depressive symptoms. Patient safety implications, such as medication errors, are also discussed. Evidence on burnout among family medicine residents and on the wellness of primary care teams and staff is summarized, together with potential differences across practice models. Findings from Turkish Family Health Centers are integrated to strengthen local relevance. Finally, the chapter presents interventions, including mindfulness toolkits, workflow redesign, team-based support, and organizational policies, and proposes monitoring indicators (burnout scores, job satisfaction, error reporting, turnover) to evaluate impact.

Keywords: burnout, professional, family practice, family medicine, job satisfaction, occupational stress, primary care

1. Introduction

Burnout in primary care is not just an individual well-being issue; it is a public health problem that can affect continuity of care, access, quality, and patient safety. The World Health Organization defines burnout as an occupational phenomenon and frames it not as a clinical disease category but as a work-related syndrome/phenomenon. This emphasis underscores that, instead of looking for the problem only within the individual, we need to examine the design of the work and the health system itself [1].

Family medicine practice is the gateway to the health system because of its proximity to the population and its role as the first point of contact. Burnout at this gateway can make it harder for patients to access appointments, weaken continuity, and disrupt team functioning and morale. Ultimately, primary care's productivity and safety are affected across a wide spectrum – from immunizations and chronic disease follow-up to prenatal care and well-child visits. For this reason, it is not enough to treat burnout as merely "stress that the individual must cope with." Organizational and system-level factors such as workload, workflow, performance/incentive structures, the burden of digital documentation, and a safe working environment must be made visible [2, 3].

From a public health perspective, burnout is not only an outcome but also an early warning indicator: it reflects workforce sustainability, service quality goals, and the system's resilience to crises such as natural disasters, pandemics, and economic fluctuations. Therefore, monitoring burnout is meaningful not only for worker health but also for the public's access to primary care and for equity goals. A systems approach shows that burnout is too multifactorial to be resolved through a "personal resilience" narrative alone [3].

The limitations of the individual resilience narrative are especially important. When resilience is reduced to personal skills alone, the design of work, organizational culture, and policy-level determinants become invisible. In contrast, workplace mental health-supporting approaches describe organizational responsibilities, such as reducing risks at their source, ensuring employee participation, and improving access to support services. Employer guidelines on managing workplace stress similarly prioritize changing the conditions that produce stress [2, 4].

The aim of this chapter is to address burnout in family medicine practice across the following domains: definition, prevalence, determinants, measurement, outcomes, and intervention strategies.

2. Definition and dimensions of burnout

Burnout is commonly understood as a syndrome associated with chronic workplace stress, especially in professions grounded in sustained interpersonal work. In the classic framework, three core dimensions stand out: emotional exhaustion (loss of energy, feeling drained), depersonalization/cynicism (emotional distancing and negative attitudes toward patients, service recipients, and the work itself), and a reduced sense of personal accomplishment (a decline in perceived competence and effectiveness). Together, these dimensions highlight that burnout is not simply "being tired" but also a form of erosion in emotions, attitudes, and professional self-worth [5].

The WHO's ICD-11 framework positions burnout as an occupational phenomenon. In clinical practice, this has two important implications:

- Burnout should be addressed primarily by improving working conditions, rather than being labeled as a medical diagnosis.
- Because symptoms can overlap with conditions such as clinical depression and anxiety, professional evaluation is warranted when clinical warning signs are present.

Systematic reviews examining burnout prevalence among physicians have shown not only substantial measurement heterogeneity but also meaningful differences in clinical interpretation [1, 6].

In primary care practice, these dimensions may show up in distinct ways. Emotional exhaustion can be fueled by continuous demand and time pressure throughout the day; depersonalization may emerge as a maladaptive form of protective distance in the setting of high patient volume; and reduced personal accomplishment can deepen when clinicians repeatedly experience limited impact in the face of complex social determinants and chronic disease burden. For this reason, context matters as much as the definition itself [3].

2.1 Distinguishing burnout from related concepts

Burnout is often discussed alongside concepts such as stress, depression, anxiety, and job dissatisfaction, and at times, they may appear to converge because they can share similar symptoms. However, burnout is not identical to any of these constructs. Stress can be understood as a process that emerges when the balance between demands and resources is disrupted; burnout is better conceptualized as a cluster of syndromic experiences that develops when this imbalance persists over time. Job dissatisfaction refers to a decline in the satisfaction one derives from work; it may be associated with burnout, but it is not sufficient on its own to explain burnout. Clinical conditions such as depression and anxiety must also be considered carefully in the differential diagnosis, given the substantial overlap in symptom profiles [2, 7].

One of the most clinically important distinctions in differential diagnosis is the extent to which symptoms remain confined to the work context. In burnout, complaints are typically concentrated within the workplace and the professional role, whereas in depression, the clinical picture may extend across multiple domains of life. That said, when there is marked hopelessness, pronounced anhedonia, thoughts of worthlessness, or suicidal ideation, attributing the presentation solely to burnout is risky; a formal clinical evaluation is essential. A study examining links among burnout, depression, and patient-safety–related outcomes in family physicians clearly illustrates the practical importance of this overlap in real-world settings [8].

In primary care, additional experiences may also be mistaken for burnout – particularly in situations that require intense emotional labor (e.g., delivering bad news, caring for survivors of violence, managing loss and bereavement). Secondary traumatic stress and compassion fatigue can resemble burnout in important ways, while also underscoring that distress may stem not only from workload but from the emotional costs of caring relationships. For this reason, accessible support mechanisms and efforts to reduce stigma become even more critical [2].

2.2 Theoretical models

From a theoretical standpoint, one of the most practical ways to understand burnout is to focus on the balance between job demands and job resources. As the number of patients and the complexity of presenting problems increase throughout the day, and as time pressure, administrative tasks, and emotional labor accumulate, demands rise. If, in response, resources such as autonomy, team support, training opportunities, regular feedback, and enabling infrastructure do not increase to the same degree, chronic stress is likely to persist, and the risk of burnout becomes more pronounced. In high-uncertainty settings such as family medicine, this balance is even more fragile: the flow of the day changes frequently, interruptions are common, and clinicians often face situations that do not unfold as planned.

The Maslach approach does more than describe the dimensions of burnout; it also invites us to look at where the fit between the person and the job breaks down. For example, when workload increases or the sense of control declines, it becomes easier to see how these mismatches can fuel burnout. In that sense, the approach moves beyond the message of "you should be more resilient" and creates space to discuss work design and organizational culture. Indeed, systems-oriented reports recommend not thinking about clinician well-being in isolation from organizational design and leadership [3].

Protective resources are not limited to individual skills. Professional identity, a sense of meaning at work, alignment with one's values, team solidarity, and a fair leadership climate can soften the impact of demanding conditions and serve as a buffer against burnout. The job satisfaction literature also shows that many key drivers of satisfaction among general practitioners are organizational and systemic. For this reason, job satisfaction is not only an outcome; it is also a legitimate target for intervention [7, 9].

3. The distinctive context of family medicine practice

Family medicine differs from many other clinical fields because of its core features: continuity (a long-term relationship with the same person), comprehensiveness (care across all ages and conditions), first contact (the entry point to the health system), coordination (linking with other levels of care), and a community-oriented focus. These characteristics can influence burnout in two directions. On the one hand, sustained relationships with patients and a sense that the work is meaningful can be protective. On the other hand, expectations to keep up with everything and the cumulative weight of uncertainty can intensify over time.

In primary care, uncertainty and a broad scope of problems are often structural parts of the work. Multimorbidity, psychosocial burden, and social determinants of health (such as poverty, migration, and vulnerability), along with major life events, are common. In many situations, diagnostic certainty and rapid resolution may not be possible. Family physicians must, therefore, manage not only biomedical decision-making but also the social and behavioral dimensions of care. This reality can substantially increase cumulative cognitive load and decision fatigue across the day.

Time pressure, frequent interruptions, administrative workload, and digital documentation/reporting requirements are among the most commonly cited stressors in primary care. Much of the work is also "invisible": reports, prescription renewals, test-result follow-ups, and phone/message traffic often do not fit within scheduled visit times and spill into after-hours work. Over time, this accumulation strains work–life balance and carries a persistent sense of unfinished tasks into the next day.

In Türkiye, the legal and regulatory framework of family medicine shapes work design directly through defined responsibilities, service organization, and documentation expectations. For this reason, any discussion of burnout should consider how regulatory duties and reporting requirements translate into day-to-day clinical practice [10, 11].

Public expectations, occasional risks of conflict or workplace violence, and the pressure to serve as the "problem-solver" create an additional, distinctive burden in family medicine. Moreover, rural–urban differences, socioeconomic inequities, and variations in resource distribution can produce markedly different working conditions even among family physicians performing similar roles. A study examining burnout and associated factors among family physicians working in Family Health Centers in Sakarya highlights how the local context in Türkiye can vary and why associated factors should be addressed in a multidimensional way [12].

The clearest answer to this section's central question is this: family medicine is different because clinical diversity, uncertainty, and social determinants converge within a high-contact, continuity-based relationship. That combination can amplify emotional, cognitive, and administrative demands simultaneously. Accordingly, burnout in family medicine is often driven not only by working too much but by working under complex, multidimensional conditions [4].

4. Epidemiology and burden: Prevalence, trends, and inequities

The literature on how common burnout is among primary care physicians is extensive, yet reported prevalence rates can vary substantially from one study to another. That variability is often driven by technical but highly consequential methodological choices: which instrument is used, what cutoffs are selected, how the sample is constructed, response rates, and, importantly, the broader context (health system design, workload, and whether data are collected during periods of crisis, such as a pandemic). A review that specifically examines the limitations in the usefulness of estimated prevalence figures for burnout in family doctors underscores the need for methodological caution when making comparisons across settings [13].

Systematic reviews across physicians overall indicate that burnout is a common problem, while also highlighting the heterogeneity in the evidence base. Meta-analyses focused on primary care show a similar pattern: meaningful differences exist across countries and institutions. Multicenter studies of European family physicians, along with more recent primary care meta-analyses, suggest that burnout is highly context-sensitive and cannot be adequately summarized by a single universal rate [6, 14–16].

National and regional studies further suggest that specific health system arrangements and working conditions may influence burnout levels. For example, a cross-sectional survey among general practitioners in the Czech Republic reported a high prevalence, while repeated survey designs within the same country allow trends over time to be monitored. Such studies make it easier to view burnout not as a one-time snapshot but as an indicator that should be tracked regularly in relation to workforce sustainability [17, 18].

Career stage also matters. Family medicine residents may exhibit distinct risk profiles due to factors such as learning pressure and role uncertainty. A nationwide cross-sectional study provides a useful example of how burnout can be measured in residents and how higher-risk groups can be identified. In addition, research examining burnout alongside differences in health status among primary healthcare professionals suggests that burnout may extend beyond the workplace and be associated with broader health outcomes [19, 20].

Inequities can function as both a cause and a consequence of burnout. In areas where vulnerable populations are concentrated, the burden of social determinants may be higher, while resources remain more limited, quickly destabilizing the demand–resource balance in family medicine. Findings from cross-sectional studies conducted in different regions of Türkiye similarly suggest that local workload, team capacity, and socioeconomic conditions can shape burnout risk [12, 21].

Macro-level shocks, such as pandemics, can increase burnout by amplifying demand and uncertainty. During these periods, both clinical risk and public anxiety rise; the family physician becomes not only a clinician but also a trusted communicator for the community. In this sense, burnout is intertwined with crisis response capacity and should be monitored at the system level [2, 3].

5. Determinants: Multilevel risk and protective factors

In this section, we examine the determinants of burnout in family medicine through a socioecological lens (individual–team–organization–system). Systematic reviews show that burnout is too multifactorial to be reduced to a single cause; at the same time, they also point to recurring patterns. Recognizing these patterns provides a practical answer to a key primary care question: where should we start, and what should we prioritize? [22]

5.1 Individual-level factors

At the individual level, sleep, chronic health conditions, caregiving responsibilities, and major life events can create vulnerability to burnout. Sleep is a particularly critical threshold: insufficient sleep can impair cognitive performance, make emotion regulation harder, and contribute to decision fatigue by steadily draining one's capacity to make judgments across the day. A study among resident physicians in Türkiye, which examined the relationship between insomnia severity and burnout, supports taking sleep seriously at both clinical and managerial levels [23].

Physical health problems, such as chronic pain or prolonged infections – may reduce a person's energy reserves, making the same work demands feel heavier and more difficult to manage. Similarly, caregiving responsibilities at home and socioeconomic stressors can deplete resources outside of work, increasing the risk of burnout. For this reason, workplace mental health frameworks consider not only what happens at work but also work–life interactions [2].

Personality traits and professional attitudes can also shape risk. Perfectionism, taking on excessive responsibility, a strong need to control everything, and difficulty setting boundaries may accelerate burnout, especially in settings where resources are limited. By contrast, setting realistic goals, cultivating self-compassion, maintaining support networks outside of work, and planning for rest can be protective. The key point, however, is that individual skills should not be expected to compensate for structural problems on their own. Individual-level strategies become more meaningful and more sustainable when they are combined with organizational and system-level changes [2, 3].

In family medicine, a sense of professional meaning and doing well at work can act as a powerful buffer. For some physicians, continuity of care, building community ties, and delivering preventive services provide strong sources of meaning that reduce the impact of difficult conditions. This area overlaps closely with the job satisfaction literature: many factors that increase job satisfaction among general practitioners (such as autonomy, support, and work–life balance) also overlap with factors that reduce burnout [7, 9].

5.2 Work/team factors

In primary care, workload is not limited to the number of patients seen. The complexity of patients, the burden of chronic illness, the need to address multiple problems within a single visit, and invisible work (reports, prescription renewals, test-result follow-up, and phone/message traffic) are major components of workload. As these components increase, time pressure intensifies, and emotional exhaustion is more easily fueled [22].

Appointment systems, frequent interruptions, and limited triage capacity are common microlevel challenges in family medicine. Interruptions increase cognitive load, may raise the risk of error, and often lead to an accumulation of unfinished work by the end of the day. Team design becomes pivotal here: nursing/midwife support, clerical support, effective triage, and task shifting can redistribute the burden away from the physician. Research on wellness and burnout among primary care clinicians and staff highlights the importance of addressing the team as a whole and shows that improvement suggestions often focus on workflow and communication [24].

When roles within the team are unclear, inefficiencies can grow, such as duplicating the same work or leaving tasks owned by no one. On especially busy days, this can escalate conflict and intensify a sense of working alone. A cross-sectional study in Türkiye, which included primary care physicians and family medicine residents, provides important local clues about team functioning and work-condition–related factors [21].

Studies examining burnout levels and associated factors among family physicians in Türkiye suggest that patient load, working conditions, and perceptions of the quality of support mechanisms may be related to burnout dimensions. The Sakarya study is valuable in highlighting that local organization and working conditions in family medicine may be linked to burnout [12].

Another microlevel area that stands out is professional fulfillment. Research comparing different practice models suggests that how work is organized (patient panel, administrative burden, payment/incentive structures) can shape both burnout and professional fulfillment. This finding points to the organization of work itself as a powerful determinant, independent of individual characteristics [25].

5.3 Organizational factors

At the organizational level, autonomy and participation in decision-making are among the most critical determinants of burnout. Rules and processes that do not fit the realities of clinical work can reduce professional autonomy; this can erode a sense of control and contribute to cynicism and burnout. Importantly, this is not limited to clinical decisions. Participatory decision-making around workflow issues, appointment planning, task distribution, and documentation responsibilities can be protective [3].

Performance pressure, feedback culture, and leadership quality are frequently reported meso-level factors. Perceptions of fairness and reward mechanisms can influence both job satisfaction and burnout. Reviews focusing on job satisfaction among general practitioners summarize that leadership and organizational climate can meaningfully shape satisfaction levels [7].

A cross-sectional study in Türkiye examining the relationship between burnout and job satisfaction among family physicians suggests that job satisfaction may be linked to burnout and that organizational conditions may influence both simultaneously. Similarly, a study in Malatya that assessed job satisfaction and burnout among primary care health workers supports the view of job satisfaction as an important indicator of organizational sustainability [26, 27].

Opportunities for professional development, protected time for training, and supportive supervision can help preserve a sense of personal accomplishment, particularly early in a career. When this area is neglected, feelings of skill erosion and diminished professional value may deepen. For this reason, strengthening the learning climate is often a core component of organizational intervention packages [3].

5.4 System-level factors

At the system level, financing and incentive structures may create volume-driven pressures. When performance indicators are poorly designed, they can lead to short visit times, increased administrative workload, and added time spent on digital documentation and reporting. These pressures become even more visible when primary care capacity is limited, deepening burnout as a systemic problem [3].

Referral pathways and coordination challenges can also drive workload in primary care. When integration with secondary and tertiary care is weak, follow-up responsibility and patient expectations often concentrate in primary care, increasing both clinical uncertainty and workload [22].

Legal and medico-legal pressures, as well as policies related to violence and workplace safety, can influence burnout at the macrolevel. A safe working environment is a foundational element of occupational health and safety. Employer guidance on workplace stress emphasizes that safe conditions and work-design adjustments are not merely matters of goodwill but institutional responsibilities [4].

In the Turkish context, the legal and administrative framework of family medicine (role definitions, service obligations, and operational rules) is essential for understanding the structural determinants of burnout. Because this framework shapes how services are organized and who is responsible for which tasks in primary care, it directly affects the balance between demands and resources [10, 11].

At the macro level, social inequities (poverty, migration, and vulnerability) increase the clinical burden. Primary care is where these inequities most visibly translate into health consequences; as a result, the emotional labor and social-navigation demands on family physicians increase. For this reason, burnout is not only about working conditions but also intersects with population health and social policy [2].

5.5 Protective factors and resilience

Although protective factors are often individualized under the label of resilience, in primary care, the strongest protection frequently comes from how the work and the team are designed. Meaning in work, alignment with professional values, and team solidarity are especially important buffers, given the continuity- and relationship-based nature of family medicine. In addition, fair leadership, psychological safety, manageable workloads, and realistic performance targets help institutionalize resilience rather than leaving it to individual effort [2, 3].

Within this framework, job satisfaction can be seen as both an outcome and a resource. Evidence shows that factors that increase job satisfaction among general practitioners (autonomy, work–life balance, professional development, and team support) substantially overlap with factors that reduce burnout. This overlap suggests that interventions can be designed not only to reduce burnout but also to intentionally strengthen job satisfaction [7, 9].

6. Clinical presentation, differential diagnosis, and measurement

6.1 Symptoms and warning signs

Burnout rarely appears overnight. It typically develops gradually and becomes more visible as workloads accumulate. Emotionally, clinicians may experience irritability, hopelessness, loss of motivation, and empathy fatigue. Cognitively, common signs include reduced concentration, decision fatigue, forgetfulness, and a sense of operating on autopilot. Behaviorally, avoidance, procrastination, a shorter or sharper communication style, decreased performance, and increased absenteeism may stand out. Physically, sleep disturbances, headaches, gastrointestinal complaints, and more diffuse somatic symptoms can accompany the picture [23].

In primary care, some warning signs may show up more clearly at the level of professional identity: increasing use of cynical or labeling language toward patients, a loss of meaning in work, reduced motivation to sustain continuity relationships, and emerging thoughts of leaving the profession. These signals suggest that burnout is not only an emotional strain; it can also shape professional behaviors and the quality of care [3].

6.2 Differential diagnosis and comorbidities

Depression and anxiety disorders are often the first conditions to consider in the differential diagnosis. Burnout and depression can overlap at the symptom level; however, it is important to remember that depression may extend across many domains of life. When symptoms such as suicidal ideation, pronounced anhedonia, or intense guilt are present, it is not safe to conclude this is just burnout; urgent clinical assessment is warranted. A study examining the relationship among burnout, depressive symptoms, and patient-safety-related outcomes (including medication errors) among family physicians illustrates that the need for clinical evaluation and support cannot be explained solely as job dissatisfaction [8].

Posttraumatic responses, secondary traumatic stress, and compassion fatigue should also be considered, particularly in contexts involving violence, abuse, bereavement, or intense emotional contact. Screening for substance use and other risky coping behaviors is likewise important. This approach should be implemented using nonstigmatizing language and by making support options (e.g., counseling services, workplace support programs) visible and easy to access [1].

6.3 Measurement tools and practical screening

One of the most widely used instruments for measuring burnout is the Maslach Burnout Inventory (MBI). Its three-dimensional structure supports comparisons across studies; however, prevalence estimates can be influenced by differences in cutoff points and by the use of different versions of the instrument. As a result, the proportion classified as high burnout in one study may change substantially in another study using different thresholds [5, 13].

In Türkiye, the adaptation of the MBI has provided a long-standing reference framework in the field. Local validity work and linguistic adaptation are important for interpreting scores more appropriately in the Turkish context [28].

Alternative instruments conceptualize burnout through different components. The Copenhagen Burnout Inventory (CBI), for example, evaluates personal, work-related, and client-related burnout separately, which can make the burden of the care relationship more visible. A newer tool, the Burnout Assessment Tool (BAT), aims to measure burnout through core symptoms; the Turkish adaptation of the BAT provides psychometric support for its use in Türkiye [29–31].

When rapid, pragmatic screening is needed, brief measures can be useful for monitoring and for internal quality-improvement cycles. Turkish validity and reliability work on short surveys, such as Mini Z 2.0, offers a practical option for quick screening and follow-up. In addition, tools that assess psychosocial working conditions (such as COPSOQ-3) and scales that evaluate perceived occupational stress can help identify upstream contributors to burnout [32–34].

Before selecting a measurement strategy, the purpose should be clearly defined: Is the goal clinical screening, internal improvement, or research? For research, standardization may be essential for comparability; for internal improvement, tracking change over time and generating actionable feedback may be more important. Studies that assess work satisfaction, stress, and burnout together suggest that these indicators complement one another [35].

Organizational monitoring should not be limited to surveys alone. Workforce indicators such as turnover, absenteeism, overtime, patient complaints, incident/error reporting, and appointment delays can help track how burnout is reflected at the system level. Measurement should be used for improvement rather than punishment, and principles of anonymity and trust must be protected [2, 3].

7. Effects of burnout on physicians, patients, and the health system

7.1 Effects on physicians

At the physician level, burnout is associated with lower job satisfaction, the intention to leave, disengagement from the profession, and shifts in career plans. The job satisfaction literature indicates that factors such as autonomy and work–life balance are critical for sustainability, and that declines in job satisfaction can weaken organizational commitment and continuity of care [7, 9].

Burnout is not always experienced only as exhaustion; it may also be felt as a loss of professional fulfillment. A study comparing burnout and fulfillment rates across different practice models suggests that lower administrative burdens and greater perceived control may increase fulfillment. This finding supports designing interventions not only to reduce symptoms but also to strengthen sources of meaning and fulfillment at work [25].

From a mental health perspective, chronic burnout may co-occur with depressive symptoms. A study evaluating burnout and depression among family physicians – along with patient-safety–related outcomes such as medication errors – indicates that, in some cases, burnout may intersect with more complex clinical risks [8].

The relationship between burnout and physical health should not be overlooked. Research examining burnout alongside differences in health status among primary healthcare professionals supports the consideration of burnout in conjunction with quality of life and perceived health [20].

7.2 Patients and quality of care

One of the most immediate pathways through which burnout can affect patient care is the quality of communication. Reduced empathy, impatience, and more mechanical encounters can undermine patient satisfaction and the trust relationship. Because continuity is central to family medicine, these changes may become apparent quickly [3].

In terms of patient safety, evidence suggests burnout may be associated with a higher risk of medical errors; however, causality should be framed cautiously. Many factors that increase error risk – interruptions, time pressure, and cognitive load – also contribute to burnout. For that reason, burnout can be viewed as an early warning indicator from a patient-safety perspective. A study examining the relationship among burnout, depression, and medication errors in family physicians provides an important example for discussing this link in the primary care context [8].

Continuity and coordination are defining quality dimensions of primary care. Burnout may erode continuity through appointment cancellations, absenteeism, and frequent staff turnover. This erosion can have indirect but meaningful effects on chronic disease management and preventive services. Therefore, monitoring burnout indicators within quality-improvement programs aligns well with clinical goals [3].

7.3 System-level effects

At the system level, burnout can translate into workforce losses, erosion of primary care capacity, and weakened service sustainability. In areas where retaining primary care physicians becomes difficult, inequities may deepen – because disruptions in access and continuity disproportionately affect vulnerable populations. In this sense, burnout is a public health problem that is directly linked to equity goals [3].

The cost implications are often not immediately visible, but indirect effects accumulate over time: absenteeism, turnover, onboarding and training costs for new staff, inefficiency, and repeated visits. A study assessing wellness levels and improvement suggestions among primary care providers and staff indicates that organizations may achieve meaningful gains even through small workflow adjustments, but that durable impact generally requires system-level changes [24].

Similarly, a study comparing burnout and professional fulfillment across practice models suggests that system design, administrative burden, financing, and patient panel structure may be key drivers of outcomes. Findings like these reinforce that a single solution focused only on individual training is unlikely to be sufficient in policy discussions [25].

8. Prevention and intervention strategies

The most effective approach to preventing and reducing burnout is multicomponent and organization/system-oriented. Meta-analyses evaluating interventions to reduce physician burnout suggest that both individual and organizational initiatives can be beneficial, but organizational redesign is especially important for sustainable impact. Systematic reviews of workplace interventions among healthcare professionals similarly indicate that one-off trainings have limited reach, whereas changes in work design and working conditions may be more influential [36–38].

Two points are worth keeping in mind when interpreting the intervention evidence. First, many burnout intervention studies were conducted in hospital settings; when translating findings to primary care, differences in workflow, team structure, and patient panel characteristics must be considered. Second, approaches that appear most effective tend to share a common feature: they produce tangible changes in clinicians' day-to-day work, such as improved scheduling flow, reduced administrative burden, clearer task-sharing within the team, visible leadership support, and stronger psychological safety. Meta-analyses and workplace-intervention reviews emphasize that individual programs may help, but lasting gains typically come from organizational changes that improve working conditions. For this reason, an intervention plan should combine individual and system components within the same package [36–38].

8.1 Primary prevention: Work design and workload management

Primary prevention aims to reduce risk before burnout develops. In family medicine, two of the most impactful levers are visit length and panel size. As clinical complexity increases, visit time and team support should increase accordingly; otherwise, the workday can become defined by a chronic sense of never catching up. Improving referral pathways and coordination processes is also part of primary prevention: balancing tasks that accumulate in primary care helps protect overall system capacity [3].

Small workflow adjustments can meaningfully reduce cognitive load – for example, managing interruptions, using standard protocols, creating templates for repetitive tasks, and defining clear responsibility for follow-up processes. Employer guidance on workplace stress recommends reducing risks at their source; this shifts the focus from "coping with stress" to designing processes that generate less stress in the first place [4].

Task-sharing and team-based care reduce the concentration of workload on the physician. Strengthening triage, assigning paperwork/report-related tasks to appropriate staff, using standard protocols, and optimizing digital processes (including reducing unnecessary clicks) can reclaim clinical time. Studies of wellness in primary care teams show that many frontline suggestions focus precisely on these operational improvements [24].

A further design element is building feedback and learning loops. If process indicators – such as appointment delays, phone traffic, and time spent on reporting – are tracked routinely, problems can be corrected before they escalate. This approach aligns with quality improvement and helps ensure burnout is not treated as inevitable [3].

8.2 Secondary prevention: Early identification and support

Secondary prevention focuses on identifying early warning signs and providing support. Periodic internal monitoring (e.g., brief surveys, focus groups) and safe reporting channels are central at this stage. The goal of measurement is not to generate performance scores but to identify risk areas and guide improvement [3].

Peer support, supervision, and Balint groups can be particularly helpful in primary care, where emotional labor and relationship-based care are prominent. Accessible counseling services that reduce stigma are also part of secondary prevention. The WHO guideline on mental health at work recommends that employers structure these supports and make access easier [2].

Another dimension of early identification is recognizing high-risk transition periods: starting a new job, moving to a new region, organizational mergers, or changes in performance metrics may increase burnout risk. During these transitions, mentorship, role clarification, and protected learning time can prevent the early accumulation of strain [3].

8.3 Tertiary prevention: Supporting clinicians experiencing burnout

Tertiary prevention aims to support clinicians who are already experiencing burnout and to reduce functional impairment. Job accommodations (temporary task adjustments, flexible scheduling, reducing nonclinical workload), a structured return-to-work plan, and referral to mental health services when needed are key steps. The process should be restorative rather than punitive, with confidentiality and voluntariness protected [2].

In high risk situations (significant depression, suicidal ideation, severe insomnia, substance use), timely clinical evaluation and appropriate specialist care should take priority. A study examining depressive symptoms and patient-safety outcomes alongside burnout among family physicians suggests that burnout may intersect with more complex clinical risks in some cases [8].

During recovery, gradually increasing workload and proactively planning team support matter. If the process is managed with pressure for a rapid return to full capacity, the risk of relapse may rise. Organizational flexibility at this point protects the clinician and reduces long-term workforce loss [3].

8.4 Individual-level interventions: Getting the dose right

Individual-level interventions can include stress management, sleep optimization, cognitive–behavioral techniques, and mindfulness-based programs. A systematic review and meta-analysis of mindfulness-based interventions among primary healthcare professionals suggest potential improvements in some dimensions of burnout; however, effect sizes are often small to moderate. Therefore, individual interventions should be positioned as complements to, rather than substitutes for, organizational and system changes [36, 39].

A study evaluating an evidence-based mindfulness toolkit implemented in primary care provides an example of how structured, accessible programs can be feasible in real-world practice. Such toolkits may include brief practices, microbreaks that fit within the clinical day, stress awareness, and emotion regulation strategies. Their impact may increase when participation is actively facilitated, and leadership support is visible [40].

Skills such as boundary-setting, time management, and professional coaching may also be helpful. Yet, their effectiveness is constrained by structural realities such as visit length, task distribution, and leave policies. The core message remains: do not place responsibility solely on the individual; make the system visible [3].

Clinician well-being strategies are also closely linked to job satisfaction and sources of professional fulfillment. Value-congruent clinical practice, learning opportunities, and professional development can strengthen resilience and serve as a bridge between individual and organizational interventions [7, 9].

8.5 Organizational leadership and culture

Organizational leadership can function as an "invisible determinant" of burnout. Fairness, transparency, and participatory decision-making do more than improve satisfaction – they strengthen trust and perceived control, which can reduce burnout. A culture of feedback and recognition can support a sense of meaning, especially under a heavy workload [3, 7].

Psychological safety refers to a climate in which team members can voice concerns, identify error risks, and share improvement ideas without fear of punishment. This culture aligns closely with patient-safety goals. Reviews of workplace well-being interventions highlight leadership and work climate as critical components of many programs [38].

Zero tolerance for violence and functioning safety protocols are foundational elements of occupational health and safety in primary care. Safety includes not only physical protections but also psychosocial support after incidents, as well as mechanisms that protect staff during legal processes [2, 4].

At the organizational level, well-being programs should extend beyond training to include workflow and resource management. Primary care wellness studies show that staff improvement suggestions often focus on concrete changes in how work is carried out, supporting the value of participatory mechanisms that genuinely incorporate frontline input [24].

8.6 Policy-level recommendations: A public health set of actions

At the policy level, the most critical area is primary care workforce planning and capacity management. Without an adequate number of physicians and support staff, even the best individual programs will have limited impact. Financing and performance metrics should be rebalanced to target not only volume but also quality, continuity, and team well-being [2, 3].

Leave, flexibility, and parenting supports help protect work–life balance and may reduce burnout, particularly early in a career. A nationwide cross-sectional study of burnout among family medicine residents helps make the support needs of this group more visible [19].

Reducing data burden and trimming unnecessary reporting can lower the clinician cost of digital transformation. Measurement matters here as well: psychosocial risk tools such as COPSOQ-3 can track working conditions, and stress indicators can be used as early-warning signals at the policy level [33, 34].

Comparisons showing that the organization of primary care work may relate to burnout and professional fulfillment encourage policymakers to evaluate alternative practice models. Higher professional fulfillment may support workforce retention. [25]

In Türkiye, the legal and administrative framework of family medicine serves as a starting point for policy discussions. Role definitions, reporting obligations, and service organization shape how much workload primary care must handle and with which resources. Burnout policy, therefore, needs to be addressed alongside regulations, incentives, and safety policies [10, 11].

Ten low-cost, practical changes for a family health center:

- A 10-minute team huddle at the start of the day to review workload and role assignments.
- Managing protected, interruption-free time blocks for critical tasks
- A triage flow with dedicated time slots for prescription renewals or report requests
- Standard response templates, educational materials, and a centralized channel for common patient questions
- Predefining task-sharing for immunizations and chronic disease follow-up
- Predefining task-sharing for patient education and monitoring activities
- A brief burnout check-in (approximately once every three months)
- A structured onboarding plan for newly starting physicians
- Nonpunitive incident/problem feedback mechanisms
- Buffer time for scheduled visits to prevent crowding and backlogs

Workflow pitfalls that increase burnout: a checklist for primary care managers:

- Is there adequate support for reporting and e-documentation workload?
- Is there a clear distribution of tasks for outreach calls and follow-up invitations?
- Are team roles and responsibilities documented in writing?
- Is there a triage mechanism for non-urgent requests?
- Is a culture of feedback, recognition, and learning functioning effectively in practice?
- Is there a protocol for threats or violence, and is it operational?
- Is leave managed in line with the relevant regulations?
- Are warning signals (e.g., rising absenteeism, disruptions due to turnover) being monitored?

9. Program design and evaluation in practice

9.1 Steps in designing an intervention

Programs aimed at reducing burnout should be designed not as one-time trainings but as continuous improvement cycles. A systems approach starts with the recognition that the problem is not located only within the individual but also in the design of work and the organization itself; that recognition is the foundation of intervention design [3].

The process begins with a problem analysis. Anonymous surveys assessing burnout, job satisfaction, and stress can be combined with focus groups and process mapping. Given the limitations of prevalence estimates, it is important to remember that within-organization benchmarking over time (tracking change) is often more meaningful than comparisons across different organizations [13, 32, 34].

Next comes prioritization. Using an impact/feasibility matrix, teams identify a small number of high-burden processes to address first. Participation of team members is essential at this stage because it increases ownership and strengthens implementation. The WHO guideline on mental health at work emphasizes employee participation and the structuring of support mechanisms [2].

Selected interventions should, whenever possible, begin as small pilots with rapid feedback. For example, appointment buffers, redesigned triage flow, or streamlined reporting can produce measurable process indicators in a short time. In this way, the program can expand based on realistic, observable gains [3].

9.2 Monitoring and evaluation indicators

Monitoring and evaluation should include process measures as well as outcome measures. Outcome indicators may include burnout scores, job satisfaction, and intention to leave [5]. Process indicators may include appointment delays, time spent on administrative tasks, and overtime. System indicators may include turnover, absenteeism, patient complaints, and incident/error reporting. Research assessing work satisfaction, stress, and burnout together supports selecting indicators in an integrated, comprehensive way [29, 31, 35].

When choosing measurement tools, organizations should be careful not to create an additional burden. Frequent and lengthy surveys can lead to measurement fatigue. For this reason, brief screeners (such as Mini Z 2.0) can be paired with less frequent, more comprehensive assessments [31–33].

9.3 Ethical principles and data security

Monitoring should be voluntary and anonymous, and results should not be used to punish individuals. The purpose is improvement – making risks visible so they can be addressed. Trust is a prerequisite for program sustainability; without it, response rates fall, and the highest-risk groups may become invisible [2, 3].

Data security is not only a technical issue; it is a key determinant of employee trust. In internal reporting systems, separating identifying information, reducing the risk of re-identification in small units, and sharing results transparently are all important. In addition, if high-risk clinical situations are identified, safe referral pathways (psychological support, specialist assessment) must be in place [2].

10. Conclusions

Burnout in family medicine is a public health issue linked to work design, team capacity, and the sustainability of the health system. The risk may be high for primary care professionals because uncertainty, comprehensive scope, and the expectation of continuity can generate sustained strain. Solutions must be equally multilevel: the most durable impact emerges when organizational changes and policy-level improvements are combined with individual support programs.

The core approach of this chapter is not to normalize burnout or ignore it, but to measure it, talk about it openly, and improve the design of work. In practice, the quickest gains often come from small workflow adjustments, while the most lasting gains typically arise from system-level levers such as financing, performance metrics, team capacity, and safe working conditions. When these levers are addressed together, both clinician well-being and the sustainability of primary care services can be strengthened.

In summary:

- Measure burnout for improvement; do not use measurement as punishment.
- Treat workload as more than just patient volume by addressing invisible work and reducing avoidable interruptions.
- Team design is an intervention: task-sharing and effective triage reduce physicians' burden.
- Individual programs can help balance strain, but the greatest impact comes from work design and system reforms.

Acknowledgments

During the preparation of the English version of this chapter, the author used artificial intelligence (AI) support for Turkish-to-English translation, spelling and grammar checks, and improving the language fluency and readability of the translated text. The AI assistance was limited to language editing; the intellectual content, interpretation, and final wording were reviewed and approved by the author, who takes full responsibility for the final text.

Conflict of Interest

The author declares no conflict of interest.

Notes/thanks/other declarations

None.

Author details

Neslişah Gürel Köksal
Department of Family Medicine, Giresun University, Giresun Training and Research Hospital, Giresun, Turkey

*Address all correspondence to: neslisahgurel@hotmail.com

References

[1] World Health Organization. Burn-out an "occupational phenomenon": International Classification of Diseases [Internet]. 2019 May 28. Available from: https://www.who.int/news/item/28-05-2019-burn-out-an-occupational-phenomenon-international-classification-of-diseases [Accessed: 2026-March-02]

[2] World Health Organization. Guidelines on mental health at work [Internet]. 2022 Sep 28. Available from: https://www.who.int/publications/i/item/9789240053052 [Accessed: 2026-March-02]

[3] National Academy of Medicine. Why & How to Take a Systems Approach: Taking Action Against Clinician Burnout: A Systems Approach to Professional Well-Being [Internet]. 2020. Available from: https://nam.edu/wp-content/uploads/2020/09/4.-NAM-Taking-Action-Against-Clinician-Burnout-systems-approach.pdf [Accessed: 2026-March-02]

[4] Occupational Safety and Health Administration (OSHA). Workplace Stress – Guidance and Tips for Employers [Internet]. Available from: https://www.osha.gov/workplace-stress/employer-guidance [Accessed: 2026-March-02]

[5] Maslach C, Jackson SE. The measurement of experienced burnout. Journal of Organizational Behavior. 1981;**2**(2):99–113

[6] Rotenstein LS, Torre M, Ramos MA, et al. Prevalence of burnout among physicians: A systematic review. JAMA. 2018;**320**(11):1131–1150. DOI: 10.1001/jama.2018.12777

[7] Van Ham I, Verhoeven AA, Groenier KH, Groothoff JW, De Haan J. Job satisfaction among general practitioners: A systematic literature review. European Journal of General Practice. 2006;**12**(4):174–180. DOI: 10.1080/13814780600994376

[8] Abd Elsadek DF, Kassem AB, ElKhwsky F, El Sayed I. Burnout, depression, and medication errors among family physicians. Scientific Reports. 2025;**15**(1):43389. DOI: 10.1038/s41598-025-29450-z

[9] Deng Q, Liu Y, Cheng Z, et al. Global job satisfaction and fluctuation among community general practitioners: A systematic review and meta-analysis. BMC Health Services Research. 2024;**24**:378

[10] Türkiye Cumhuriyeti. Aile Hekimliği Kanunu (Kanun No: 5258) [Internet]. Available from: https://hsgm.saglik.gov.tr/depo/Mevzuat/Kanunlar/Aile_Hekimligi_Kanunu_5258.pdf [Accessed: 2026-March-02]

[11] Türkiye Cumhuriyeti Sağlık Bakanlığı. Aile Hekimliği Uygulama Yönetmeliği [Internet]. Available from: https://www.saglik.gov.tr/TR-10516/aile-hekimligi-uygulama-yonetmeligi.html [Accessed: 2026-March-02]

[12] Şerik B, Erdoğan N, Ekerbiçer HÇ, et al. Sakarya'da aile sağlığı merkezlerinde çalışan aile hekimlerinin tükenmişlik düzeyleri ve ilişkili faktörler. Sakarya Medical Journal 2016;**6**:76–82

[13] McCammon LC, Gillen P, Kernohan WG. Explaining and

addressing the limitations in usefulness of available estimated prevalence figures relating to burnout in family doctors: Evidence from a systematic scoping literature review. Journal of Psychiatric Research. 2023;**158**:261–272. DOI: 10.1016/j.jpsychires.2022.12.013

[14] Soler JK, Yaman H, Esteva M, et al. Burnout in European family doctors: The EGPRN study. Family Practice. 2008;**25**(4):245–265. DOI: 10.1093/fampra/cmn038

[15] Karuna C, Palmer V, Scott A, Gunn J. Prevalence of burnout among GPs: A systematic review and meta-analysis. British Journal of General Practice. 2022;**72**(718):e316–e324. DOI: 10.3399/BJGP.2021.0441

[16] Beltrán-Gómez E, Pujol-de Castro A, Vaquero-Cepeda P, Catalá-López F. Prevalencia de burnout en profesionales de atención primaria del Sistema Nacional de Salud: Revisión sistemática y metaanálisis. Gaceta Sanitaria. 2025;**39**:102526. DOI: 10.1016/j.gaceta.2025.102526

[17] Štěpánek L, Patel MS, Horáková D, Juríčková L, Býma S. High prevalence of burnout syndrome in Czech general practitioners: A cross-sectional survey. Preventive Medicine Reports. 2023;**36**:102502. DOI: 10.1016/j.pmedr.2023.102502

[18] Štěpánek L, Horáková D, Král N, Štěpánek L, Býma S. Burnout syndrome among general practitioners in the Czech Republic: A repeated survey study. BMC Primary Care. 2024;**25**(1):421. DOI: 10.1186/s12875-024-02675-z

[19] Treister-Goltzman Y, Samson T, Rosenberg R, et al. Burnout among family medicine residents: A cross-sectional nationwide study. Israel Journal of Health Policy Research. 2024;**13**(1):5. DOI: 10.1186/s13584-024-00591-2

[20] Ferreira PL, Raposo V, Tavares AI, Pinto A. Burnout and health status differences among primary healthcare professionals in Portugal. BMC Family Practice. 2021;**22**(1):81. DOI: 10.1186/s12875-021-01425-9

[21] Altan S, Şahin MK. Samsun'da aile sağlığı merkezlerinde çalışan hekimlerde ve aile hekimliği asistanlarında tükenmişlik ve ilişkili faktörler: Kesitsel bir çalışma. Turkish Journal of Family Medicine and Primary Care. 2023;**17**(1):68–78. DOI: 10.21763/tjfmpc.1163483

[22] Shoman Y, El May E, Marca SC, et al. Predictors of occupational burnout: A systematic review. International Journal of Environmental Research and Public Health. 2021;**18**(17):9188. DOI: 10.3390/ijerph18179188

[23] Balki E, Gürel Köksal N. Araştırma görevlisi doktorların tükenmişlik düzeyi ile uykusuzluk şiddeti arasındaki ilişkinin incelenmesi: Kesitsel araştırma. Turkiye Klinikleri Journal of Health Sciences. 2026;**11**(1):280–287

[24] Cunningham AT, Waters A, Shah D, Arefi P, Sifri RD. Primary care provider and staff wellness and burnout levels and suggestions to improve wellness: Analysis of survey findings. American Journal of Medical Quality. 2024;**39**(5):209–219. DOI: 10.1097/JMQ.0000000000000201

[25] Boylan ME, Hurley DM. Comparison of burnout and fulfillment rates between physicians in direct primary care and other practice models. Southern Medical Journal. 2025;**118**

(5):275–280. DOI: 10.14423/SMJ.0000000000001821

[26] Çeleğen İ, Çetin Dağlı S. Factors related to levels of burnout and job satisfaction in family physicians (cross-sectional research). Genel Tıp Dergisi. 2024;**34**(3):296–300

[27] Cagan O, Gunay O. The job satisfaction and burnout levels of primary care health workers in the province of Malatya in Turkey. Pakistan Journal of Medical Sciences. 2015;**31**(3):543–547. DOI: 10.12669/pjms.313.6795

[28] Ergin C. Doktor ve hemşirelerde tükenmişlik ve Maslach Tükenmişlik Ölçeğinin uyarlanması. In: VII Ulusal Psikoloji Kongresi Bilimsel Çalışmaları; 22-25 September 1992; Ankara. Ankara: VII Ulusal Psikoloji Kongresi Düzenleme Kurulu ve Türk Psikologlar Derneği; 1992

[29] Kristensen TS, Borritz M, Villadsen E, Christensen KB. The Copenhagen Burnout Inventory: A new tool for the assessment of burnout. Work & Stress. 2005;**19**(3):192–207. DOI: 10.1080/02678370500297720

[30] Schaufeli WB, Desart S, De Witte H. Burnout Assessment Tool (BAT)-development, validity, and reliability. International Journal of Environmental Research and Public Health. 2020;**17**(24):9495. DOI: 10.3390/ijerph17249495

[31] Koçak ÖE, Gençay O, Schaufeli WB. BAT-TR: Tükenmişlik Ölçme Aracı'nın (BAT) Türkçeye uyarlanması. Studies in Psychology. 2022;**42**(3):509–549. DOI: 10.26650/SP2020-799817

[32] Kaçmaz Ersu N, Bakırarar B. Mini Z 2.0 klinisyen iş hayatı anketinin hekimler arasında Türk geçerliliği ve güvenilirliğinin değerlendirilmesi. Journal of Health Sciences and Medicine. 2025;**8**(5):759–764. DOI: 10.32322/jhsm.1690010

[33] Şahan C, Baydur H, Demiral Y. A novel version of Copenhagen Psychosocial Questionnaire-3: Turkish validation study. Archives of Environmental & Occupational Health. 2018;**74**:297–309. DOI: 10.1080/19338244.2018.1538095

[34] Yıldırım M, Dilekçi Ü, Marcatto F, Gómez-Salgado J. Validation of a Turkish translation of the Perceived Occupational Stress Scale and measurement invariance across Turkish and Italian workers. Risk Management and Healthcare Policy. 2024;**17**:261–268. DOI: 10.2147/RMHP.S437312

[35] Linzer M, Smith CD, Hingle S, et al. Evaluation of work satisfaction, stress, and burnout among US internal medicine physicians and trainees. JAMA Network Open. 2020;**3**(10):e2018758. DOI: 10.1001/jamanetworkopen.2020.18758

[36] West CP, Dyrbye LN, Erwin PJ, Shanafelt TD. Interventions to prevent and reduce physician burnout: A systematic review and meta-analysis. The Lancet. 2016;**388**(10057):2272–2281. DOI: 10.1016/S0140-6736(16)31279-X

[37] Panagioti M, Panagopoulou E, Bower P, et al. Controlled interventions to reduce burnout in physicians: A systematic review and meta-analysis. JAMA Internal Medicine. 2017;**177**(2):195–205. DOI: 10.1001/jamainternmed.2016.7674

[38] Cohen C, Pignata S, Bezak E, Tie M, Childs J. Workplace

interventions to improve well-being and reduce burnout for nurses, physicians and allied healthcare professionals: A systematic review. BMJ Open. 2023;**13**(6):e071203. DOI: 10.1136/bmjopen-2022-071203

[39] Salvado M, Marques DL, Pires IM, Silva NM. Mindfulness-based interventions to reduce burnout in primary healthcare professionals: A systematic review and meta-analysis. Healthcare (Basel). 2021;**9**(10):1342. DOI: 10.3390/healthcare9101342

[40] Christensen AJ, Virnig JP, Case NL, et al. Addressing burnout in the primary care setting: The impact of an evidence-based mindfulness toolkit. Military Medicine. 2023;**189**(Suppl 1):64–70. DOI: 10.1093/milmed/usad277

Chapter 6

Burnout and Depression in Sports

Alexander Schorb

Abstract

Mental symptoms and disorders in competitive sports can reduce performance and may occur as sport-specific and non-specific disorders. Unrecognized or inadequately treated mental health symptoms and disorders in athletes can have serious health consequences. The promotion of mental health is not yet an integral part of the care structures in competitive sports. Competitive success founds social status of athletes and contributes significantly to their self-esteem. In the case of participation loss or injury, the implicit or explicit pressure to restore function and performance quickly poses a particular challenge. Appropriate mental health care concepts can support early and professional diagnosis in sports. Burnout is a concept that could prove suitable for supporting early diagnosis. Burnout is not a separate diagnostic category and does not appear as such in medical psychiatric classification systems. There are numerous burnout scales that summarize a total of approximately 130 different symptoms and complaints under the current burnout concept. Excerpts from the concept can be used to observe subclinical symptoms or stress tendencies in athletes, which, when embedded in appropriate mental health care concepts, support the promotion of mental health in sports.

Keywords: sports psychiatry, competitive and elite sports, mental health in sports, Athlete Burnout Questionnaire (ABQ), Synergetic Navigation System (SNS)

1. Introduction

Burnout and depression can occur in competitive sports. However, competitive athletes are less likely to seek professional help [1]. Competitive sports offer those affected little opportunity to develop an alternative to the role model of an athlete [2]. Since the careers of athletes usually begin in childhood and adolescence, they are exposed to the prevailing pressure to perform at a young age and are compared and selected on the basis of their athletic performance. Competitive success confers social status within the competitive sports system and contributes significantly to the athlete's self-esteem [2]. Due to early and intense involvement in sports and a lack of alternatives to an athletic identity, athletic performance is used as a measure of self-esteem [3]. Self-esteem and identity are primarily generated by athletic performance and, above all, by success [1]. Athletes often only turn to their coaches when mental health problems become a measurable limitation on their performance [1]. However, treatment should be started in good time before performance declines, as soon as subclinical symptoms appear. It is important to create good support structures in which athletes can receive treatment at an early stage or participate in preventive projects to promote mental health [1, 4]. However, athletic success and mental health should not be a contradiction [5]. This chapter presents the concepts of burnout and depression in sports, as well as diagnostics and specialized forms of care, concepts, and treatment. In sports, it is important to provide adequate care structures so that athletes can receive treatment at an early stage or are already involved in prevention projects to promote mental health [1].

2. Mental health and burnout in sports

Mental health symptoms in competitive sports can manifest as sport-specific and non-sport-specific disorders [6]. They can reduce performance, increase the risk of physical injury, and subsequently prolong rehabilitation [7]. Unrecognized or inadequately treated mental health symptoms and disorders in athletes can have serious health and, at times, existential consequences [6]. This also applies to burnout and depression in sports. Burnout in sports is a serious phenomenon. Studies show a high prevalence of up to 9% among young elite athletes in particular, with almost a third experiencing significant stress [8]. Symptoms include physical and emotional exhaustion, sports devaluation, and reduced athletic accomplishment. For several decades, the topic of burnout in sports has been attracting increasing interest. The number of burnout studies in sports has risen steadily [9, 10].

The term "burnout" describes a person's performance-related exhaustion. It encompasses the feeling of losing personal control (self-sacrificially) in one's career and life, as well as having difficulty keeping up with the pace (in a world characterized by acceleration). Psychoanalyst Herbert J. Freudenberger first coined the term "burnout" in 1974 [11]. He understood it to mean a stressful state of emotional exhaustion resulting from a conflict between external and internal demands in everyday working life. He had no intention of introducing a new category of mental disorders. Maslach and Jackson expanded the original burnout concept into a general concept of occupational and organizational psychology. They defined three fundamental, interrelated dimensions: *emotional exhaustion, depersonalization* (or cynicism), and *reduced personal accomplishment* (or performance dissatisfaction) [12].

Emotional exhaustion occurs when people are under high emotional stress in their jobs. They invest a lot of work but receive relatively little recognition and a sense of achievement in return. The second dimension, *depersonalization* (or cynicism), develops as a protective and defensive function in order to devalue the (overly) demanding task and distance oneself from it, possibly also with bitterness about prevailing working conditions. This results in reduced work performance, feelings of failure, and *performance dissatisfaction* [13]. Stress-inducing exogenous factors are related to the (working) environment (e.g., an unsatisfactory cost-benefit ratio). In addition, personal disposition plays a role. This includes perfectionism and the inability to set boundaries.

The Maslach Burnout Inventory (MBI) is the most commonly used measurement tool in studies worldwide for determining the severity of (work-related) subjective complaints. However, there are also numerous other burnout scales that combine a total of approximately 130 different symptoms and complaints under the current burnout concept. Conceptually, it remains unclear which primary and secondary symptoms must be present for burnout to be diagnosed and how the individual degrees of severity of the primarily subjective complaints are to be defined. Burnout is not a separate diagnostic category and does not appear as such in the psychiatric classification systems used in medicine (DSM-5, ICD-10/11) [13, 14]. In ICD-10, burnout can be coded under factors that influence health status and lead to the use of health services. Accordingly, the syndrome can be marked without depicting a defined disorder or disease. Thus, in the ICD-10 code Z.73, "*problems associated with difficulties in coping with life*" can be noted, and "*burnout synonymous with a state of total exhaustion*" can be specifically recorded under Z.73.0, even if no other mental disorder can be diagnosed [13, 14] . A consensus statement by the German Society for Psychiatry, Psychotherapy, and Psychosomatics (DGPPN) differentiates between burnout as temporary work overload and burnout as long-term work overload without diagnostic status as a disease according to ICD-10, but as a problem-oriented risk condition with work-related subjective suffering. In addition, burnout symptoms are also differentiated as triggers of mental disorders or somatic illnesses and burnout symptoms as integral or early symptoms of mental disorders or somatic illnesses [14, 15].

The cardinal symptom of burnout, persistent *emotional exhaustion* with ongoing fatigue, is the most significant factor relevant to the disorder, but it is diagnostically nonspecific. In individual cases, the symptom can be attributed equally to several mental disorders and also to physical illnesses:

2.1 Depression

If the diagnostic criteria for depression are met, the diagnosis should be made and not mislabeled as burnout. This is also an essential prerequisite for indicating pharmacological and psychotherapeutic treatment. In terms of differential diagnosis, a distinction must be made between *dysthymia*, a mood disorder that persists for several years, can vary in intensity, and is sometimes accompanied by considerable subjective suffering and psychosocial disabilities. Also, in cases of *atypical depression* (dysphoria, preserved mood reactivity to positive events, hyperphagia, hypersomnia, leaden heaviness in the arms and legs, increased interpersonal sensitivity, and touchiness) or *seasonal depression* (great overlap with atypical depression without particular sensitivity to criticism or rejection), the symptom of *emotional exhaustion* can be very prominent. Differential diagnoses must also be made, particularly with regard to *bipolar depression*.

2.2 Neurasthenia

Persistent and distressing complaints of increased fatigue after mental exertion, or complaints of physical weakness and exhaustion after minimal exertion, should also suggest neurasthenia in the differential diagnosis. Other signs may include an inability or lack of effectiveness in coping with daily tasks, irritability, joylessness, general insecurity, and concern about declining well-being, accompanied by two or more of the following symptoms: Muscle discomfort and pain, dizziness, tension headaches, sleep disturbances, inability to relax, irritability, and dyspepsia. The autonomic and psychological symptoms are not persistent or severe enough to meet the criteria for a specific disorder in the classification. The symptoms cannot be explained by the presence of organic mental disorders, depressive disorders, or anxiety disorders. Key features are fatigue and weakness, as well as *concern* about reduced mental and physical performance.

Persistent *emotional exhaustion,* accompanied by ongoing fatigue, can also occur nonspecifically in the context of the following disorders:

- *Anxiety disorders*
- *Somatoform disorders*
- *Functional body syndromes*
- *Physical illnesses*

In medicine, differentiated examinations and guideline-oriented diagnostics are necessary in order to provide appropriate professional treatment. Athletes are often burdened by stress and pressure. Therefore, it is also useful to reflect on stress and strain for the prevention and early detection of disorders. This can be done as part of sports psychiatric support and supplemented by psychological measurements for recovery-stress diagnostics [15–17], or as part of prevention projects in sports [1].

3. Application of the burnout concept in sports

In a study involving soccer coaches, a fundamental distinction is made between highly stressed and low recovery, highly stressed and high recovery, low stressed and low recovery, and low stressed and high recovery. Coaches who are highly stressed and have low recovery levels show significantly higher burnout scores. In contrast, coaches who are low stressed and have high recovery levels appear to be least at risk of burnout [17, 18]. The Burnout Prevention Questionnaire for soccer coaches can be used to identify stress and strain at an early stage and to take appropriate preventive measures. Stress and strain among coaches are recorded in three dimensions (see **Tables 1** and **2**).

A *pre-burnout*, caused by persistent fatigue, for example, serves as an early warning sign. *Resources* help to counteract potential stress and develop recovery strategies. The *burnout* scale is used to measure stress levels.

Another study on the psychological stress experienced by soccer coaches showed that recovery phases are particularly important during the course of a season (the weeks during the winter and summer breaks). It is equally important to build up long-term, effective resources that can be drawn on when needed [18, 19].

Dimensions	Scale
Pre-burnout	Exhaustion, physical strain, disrupted rest periods, disrupted leisure time
Ressources	Social recovery, somatic recovery, general recovery, sleep, being in shape
Burnout	General stress, emotional stress, social stress, emotional exhaustion, loss of meaning, amotivation

Table 1.
Burnout prevention questionnaire for soccer coaches.

Dimensions	Function
Pre-burnout	→ Early detection
Ressources	→ Recovery strategies
Burnout	→ Recording of the load

Table 2.
Dimensions and functions in the burnout prevention questionnaire for soccer coaches.

In summary, stress requires recovery. It is helpful to know how to recover. Recovery must be part of long-term planning. Recovery varies from person to person. It is helpful to consciously address the topic of recovery and to be aware of the available options. A balance between stress and recovery is beneficial.

4. Real-time monitoring with the Synergetic Navigation System (SNS) in sports

Regeneration is particularly essential for athletes. Procedures and documentation systems for recording stress levels in athletes are especially helpful for the prevention and early detection of disorders. Real-time monitoring of change processes with the Synergetic Navigation System (SNS) can be used [1]. The SNS is an internet-based system used to record, visualize, and analyze change processes and their nonlinear trajectories [19–22]. It can be applied in diverse fields like psychotherapy, coaching, team development, and sports [22]. The visualization and evaluation of the processes enable collaborative process feedback between therapists and athletes, as well as data-driven management of therapy, training, and change processes. Questionnaires used for high-frequency self-assessments (e.g., day by day) provide data and time series analysis that can be used for reflection. In particular, they are used to visualize and conceptualize change processes in the data [23]. The SNS can be used as a tool to guide effort, training, and competition management to prevent non-functional overreaching and overtraining [1, 22–25]. Furthermore, it is suited to promote performance and stabilize the psychological structure [1, 20–25].

5. Sports psychiatric diagnostics

Early medical intervention is only possible if the indication for treatment can be made at an early stage. In order to make such an indication at an early stage, knowledge of those affected within the framework of ongoing care is essential. The specific aspects of competitive sports and certain sports-specific phenotypes of mental disorders often go beyond the scope of traditional psychiatric expertise. Sport-specific stress and overload [8], performance impairments and disorders, and possible overtraining conditions must also be taken into account [24, 25]. To meet the various requirements, the international societies for sports psychiatry (SGSPP, DGSPP, and ISSP) have developed specific training courses to address the different requirements and needs of those involved. In an article by Claussen et al. from 2020, the SGSPP's "Curriculum Sport Psychiatry and Psychotherapy" is presented as an example [25, 26].

The Sport Mental Health Assessment Tool 1 (SMHAT-1) is currently used for psychiatric screening in Olympic sports [26, 27]. It ensures a comprehensive psychological assessment of athletes. However, the predictive validity of its triage varies depending on the area of mental health (5% to 60% false-negative results), while the complete algorithm is very time-consuming for routine examinations. A shorter, more economical alternative using items obtained in the SMHAT-1 was recently validated as AMHS-18 [27, 28]. The AMHS-18 is a time-saving tool for assessing the mental health of athletes. It offers a practical alternative to the SMHAT-1, especially in situations where time and resources are limited or when athletes are assessed more regularly. The Polish Olympic Sports Federation recently published the ATHLETE MENTAL HEALTH SCREENING AND SUPPORT SYSTEM [28, 29]. It consists of four steps: 1. Initial Meeting, 2. Questionnaire Administration, 3. Brief Clinical Intake Interview, 4. Post-Interview Feedback and Mental Health Recommendations.

In the D-A-CH region (German-speaking region), a model for structured, multi-stage psychiatric diagnosis in competitive sports is currently being developed, which includes a basic psychiatric assessment as part of the annual or semi-annual sports medical examination (PBA-Sport) [29]. As part of this, a three-stage diagnostic procedure is to be implemented, involving an assessment of the extent of impairments, mental functioning, general self-efficacy expectations, and resilience in the first stage, a structured interview on psychiatric complaints in the second stage, and symptom- and disorder-specific diagnostics in the third stage [29, 30]. The first step includes defined red flags that indicate an immediate need for clarification.

6. Mental health care concepts in sports

The current practice of sports psychiatry and sports psychotherapy care is heterogeneous. It is recommended that sports psychiatric expertise be available both in clubs and at the association level. This can be integrated into special care concepts that also take performance factors into account, for example [1]. In principle, however, psychiatrists should not only be consulted for the treatment of disorders but also in advance for preventive and differential diagnostic interventions, as athletes could then also be supported within the system [30, 31]. It is not uncommon for disorders to be treated relatively late due to a lack of expertise within the system [30, 31]. **Table 3** shows a concept for mental health care in sports [1].

7. Athlete burnout

Early detection is very important, especially when it comes to the complex symptoms of burnout. Raedeke defines athlete burnout as a multidimensional syndrome characterized by *emotional and physical exhaustion*, *devaluation of sports*, and *dissatisfaction with athletic performance* [31–33]. Because the field of sports cannot be compared one-to-one with the work-related problems of a company, Raedeke reinterpreted the underlying dimensions. The *devaluation of sports* replaces the dimension of *depersonalization* (or cynicism). Accompanied by

Mental health care and prevention in sports			
	Contents	**Goal**	**Method**
Mental health care and prevention to maintain and improve performance			
Primary prevention	Education + early detection	Prevent the development of a disorder = Health of the athletes	Medical education + advice Preventive sports psychology Psychiatric screening SNS
Secondary prevention	Early detection in risk groups	Early treatment of a disorder with knowledge of sport-specific risk profiles and typical disorder patterns	Targeted investigations SNS
	Risk assessment for the occurrence of injuries	Data-based approach to injury prevention	SNS
Mental health care and prevention to restore performance			
Tertiary prevention	Prevention of the recurrence of **disorders** and **injuries**	Prevent the recurrence of a **disorder** or **injury** on return to play	Structured and accompanied return to play SNS
Mental health care and prevention based on guidelines			
Quaternary prevention	Preventing overdiagnosis and overtreatment	Guideline-based and economical care	Medical psychiatric expertise

Table 3.
Mental health care concept in sports [1].

persistent complaints, athletes subsequently develop a negative attitude toward sports. As a result, athletes distance themselves emotionally from it [33–35]. In addition, Raedeke supplements the factor of *emotional exhaustion* with the physical component, as physical exertion plays an essential role in sports (see **Figure 1**).

The Athlete Burnout Questionnaire [32, 33] measures three dimensions of athlete burnout: *emotional/physical exhaustion*, *devaluation of sports*, and a *reduced sense of accomplishment*. The 21-item ABQ is based on Raedeke's (1997) preliminary burnout scale and items adapted from Eades (1990) burnout inventory [35, 36].

The Athlete Burnout Questionnaire [32, 33]

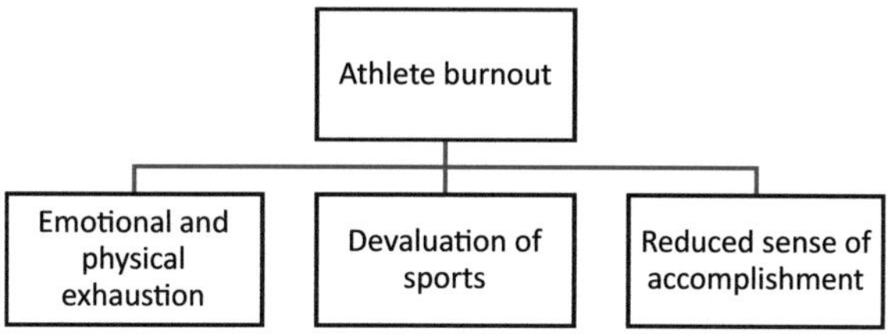

Figure 1.
Athlete burnout [33].

1. *Emotional and physical exhaustion*
   This component measures the feeling of fatigue, depletion, and physical weariness resulting from training and competition.
   Indicators include:

- Feeling drained even after rest
- Physical fatigue interfering with daily activities
- Loss of enthusiasm for training

2. *Devaluation of sports*
   This aspect reflects a negative attitude toward the sport, resulting in a loss of interest or motivation.
   Indicators include:

- Dreading training sessions
- Losing passion for competition
- Viewing sports as a chore rather than an enjoyable activity

3. *Reduced sense of accomplishment*
   This dimension measures feelings of inefficacy or a lack of achievement despite efforts.
   Indicators include:

- Belief that performance is not improving
- Feeling unsuccessful regardless of effort
- Decreased confidence in abilities

A more general definition of burnout in athletes comes from Smith [36, 37]. According to this definition, burnout is a psychological, emotional, and physical withdrawal from a once "beloved" sport as a result of excessive stress.

Due to the generally nonspecific symptoms of burnout syndrome, a differentiated sports psychiatric diagnosis should be sought at an early stage in order to diagnose the corresponding clinical pictures in accordance with valid medical classification systems and guidelines, and to be able to treat them early. The burnout concept can also be used to support and monitor athletes with regard to subclinical psychological symptoms related to training load and other stresses. In this case, monitoring with the SNS, including items from the ABQ, is recommended [1, 7].

8. Adjustment disorders in sports

In sports, it is always important to consider the possibility of adjustment disorders when making a diagnosis.

8.1 Adjustment disorder

Adjustment disorders are relatively common in sports. An adjustment disorder is a reaction to a stressful event, which can lead to depressive reactions or social behavior disorders. An adjustment disorder occurs when new stresses are difficult to accept or when those affected are unable to adapt adequately to a new life situation. An adjustment disorder is characterized by a pronounced feeling of subjective distress and emotional impairment. Social relationships and performance are temporarily limited. Those affected may develop a high level of psychological distress. Triggering stresses include, for example, professional conflicts, contract disputes, legal disputes, family problems, financial difficulties, but also disputes with sports management and coaches, teammates, injuries, selection, and the end of a career.

The decisive factor in the development of an adjustment disorder is the subjective experience of stress in connection with exceeding the individual stress limit, as well as the available resources and coping strategies.

Athletes are generally under pressure to succeed, exposed to physical strain, and must expect to be selected if they fail to achieve success. Constant pressure and permanent stress, experienced as excessive demands, frustration, and hurt feelings in the event of failure, are conducive to the development of disorders. Other stress factors for athletes sometimes include pronounced perfectionism, weight standards, or disorganization due to ADHD. A lack of career alternatives can also be a contributing factor.

9. Athlete personality

Athletes have generally learned to demonstrate *mental strength* during competition. This is characterized by willpower, self-discipline, and perseverance, as well as the ability to perform when it matters while remaining calm, composed, focused, and highly concentrated. Regardless of this, mental vulnerability or even a mental disorder may still exist. Those affected may have worked on their competitive personality for years and may not have developed other important personality functions to the same extent, which can lead them to feel more stressed, overwhelmed, or attacked in everyday situations. It is important to distinguish between mental strength and mental health. Mental strength should not be equated with mental health [37]. In competitive sports, it is common practice to deny one's own limits of mental resilience, as well as the occurrence of physical pain. This promotes the development of mental disorders [37]. Sports psychiatry, as a medical discipline, can help to recognize such connections in competitive sports and to address them in addition to existing support structures [1, 37]. The aim is to identify mental disorders at an early stage and treat them professionally [1]. In the long term, sports psychiatric support also leads to performance optimization and improvement, as a successful athletic career is usually only possible in the long term with stable mental health [1]. Furthermore, it can prevent premature career breaks, crises, and personal disasters.

10. Methods for coping with burnout and depression in sports

Physiological symptoms of burnout in sports, often linked to overtraining syndrome, include chronic fatigue that persists despite rest, decreased performance, and increased resting heart rate or blood pressure [24, 25]. Athletes may experience persistent muscle soreness, prolonged recovery times, loss of appetite, weight loss, and frequent illnesses due to a suppressed immune system [24, 25]. Body weight, maximum oxygen uptake (VO2max), and libido may decrease, as may muscle glycogen stores, which can lead to increased muscle tone and a higher incidence of muscle injuries. Signs and symptoms of burnout also include cognitive issues such as difficulty in concentration or forgetfulness, and emotional issues such as disinterest, moodiness, irritability, as well as low self-esteem, increased anxiety, and depression as a result of falling short of sports demands [8, 25]. All of these symptoms should be monitored in athletes. Athletic trainers can help in identifying and preventing burnout in athletes through an awareness of the signs and symptoms, and through communication with coaches and strength staff to monitor the athletes. Real-time monitoring can also be performed, for example, using the Synergetic Navigation System (SNS) [1].

The treatment of burnout in sports requires a holistic approach that combines a reduced training load, targeted recovery, and psychological support [8, 25]. Key factors include reducing performance pressure, getting enough sleep, practicing relaxation techniques (such as yoga or meditation), and engaging in non-competitive, recreational physical activities. An individualized training plan, often developed in consultation with a sports psychiatrist or sports psychologist, helps restore balance.

The treatment of burnout, combined with depression, requires a combination of medication with antidepressants, psychotherapy, stress management, and relaxation techniques. In severe cases, treatment should take place in a clinical setting.

To prevent burnout in sports, it is important for training to be varied, and athletes should have at least 1 to 2 days off per week from competitive athletics, sport-specific training, and competitive practice to allow them to recover both physically and psychologically. The weekly training time, number of repetitions, or total distance should not increase by more than 10% each week. The athletes should take at least 2 to 3 months away from a specific sport during the year. The focus of sports participation should also be on fun, skill acquisition, safety, and sportsmanship. Athletes should have access to information about appropriate nutrition and fluids, sports safety, and stress management [25].

Acknowledgments

OpenAI was used for language refinement, and clarification of phrasing.

DOI: http://dx.doi.org/10.5772/intechopen.1015610

Author details

Alexander Schorb
Department of Sports Psychiatry and Sports Psychotherapy, Paracelsus Medical University Salzburg, University Hospital of Psychiatry, Psychotherapy and Psychosomatics, Salzburg, Austria

*Address all correspondence to: a.schorb@salk.at

References

[1] Schorb A, Häfelinger U, Pesicka M, Kohl S, Karus Kaiser A, Schiepek G, Aichhorn W. Promoting mental health care to reach optimal performance in sports. Sports Psychiatry. 2025;1–6. DOI: 10.1024/2674-0052/a000106

[2] Halioua R, Wyssen A, Karrer Y, Matter Brügger S, Milos G, Munsch S. Psychische Erkrankungen im Leistungssport: Gestörtes Essverhalten und Essstörungen. Chapter 28. In: Claussen MC, Seifritz E, editors. Lehrbuch der Sportpsychiatrie und -psychotherapie. Psychische Gesundheit und Erkrankungen im Leistungssport Hogrefe Verlag (Bern). 1. Auflage. Hogrefe; 2022. 347–375

[3] Gugutzer R. Sport. In: Handbuch Körpersoziologie. Band 2, Forschungsfelder Und Methodische Zugänge. Gugutzer R, Klein G, Meuser M, H, Wiesbaden: Springer Fachmedien; 2017. p. 303–317

[4] Claussen MC, Gonzalez Hofmann C, Schneeberger AR, Seifritz E, Schorb A, Allroggen M, Freyer T, Helmig F, Niebauer J, Hefert J, Klostermeier E, Fröhlich S, Scherr J. Position paper: Sports psychiatric care provision in competitive sports. Deutsche Zeitschrift Für Sportmedizin. 2021;**72**:316–322. DOI: 10.5960/dzsm.2021.503

[5] Claussen MC, Currie A, Koh Boon Yau E, Nishida M, Martínez V, Burger J, Creado S, Schorb A, Nicola RF, Pattojoshi A, Menon R, Glick I, Whitehead J, Edwards C, Baron D. First international consensus statement on sports psychiatry. Scandinavian Journal of Medicine & Science in Sports. 2024;**34** (4):e14627. DOI: 10.1111/sms.14627

[6] Claussen MC, Seifritz E (Hrsg.) Lehrbuch der Sportpsychiatrie und -psychotherapie. Psychische Gesundheit und Erkrankungen im Leistungssport. Hogrefe Verlag (Bern) Hogrefe 1. Auflage: 2022

[7] Schiepek G, Schorb A, Schöller H, Aichhorn W. Prediction of sports injuries by psychological process monitoring. Sports Psychiatry. 2023;1–8. DOI: 10.1024/2674-0052/a000038

[8] Schorb A, Aichhorn J, Schiepek G, Aichhorn W. Burnout in adolescent elite athletes: A pilot study on an Austrian student sample. Sports Psychiatry. 2023;**2**(2):51–56. DOI: 10.1024/2674-0052/a000046

[9] Goodger K, Gorely T, Lavallee D, Harwood C. Burnout in Sport: A Systematic Review. The Sport Psychologist. 2007;**21**:127–151

[10] Altfeld S, Kellmann M. Burnout bei Trainern. Zeitschrift Für Sportpsychologie. 2013;**20**:47–58

[11] Freudenberger HJ. Staff burn-out. Journal of Social Issues. 1974;**30** (1):159–165. DOI: 10.1111/j.1540-4560.1974.tb00706.x

[12] Maslach C, Jackson SE. Burnout in health professions: A social psychological analysis. In: Sanders GS, Suls J, editors. Social Psychology of Health and Illness, Erlbanm, Hillsdale. Hillsdale, NJ Lawrence Erlbaum Associates; 1982. p. 227–251

[12] Burisch M. Das Burnout-Syndrom: Theorie der Inneren Erschöpfung. Berlin: Springer; 2006

[13] Kapfhammer HP. Burnout-anerkannte psychische Störung oder klärungsbedürftige Beschwerden? ÖGPB-Newsletter 5/2018

[14] DGPPN. Positionspapier der Deutschen Gesellschaft Für Psychiatrie, Psychotherapie und Nervenheilkunde (DGPPN) Zum Thema Burnout. Berlin. Herausgeber: Deutsche Gesellschaft für Psychiatrie, Psychotherapie und Nervenheilkunde (DGPPN) im Selbstverlag: 2012

[15] Kellmann M, Kallus KW. Der Erholungs-Belastungs-Fragebogen Für Sportler, Handanweisung. Frankfurt: Verlag Swets Test Services; 2000

[16] Kellmann M, Kallus KW. The Recovery-Stress Questionnaires. User Manual. Frankfurt am Main: Pearson Assessment & Information GmbH; 2016

[17] Altfeld S, Kellmann M. Are German coaches highly exhausted? A study of differences in personal and environmental factors. International Journal of Sports Science & Coaching. 2015;**10**:637–654

[18] Kellmann M, Schaffran P, Hummels J. Psychische Gesundheit von Fußballtrainern: Wann wird es eng? BDFL-Journal. 2017;**53**:16–21 Herausgeber: Bund Deutscher Fußball-Lehrer e.V. (BDFL)

[19] Schiepek G, Strunk G. The identification of critical fluctuations and phase transitions in short term and coarse-grained time series – A method for the real-time monitoring of human change processes. Biological Cybernetics. 2010;**102**(3):197–207. DOI: 10.1007/s00422-009-0362-1

[20] Schiepek G, Stöger-Schmidinger B, Kronberger H, Aichhorn W, Kratzer L, Heinz P, Viol K, Lichtwarck-Aschoff A, Schöller H. The Therapy Process Questionnaire. Factor analysis and psychometric properties of a multidimensional self-rating scale for high-frequency monitoring of psychotherapeutic processes. Clinical Psychology & Psychotherapy. 2019;**26**:586–602. DOI: 10.1002/cpp.2384

[21] Schiepek G, Schöller H, Aichhorn W, Kratzer L, Goditsch H, Viol K. Prozessmonitoring in der Psychotherapie: Der Therapie-Prozessbogen und seine psychometrischen Eigenschaften. Familiendynamik. 2022;**47**(3):210–224. DOI: 10.21706/fd-47-3-210

[22] Schiepek G, Schorb A, Schöller H, Aichhorn W. Prediction of sports injuries by psychological process monitoring. Sports Psychiatry. 2023; 1–8. DOI: 10.1024/2674-0052/a000038

[23] Schiepek G. Prozessfeedback und Prozesssteuerung in der Psychotherapie. Erfahrungen Mit Dem Synergetischen Navigationssystem (SNS) Psychopraxis. neuropraxis. 2022;**25**:323–331. DOI: 10.1007/s00739-022-00843-3

[24] Schorb A, Niebauer J, Aichhorn W, Schiepek G, Scherr J, Claussen MC. Overtraining from a sports psychiatry perspective. Deutsche Zeitschrift Für Sportmedizin. 2021;**72**:271–279. DOI: 10.5960/dzsm.2021.496

[25] Claussen MC, Imboden C, Seifritz E, Hemmeter U, Gonzalez Hofmann C. SGSPP-Curriculum Sportpsychiatrie und -psychotherapie: Stufe 1. Swiss Archives of Neurology Psychiatry and Psychotherapy. 2020;**171**(3). DOI: 10.4414/sanp.2020.03111

[26] Gouttebarge V, Bindra A, Blauwet C, Campriani N, Currie A, Engebretsen L, Hainline B, Kroshus E, McDuff D, Mountjoy M, Purcell R, Putukian M, Reardon CL, Rice SM, Budgett R. International Olympic Committee (IOC) Sport Mental Health Assessment Tool 1 (SMHAT-1) and Sport Mental Health Recognition Tool 1 (SMHRT-1): Towards better support of athletes' mental health. British Journal of Sports Medicine. 2021;**55**(1):30–37. DOI: 10.1136/bjsports-2020-102411

[27] Waleriańczyk W, Wójcik K, Konopka K, Lisek G, Iwaszkiewicz E, Krysztofiak H, Krzywański J, Zawadzki B. Shorter, faster, but still accurate: Using ant colony optimisation to develop and validate the Athlete Mental Health Screener-18 (AMHS-18) as a brief alternative to Sport Mental Health Assessment Tool 1 (SMHAT-1). British Journal of Sports Medicine. 2026;**60**:505–513. DOI: 10.1136/bjsports-2025-110881

[28] Waleriańczyk W, Lisek G, Wójcik K, Konopka K, Iwaszkiewicz E, Krzywański J, Krysztofiak H, Poczwardowski A. Taking the best from the two worlds: The benefits of combining athlete mental health screening with brief clinical intake interviews. British Journal of Sports Medicine. 2026;111155. DOI: 10 .1136/bjsports-2025-111155

[29] Gonzalez Hofmann C, Wyssen A, Schorb A, Allroggen M, Dallmann P, Schmidt RE, Graffius S-T, Niebauer J, Herfert J, Fröhlich S, Scherr J, Claussen MC. Sports psychiatric examination in competitive sports. Deutsche Zeitschrift Für Sportmedizin. 2021;**72**:307–315. DOI: 10.5960/dzsm.2021.502

[30] Schorb A. Conference report: 3rd International Conference on Sports Psychiatry, Salzburg, Austria, October 17-18, 2025. Sports Psychiatry. 2025;**4**(4):215–225. DOI: 10.1024/2674-0052/a000125

[31] Raedeke TD. Is Athlete burnout more than just stress? A sport commitment perspective. Journal of Sport and Exercise Psychology. 1997;**19**(4):396–417

[32] Raedeke TD, Smith AL. Development and preliminary validation of an athlete burnout measure. Journal of Sport and Exercise Psychology. 2001;**23**:281–306

[33] Raedeke TD, Lunney K, Venables K. Understanding athlete burnout: Coach perspectives. Journal of Sport Behavior. 2002;**25**(2):181–206

[34] Lemyre PN, Roberts GC, Stray-Gundersen J. Motivation, overtraining, and burnout: Can self-determined motivation predict overtraining and burnout in elite athletes? European Journal of Sport Science. 2007;**7**(2):115–126

[35] Eades AM. An Investigation of Burnout of Intercollegiate Athletes: The Development of the Eades Athlete Burnout Inventory. Berkeley: University of California; 1990

[36] Smith RE. Toward a cognitive-affective model of athletic burnout. Journal of Sport Psychology. 1986;**8**(1):36–50

[37] Markser VZ, Bär KJ. Seelische Gesundheit Im Leistungssport. Schattauer Verlag; 1. Aufl; 2019

Chapter 7

Academic Burnout and School Performance Among Adolescents: Concepts, Measurement and Evidence

José Ángel Hernández-Mariano, Erick Ordoñez-Villordo, Rocío Castilllo-Díaz, Fani Villa-Rivas, Nadia Velázquez-Hernández, Miguel Trujillo-Martínez, Edith Araceli Cano-Estrada, Dulce Milagros Razo-Blanco-Hernández, María Alicia Mejía-Blanquel and Juan Carlos Fernando Sánchez-Velázquez

Abstract

Academic burnout has emerged as a significant concern during adolescence, a developmental stage characterized by increasing academic demands and complex psychosocial challenges. This review synthesizes current evidence on the association between academic burnout and academic performance among adolescents, with particular attention to its educational and public health implications. Following a systematic selection process, 20 studies were included, encompassing both cross-sectional and longitudinal designs across diverse cultural and educational contexts. Overall, the evidence consistently indicates that higher levels of academic burnout are associated with poorer academic outcomes, including lower grade point averages and reduced performance on standardized assessments. Although the magnitude of these associations is generally small to moderate, their consistency across studies suggests that burnout constitutes a meaningful correlate of academic functioning. Longitudinal findings further indicate that the relationship between burnout and academic performance is dynamic and potentially bidirectional: in some cases, burnout precedes declines in performance, whereas in others, academic difficulties increase vulnerability to burnout. Beyond immediate educational outcomes, academic burnout may carry long-term implications by shaping educational attainment, future employment opportunities, and broader socioeconomic trajectories. From a public health perspective, these findings underscore the importance of early identification and prevention strategies targeting burnout during adolescence. Addressing academic burnout may contribute not only to improved academic achievement but also to a healthier transition into adulthood and the workforce. Overall, this review positions academic burnout as a shared concern for both education and public health, highlighting the need for integrated, life-course-oriented approaches in research, policy, and practice.

Keywords: academic burnout, academic performance, adolescents, mental health, public health, educational outcomes

1. Introduction

Adolescence is a period marked by profound changes that extend well beyond biological maturation [1, 2]. As young people move through secondary and high school, they face increasing academic demands, higher expectations, and greater pressure regarding future educational and occupational pathways [3]. During this stage, school performance becomes a central concern for students, families, and educational systems, as it is closely linked to later academic opportunities, psychosocial well-being, and long-term life trajectories [4].

Within this demanding context, the concept of academic burnout has gained increasing attention as a means of understanding how some students respond to sustained academic stress [5]. Academic burnout refers to a pattern of emotional exhaustion related to schoolwork, a cynical or detached attitude toward learning, and a diminished sense of educational efficacy [6]. Rather than reflecting a transient reaction to examinations or short-term academic pressure, burnout is generally understood as the result of prolonged exposure to academic demands that exceed students' coping resources [7].

Previous evidence suggests that academic burnout is associated with academic performance [8, 9]. Students experiencing higher levels of burnout or disengagement may struggle to maintain motivation, focus, and sustained academic effort, potentially leading to lower academic achievement [10]. Conversely, a strong sense of academic efficacy may act as a protective factor, helping students maintain their academic performance despite high demands [11, 12].

It is worth noting that most research on academic burnout has focused on undergraduate students, for whom the demands of academic autonomy and self-regulation are particularly relevant [10–14]. Less attention has been paid to middle and high school students, even though this developmental stage can represent a period of heightened vulnerability. From a neurodevelopmental perspective, adolescence is characterized by an imbalance between the relatively early maturation of the limbic system, involved in emotional processing and reward sensitivity, and the still-developing prefrontal cortex, which supports executive functions such as planning, self-regulation, and long-term decision-making [17]. This imbalance can limit adolescents' ability to anticipate the long-term consequences of their behaviors fully and to regulate academic stress effectively. As a result, sustained academic demands during this stage can have a greater emotional impact, increasing vulnerability to academic burnout and its potential consequences for academic performance [5, 7, 9].

Furthermore, the existing literature on academic burnout among adolescents is characterized by considerable methodological heterogeneity. Studies differ not only in how burnout is operationalized and analyzed but also in how academic performance is conceptualized and measured [15–17]. Some investigations adopt variable-centered approaches, examining linear associations between burnout dimensions and indicators of school performance using correlations or regression models [18, 21, 22]. In contrast, others rely on person-centered approaches, identifying distinct burnout or motivational profiles and comparing academic outcomes across groups [23–25]. At the same time, burnout is frequently examined alongside broader constructs such as stress, engagement, or general well-being, making it difficult to isolate its specific relationship with academic achievement [26, 27]. Together, these differences hinder the synthesis of findings and limit the comparability of results across studies, underscoring the need for integrative work explicitly focused on adolescents and measurable indicators of school performance in secondary and high school settings.

Against this background, this chapter aims to synthesize the available evidence on the association between academic burnout and school performance among adolescents enrolled in secondary and/or high school education. By integrating findings from studies using validated burnout measures and quantitative analytical approaches, including both variable-centered and person-centered designs, this chapter seeks to provide a coherent overview of current knowledge, highlight methodological challenges, and identify directions for future research and educational practice.

2. Conceptualization and measurement of academic burnout and academic achievement

Burnout syndrome is a condition characterized by emotional exhaustion, loss of interest in work, and a reduced sense of personal accomplishment, resulting from prolonged exposure to high levels of work-related stress. Initially, burnout was primarily described among healthcare professionals, reflecting the physical and emotional demands of caring for others [28, 29].

Over time, the concept of burnout was extended beyond occupational settings to the academic context, recognizing that students may also experience sustained periods of stress related to educational demands. Similar to employees, students are required to attend classes, complete assignments within strict deadlines, and successfully pass examinations, often under conditions of continuous evaluation and performance pressure [30, 31]. As a result, academic burnout emerged as an adaptation of the occupational burnout framework to capture students' responses to chronic academic stress [13].

In educational settings, academic burnout is generally conceptualized as a multidimensional construct encompassing emotional exhaustion, cynicism or disengagement, and reduced academic efficacy. Emotional exhaustion reflects feelings of being emotionally drained and overwhelmed by academic demands. Cynicism or disengagement refers to a distant, indifferent, or hostile attitude toward schoolwork and learning activities. Reduced academic efficacy captures students' perceptions of diminished competence and effectiveness in their educational roles [13].

In the adolescent population, academic burnout has increasingly been used to describe a pattern of emotional, cognitive, and motivational strain associated with sustained academic demands rather than temporary academic pressure [32].

Importantly, academic burnout is not understood as a short-term reaction to isolated stressors, such as examinations or deadlines, but rather as the result of prolonged exposure to academic demands that, over time, exceed students' coping capacities [5, 13]. During adolescence, these demands often occur within highly structured educational environments characterized by frequent assessments, performance comparisons, and expectations from teachers, families, and peers. Such conditions may intensify the emotional and motivational components of burnout, particularly among students who perceive limited control over academic demands [3, 9].

The assessment of academic burnout syndrome in adolescents has relied primarily on self-report instruments, most of which are adaptations of measures developed initially for occupational settings [33]. The Maslach Burnout Inventory–Student Survey is one of the most widely used tools, operationalizing burnout through the dimensions of emotional exhaustion, cynicism, and academic efficacy [32]. Other instruments, such as the School Burnout Inventory and its adaptations, have also been applied, particularly in European studies [32]. While these instruments share a common conceptual framework, differences in item wording, scale structure, and scoring procedures contribute to variability across studies.

In student populations, an additional challenge is the lack of clearly defined, universally accepted cutoff points for academic burnout. Unlike occupational settings, where threshold values have been proposed to classify burnout severity, most student-oriented instruments conceptualize burnout as a continuous construct [6, 29, 32]. When categorical classifications are used, cutoff points often vary across studies and are frequently derived from sample-specific distributions or regional norms [5, 34]. As a result, prevalence estimates and comparisons across studies are sensitive to the criteria applied and may differ substantially across educational systems and cultural contexts [35, 36].

Importantly, this variability is not limited to the definition of cutoff points. Further heterogeneity arises from how burnout is operationalized in the analysis. Some studies examine burnout as a global construct, while others analyze its individual dimensions separately [28]. This distinction is relevant, as different dimensions may capture distinct aspects of students' academic experiences and psychological functioning. Emotional exhaustion and cynicism often reflect disengagement from schoolwork, whereas academic efficacy is more closely linked to students' perceived competence and self-confidence [13].

Beyond measurement, studies also differ in their methodological approach. Variable-centered approaches conceptualize burnout as a continuous construct and examine its associations with other variables using correlational or regression-based methods. In contrast, person-centered approaches view burnout as a pattern of co-occurring characteristics within individuals and identify distinct burnout profiles using techniques such as cluster analysis or latent profile analysis. These different perspectives offer complementary ways of understanding academic burnout and contribute to the literature's conceptual and methodological diversity [9, 37].

Taken together, the conceptualization and measurement of academic burnout in adolescent populations reveal a construct that is theoretically well-defined but methodologically diverse. Variability in instruments, dimensional focus, cutoff criteria, and analytical approaches has shaped how burnout is identified and interpreted across studies [9, 38]. Recognizing these differences is essential for understanding the scope and limitations of existing evidence and for avoiding simplistic comparisons across educational contexts. This conceptual and methodological overview provides the necessary foundation for examining academic performance as the primary outcome of interest, which is addressed in the following section.

3. Academic performance in secondary and high school education

Academic performance is a central outcome in educational research and a key indicator of student progress in secondary and high school education systems. During adolescence, academic performance is closely linked to academic trajectories, access to further educational opportunities, and broader psychosocial development [3]. Hence, understanding how academic performance is conceptualized and measured is essential when examining its relationship with academic burnout.

In educational research, academic performance is most often operationalized using grade-based indicators, such as overall grade point averages or subject-specific grades [39]. These measures are typically derived from official school records and reflect cumulative academic performance over a defined period. In secondary and high school settings, grades often reflect performance in multiple areas, including core subjects such as mathematics, language arts, and science. They are frequently used as indicators of academic success [3].

In some studies, academic performance is assessed using standardized test scores, which aim to provide more uniform comparisons across students or schools [40]. These assessments can reduce variability associated with teacher grading practices, but they often reflect performance at a specific point in time rather than sustained academic functioning. Other research relies on teacher evaluations or composite indices that integrate grades across different subjects or academic periods, reflecting broader patterns of academic performance [41].

Another distinction concerns the source of performance data. While official school records are generally considered objective indicators of academic performance, several studies rely on students' self-reported grades or perceived academic performance [39]. Self-reported measures may be more readily available in large-scale surveys, but they can be influenced by recall bias, social desirability, and students' subjective perceptions of competence. Notably, these perceptions may be conditioned by burnout-related cognitions, notably reduced academic efficacy, which complicates the interpretation of associations between burnout and academic performance [6].

Academic performance in adolescence is also influenced by contextual factors that extend beyond individual ability or effort. Educational systems vary in grading standards, curriculum requirements, and assessment practices, which can affect the comparability of performance indicators across studies and settings. Furthermore, academic performance during this stage is embedded in social and institutional contexts, including classroom climate, teacher expectations, peer dynamics, and family support. These contextual influences are particularly relevant in middle and high school settings, where assessment is frequent and academic comparisons are often explicit [3].

From an analytical perspective, academic performance is variably treated as a continuous outcome, a categorical classification, or a composite score. Continuous measures offer greater sensitivity to variation in academic performance, while categorical classifications can facilitate interpretation but risk oversimplifying performance differences. The choice of outcome specifications influences both statistical modeling and substantive conclusions regarding the relationship between academic burnout and academic performance [42].

Overall, the diversity in how academic performance is conceptualized, measured, and analyzed presents significant challenges for synthesizing evidence across studies. Differences in outcome definitions, data sources, and educational contexts can influence reported associations with academic burnout and contribute to heterogeneity in findings. Therefore, a clear understanding of these considerations is essential for interpreting existing research and contextualizing the evidence reviewed in subsequent sections.

4. Approach and methods of the review

4.1 Data sources and search strategy

This review was conducted following the Preferred Reporting Items for Systematic Reviews and Meta-Analyses (PRISMA) guidelines [43]. The review protocol was registered in the International Prospective Register of Systematic Reviews (PROSPERO; registration number: CRD420251183925). Electronic searches were performed in PubMed®, Web of Science®, EBSCO, SCOPUS, and LILACS to identify epidemiological studies examining the association between academic burnout and school performance among adolescents. Search covered the period from database inception to November 5, 2025, without restrictions on publication date or language.

For studies published in languages other than English or Spanish, a professional translation service was used when necessary. Titles and abstracts of all retrieved records were independently screened by two reviewers (J.A.H.-M. and E.O.-V.) to assess potential relevance. Full texts of potentially eligible studies were subsequently reviewed in detail according to predefined inclusion and exclusion criteria. Discrepancies between reviewers were resolved through discussion and consensus.

4.2 Study selection and eligibility criteria

Eligibility criteria were defined according to the following research question: "Is the presence of academic burnout associated with school performance among adolescents enrolled in secondary and/or high school education?" Studies were included if they reported a quantitative association (e.g., correlation or regression-based estimate) between academic burnout and any indicator of educational or school performance among adolescents aged 12–18 years, using validated instruments to assess academic burnout and quantitative analytical approaches, regardless of whether academic performance constituted the primary study outcome. Both variable-centered studies (i.e., correlations or regression-based analyses) and person-centered studies (i.e., profile or cluster analyses incorporating burnout dimensions) were considered eligible, provided that academic burnout was explicitly assessed and related to academic performance outcomes. Observational study designs were eligible. Studies involving university students, qualitative designs, reviews, or reports lacking quantitative data that could be extracted were excluded. When multiple publications used the same dataset, the most recent or most comprehensive report was retained.

4.3 Data extraction and quality assessment

Data extraction was conducted independently by two reviewers (J.A.H.-M. and E.O.-V.) using a pre-piloted, standardized extraction form. The following information was extracted from each study: first author; year of publication; country; study design; sample size; participant characteristics; academic level and school grade; instrument used to assess academic burnout; indicator used to measure academic performance; and main quantitative findings (i.e., correlation coefficients, regression coefficients, odds ratios, and corresponding 95% confidence intervals).

The methodological quality of the included studies was independently assessed by the same reviewers using the Newcastle–Ottawa Scale (NOS), adapted for observational studies. The appropriate NOS version was applied according to the study design (cohort, case–control, or cross-sectional). The scale evaluates three domains: selection of study groups, comparability of groups, and ascertainment of exposure or outcome, with a maximum possible score of nine stars. Studies were classified as high quality (≥ seven stars), moderate quality (4–6 stars), or low quality (≤3 stars). Any disagreements were resolved through discussion and consensus [44].

4.4 Data synthesis and analytical approach

Due to the expected heterogeneity in study designs, measurement instruments, and analytical strategies, the findings were synthesized using a narrative approach. Although several studies reported quantitative effect estimates, a formal meta-analysis was not conducted.

Across the included studies, the only potentially comparable effect measures were Pearson correlation coefficients (r). However, these were inconsistently reported for overall academic burnout, and even fewer studies reported correlations for specific burnout dimensions. In addition, there was considerable variation in how both burnout and academic performance were defined and measured, as well as in the statistical methods used to examine their association. These differences limited the number of effect estimates that could be meaningfully compared across studies.

Given the small number of studies reporting comparable correlation coefficients and the substantial methodological and contextual heterogeneity of the evidence base, a pooled quantitative synthesis was unlikely to yield a meaningful or interpretable summary estimate. Therefore, the results were synthesized narratively, with emphasis on the direction, consistency, and relative strength of associations reported across studies.

5. What do we know so far? Findings from the review

Following the screening and eligibility process, we included 20 studies in the final synthesis (**Figure 1**). These studies provide the current evidence on the relationship between academic burnout and academic performance among adolescents.

Table 1 summarizes the characteristics of the studies included in the review. Overall, 12 of the 20 included studies employed cross-sectional designs, while the remaining studies used longitudinal designs. Most studies were conducted in Europe (n = 10), followed by Asia (n = 5), North America (n = 2), Africa (n = 2), and Oceania (n = 1). Burnout was most commonly assessed using the School Burnout

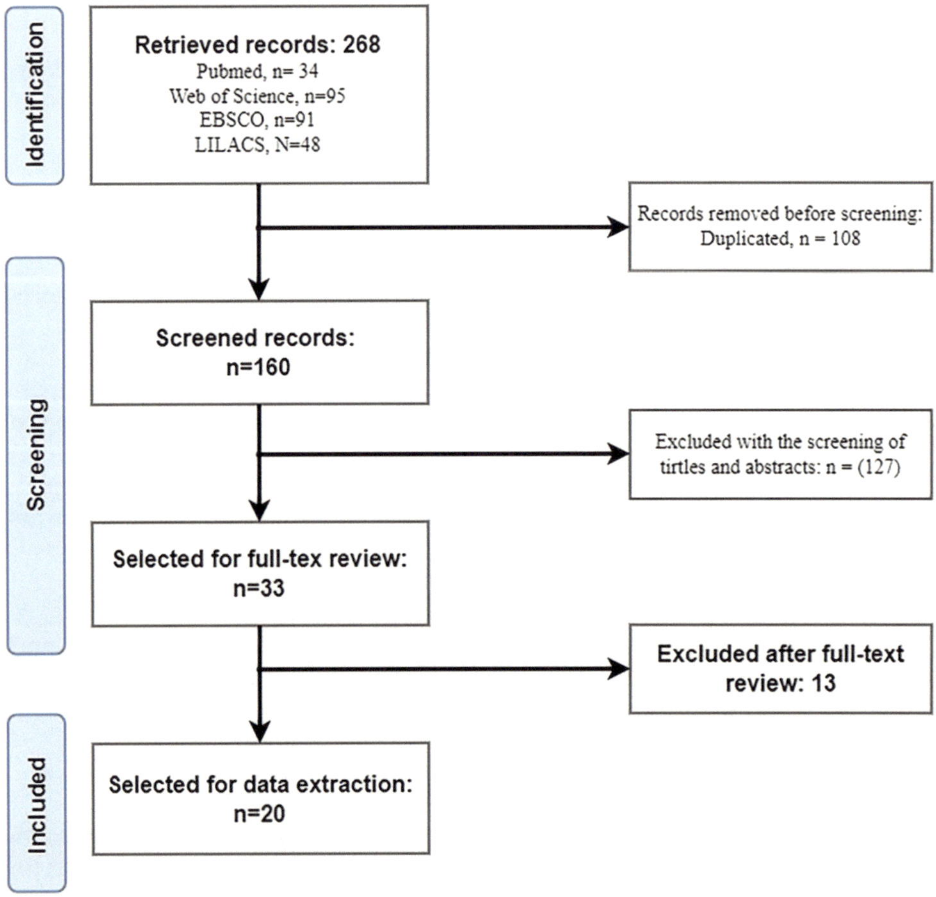

Figure 1.
PRISMA flow diagram of the study selection process.

Inventory (SBI; n ≈ 12), whereas six studies used versions of the Maslach Burnout Inventory–Student Survey (MBI-SS). A small number of studies applied alternative scales or person-centered approaches, such as burnout profiles derived from cluster or latent class analyses. Academic performance was typically measured using objective indicators, including school-record grades or standardized test scores, although a minority of studies relied on composite academic indices.

Overall, the methodological quality of the studies included was ranked from moderate to high according to the NOS. All longitudinal studies were rated as high quality, reflecting well-defined cohorts, appropriate temporal sequencing, the use of validated instruments, adequate adjustment for key confounders, and appropriate handling of missing data (**Table 2**). In contrast, cross-sectional studies showed moderate to high quality, with greater variability in their methodological rigor. The main limitations identified among cross-sectional studies included the inherent inability to establish temporal direction, limited adjustment for potential confounders beyond basic sociodemographic variables, and, in some cases, insufficiently detailed reporting of sampling procedures (**Table 3**).

Author, country and study design	n (sex)	Age (years)	School context	Burnout measurement	Academic achievement measurement	Main Findings
Oyyo et al. [18], Kenya. Cross-sectional.	714 (♂ 436; 278 ♀)	18.11 ± 1.49 [a]	Public upper secondary education – final year (Grade 12/Form 4)	MBI-SS – global score and dimensional (emotional exhaustion, cynicism, academic efficacy)	End-of-term examination grades (standardized scores)	Higher academic burnout was associated with lower academic achievement ($r = -0.24$, $p < 0.01$). Emotional exhaustion ($r \approx -0.21$) and cynicism ($r \approx -0.19$) showed negative bivariate associations, while academic efficacy remained independently associated with academic achievement in multivariable analysis ($\beta = 0.18$, $p < 0.01$).
Lee et al. [25]; Republic of Korea. Cross-sectional	338 (♂ 160; 178 ♀)	NR	Middle and high school students (school type NR; 27.2% and 72.8%, respectively)	MBI-SS – burnout profiles derived from cluster analysis (emotional exhaustion, cynicism, academic efficacy)	Self-reported Grade Point Average	Academic achievement (GPA) differed significantly across academic burnout profiles. Higher GPA was observed in well-functioning and persevering profiles, whereas lower GPA characterized distressed and laissez-faire profiles ($\eta^2 = 0.11$). GPA remained independently associated with burnout profiles in multivariable analysis ($\beta = -0.26$, $p < 0.01$).
Tuoimene et al. [23]; Finland Longitudinal study	419 (♂ 183; 236 ♀)	12–13	Elementary to lower secondary education (Grade 6–7; type NR)	SBI: burnout dimensions integrated into motivational profiles (exhaustion, cynicism, inadequacy)	Official register-based school grades (Mathematics, Finnish, Biology, Physics; scale 4–10), assessed in Grade 7.	Academic achievement differed significantly across achievement goal orientation profiles. Students who remained in mastery- and success-oriented profiles showed higher academic achievement after the transition, whereas those in indifferent and avoidance-oriented profiles showed lower grades. Changes toward maladaptive profiles were associated with poorer educational outcomes.

Author, country and study design	n (sex)	Age (years)	School context	Burnout measurement	Academic achievement measurement	Main Findings
Virtanen et al. [19]. Finland. Cross-sectional	821 (NR)	13–15	Public lower secondary school, grade NR	SBI: a continuous measure assessing exhaustion, cynicism, and inadequacy.	Self-reported GPA based on literacy, mathematics, and English grades (continuous)	School burnout was negatively associated with academic performance, with higher burnout related to lower GPA (standardized $\beta < 0$).
Teuber et al. [21]. Germany. Cross-sectional	395 (♂ 152; 242 ♀)	6.9 ± 1.25 [a]	Public upper secondary school students	SBI: continuous measure assessing exhaustion, cynicism, and reduced academic efficacy.	Grade point average from the most recent school report card, averaged across all subjects.	Academic burnout was negatively associated with academic performance ($r \approx -0.34$, $p < 0.001$)
Usán Supervía and Salavera Bordás. [22]. Spain. Cross-sectional	2652 (1389 ♂; 1283 ♀)	14.55 ± 1.70[a]	Public and private lower secondary education (four-year cycle) and upper secondary education (two-year cycle)	MBI-SS; continuous scores assessing emotional/physical exhaustion, cynicism, and academic efficacy.	Official school grades from first trimester report cards (0–10 scale)	Academic burnout showed a significant negative association with academic performance; higher levels of cynicism and exhaustion were associated with lower grades, while academic efficacy was positively associated with performance (e.g., cynicism $B \approx -0.26$; SEM correlation burnout–performance $r = -0.71$).
Evers et al. [26]. Taiwan. Longitudinal study	2462 (1293 ♂; 1169 ♀)	Baseline:13.9 Follow-up: 14.3	Public and private lower secondary education (academic year NR)	SBI: continuous composite score assessing exhaustion at schoolwork, cynicism toward school, and sense of inadequacy as a student.	Academic performance; standardized school test scores (T-scores) obtained from school records.	Academic burnout was negatively associated with academic performance (burnout–achievement $r = -0.25$ at T1 and $r = -0.22$ at T2); higher burnout predicted lower subsequent academic achievement indirectly through disturbed sleep due to social media use (burnout T1 → DSSM T2 $\beta \approx 0.10$; DSSM T1 → achievement T2 $\beta \approx -0.07$), while lower academic achievement predicted higher subsequent burnout ($\beta \approx -0.11$).

DOI: http://dx.doi.org/10.5772/intechopen.1014751

Author, country and study design	n (sex)	Age (years)	School context	Burnout measurement	Academic achievement measurement	Main Findings
Korhonen et al. [20], Finland. Cross-sectional	1,979 (sex NR)	12–16	Lower secondary education (academic year and school type NR)	SBI: continuous composite score assessing exhaustion at schoolwork, cynicism toward school, and sense of inadequacy as a student.	Academic performance; standardized test scores in reading, spelling, and mathematics.	School burnout showed a negative association with academic performance, with higher burnout correlated with lower achievement in mathematics ($r \approx -0.20$) and reading ($r \approx -0.12$).
Liou et al. (2022), Taiwan Longitudinal (three-wave cross-lagged panel study)	1301 (714 ♂; 587 ♀)	Baseline: 12.5	Public and private lower secondary schools (7th–9th grade)	SBS; continuous composite score assessing exhaustion at schoolwork, cynicism toward school, and sense of inadequacy as a student.	Academic decrement related to Internet use; perceived negative impact of Internet use on academic performance (homework, grades, sleep, attendance).	School burnout was positively associated with academic decrement over time (e.g., SB T1 → AD T2 $\beta \approx 0.08$; SB T2 → AD T3 $\beta \approx 0.09$); higher academic decrement predicted higher subsequent school burnout in early adolescence (AD T1 → SB T2 $\beta \approx 0.12$).
Altikulaç et al. [24], Finland. Cross-sectional	1,283 (sex NR)	11.0–14.7	Lower secondary education (academic year and school type NR)	SBI; continuous scores assessing exhaustion at schoolwork, cynicism toward school, and sense of inadequacy as a student, used to derive burnout profiles (person-centered approach).	Academic performance: grade point average (GPA) and mathematics grades obtained from school records.	Students with profiles characterized by high school burnout showed significantly lower GPA and mathematics grades compared with profiles characterized by low burnout and growth-oriented mindsets.

Author, country and study design	n (sex)	Age (years)	School context	Burnout measurement	Academic achievement measurement	Main Findings
Li et al. [27], China: Longitudinal study.	706 (≈387 ♂; 319 ♀)	Baseline: 10.7–14.3	Public lower secondary education (Grade 7 at baseline).	SBI: continuous composite score assessing exhaustion at schoolwork, cynicism toward school, and a sense of inadequacy as a student.	Academic achievement: school-record grades in Chinese, Mathematics, and English.	Academic burnout was negatively associated with academic achievement (i.e., burnout–achievement $r \approx = -0.30$); higher burnout predicted lower subsequent academic achievement over time ($\beta \approx = -0.10$), with effects varying according to levels of parental warmth.
Widlund et al. [45], Finland. Longitudinal study (4 waves, accelerated longitudinal design)	1,131 (sex NR)	Baseline: ~ 13; Follow-up: ~ 15	Public lower secondary schools (grades 7–9)	SBI: a self-report scale with three dimensions (exhaustion, cynicism, and inadequacy), assessed using a 6-point Likert scale. Both composite scores and subscale scores were analyzed.	Academic performance (standardized mathematics test scores)	Higher academic burnout was associated with lower mathematics performance (exhaustion $r \approx -0.22$; cynicism $r \approx -0.29$; inadequacy $r \approx -0.27$). Longitudinal analyses showed reciprocal effects between burnout dimensions and academic performance over time.
Usán Supervía et al. [22]. Cross-sectional	1,756 (897 ♂; 859 ♀)	14.53 ± 1.69[a]	Public lower secondary education (1st ESO, 338; 2nd, 436; 3rd, 567; 4th, 415)	MBI-SS; continuous subscale scores assessing emotional exhaustion, cynicism toward school, and academic efficacy	Academic performance (grade point average; mean academic grades)	Higher academic burnout was associated with lower academic performance, particularly higher emotional exhaustion ($r = -0.150$) and cynicism ($r = -0.386$). Academic efficacy was positively associated with school performance.
Usán-Supervía, Salavera Bordás and Mejías Abad [22], Spain. Cross-sectional	1756 (914 ♂; 842 ♀)	14.55 ± 1.68[a]	Public lower secondary education (1st ESO, 338; 2nd, 436; 3rd, 567; 4th, 415)	MBI-SS; continuous subscale scores assessing emotional exhaustion, cynicism toward school, and academic efficacy	Academic performance (grade point average; mean academic grades)	Higher academic burnout was associated with lower academic performance, particularly with higher emotional exhaustion ($r = -0.150$) and cynicism ($r = -0.388$), whereas academic efficacy was positively associated with school performance ($r = 0.431$).

Author, country and study design	n (sex)	Age (years)	School context	Burnout measurement	Academic achievement measurement	Main Findings
Atik and Özer (2020), Turkey. Cross-sectional	2,291 (1,239 ♂; 1,052 ♀)	NR	Public upper secondary education (9th–12th grade)	MBI-SS; continuous subscale scores assessing exhaustion, cynicism toward school, and academic efficacy	Academic achievement (school grades; fall semester grades standardized as z-scores)	Higher school burnout was associated with lower academic achievement (r = - 0.320); SEM showed a direct negative effect of school burnout on academic achievement (β = - 0.27), with additional indirect effects via school alienation and school attitudes
Özhan and Yüksel (2021), Turkey. Cross-sectional	866 (402 ♂; 440 ♀; 24 sex NR)	14–18	Public upper secondary education (10th–11th grade)	MBI-SS; continuous subscale scores assessing exhaustion at school, cynicism toward school, and academic efficacy	Academic achievement (grade point average; weighted final grades for fall semester)	Higher school burnout was associated with lower academic achievement (r = - 0.37); SEM showed a direct negative effect of school burnout on academic achievement (β = - 0.40).
Wang, Zha and Li [46], China. Longitudinal (two-wave, 1-year interval	2,481 (1,302 ♂; 1,179 ♀)	13.27 ± 0.67[a]	Public lower secondary education (7th grade)	SBI: continuous composite score assessing exhaustion from school demands, cynicism toward school, and sense of inadequacy as a student	Academic achievement (class-standardized average of Chinese, Mathematics, and English exam scores)	Academic achievement and school burnout showed reciprocal associations over time; higher baseline academic achievement predicted lower subsequent school burnout (β = - 0.243), and higher baseline school burnout predicted lower later academic achievement (β = - 0.015), with a more substantial effect from achievement to burnout.
Wang et al. [46], Finland. Longitudinal (three-wave latent growth design	362 (173 ♂; 189 ♀)	Baseline: 5.98 ± 0.15[a] Follow-up: NR	Public upper secondary education (Grades 9–11; academic track)	SBS: continuous composite score assessing exhaustion, cynicism toward school, and feelings of inadequacy	Academic achievement (grade point average; annual GPA on a 4–10 scale)	School burnout increased over time and was negatively associated with academic achievement; higher baseline GPA predicted lower initial burnout levels, while changes in school burnout were not significantly associated with changes in GPA over time

Author, country and study design	n (sex)	Age (years)	School context	Burnout measurement	Academic achievement measurement	Main Findings
Lindfors et al. (2018), Finland. Longitudinal (three-wave, multilevel design)	4,467 (2,198 ♂; 2,269 ♀)	Baseline: 13; follow-up: 16	Public lower secondary education (7th–9th grade)	SBI; continuous composite score assessing exhaustion at schoolwork, cynicism toward school, and sense of inadequacy as a student	Academic achievement (school-leaving certificate GPA; mean grades in mother tongue, mathematics, and foreign language; scale 4–10)	Higher school social capital was associated with lower school burnout and higher academic achievement. School burnout and academic achievement were negatively associated at the student level; higher burnout was longitudinally associated with lower educational achievement.
Yedemie et al. (2025); Ethiopia. Cross-sectional	395 students (sex distribution NR)	17.0 ± 3.21[a]	Public upper secondary education (Grades 11–12)	MBI-SS: emotional exhaustion, cynicism, and academic efficacy subscales	Academic achievement: GPA/ final grades obtained from school records	Emotional exhaustion was positively associated with academic achievement ($\beta = 0.10$, $p = 0.01$), while cynicism was negatively associated with achievement ($\beta = -0.07$, $p < 0.01$); engagement and resilience showed positive associations with academic achievement ($\beta \approx 0.12$), with the model explaining approximately 15% of the variance

Abbreviations: SBI, School Burnout Inventory; MBI-SS, Maslach Burnout Inventory–Student Survey; SBS, School Burnout Scale; GPA, Grade Point Average; NR, Not reported.
[a]Median ± standard deviation
Symbols: ♂, male; ♀, female.

Table 1.
Characteristics of studies included in the review examining academic burnout and academic performance among adolescents.

Author and year	Selection (4)	Comparability (2)	Exposure or outcome (3)	Global score (9)	Interpretation[a]	Comments
Wang et al. [46], Finland	3	2	3	8	High quality	This Finnish longitudinal cohort used repeated assessments and validated measures, with analyses adjusting for key confounders and school clustering. Generalizability may be limited by the focus on only academic-track students, rather than on lower-performing students.
Lindfors et al. (2018), Finland	3	2	3	8	High quality	This population-based Finnish cohort used repeated measures and register-based grades, with analyses accounting for clustering and key confounders. Slightly higher achievement in the final sample may limit generalizability to lower-performing students.
Tuomiene et al. [23]. Finland	3	2	3	8	High quality	This Finnish longitudinal cohort used repeated assessments and register-based grades with validated measures. Analyses accounted for key baseline factors and attrition, although the modest final sample and single metropolitan setting may limit generalizability.
Evers et al. [26] Taiwan	3	2	3	8	High quality	This two-wave cohort used repeated assessments and validated measures, with analyses adjusting for key covariates and attrition. The non-random school sample and short follow-up may limit generalizability and long-term conclusions.
Li et al. (2022), China	3	2	3	8	High quality	This three-wave cohort used validated burnout measures and school-record grades, with analyses adjusting for key covariates and prior levels. The sample was limited to two non-random public schools in one urban area, which may restrict generalizability.
Liou et al. (2022), Taiwan	3	2	3	8	High quality	This three-wave cohort used repeated assessments and validated measures, with analyses accounting for baseline factors and missing data. The non-random school sample and single metropolitan setting may limit generalizability.
Widlund et al. [45] Finland	4	2	2	9	High quality	This population-based cohort followed Finnish lower secondary students with repeated measures. Burnout and engagement were assessed using validated tools, mathematics performance with standardized tests, and analyses accounted for prior levels and missing data.
Wang, Zha and Li [46], China	3	2	3	8	High quality	This two-wave cohort used validated burnout measures and school-record grades, with analyses accounting for prior levels, clustering, and missing data. The sample came from three non-random urban schools, which may limit generalizability.

[a] *Global score of the Newcastle-Ottawa Scale: ≥7, high quality; 4 to 6, moderate quality; and ≤3, low quality.*

Table 2.
Quality assessment of longitudinal studies using the Newcastle–Ottawa Scale (NOS).

Author and year	Selection (5)	Comparability (2)	Exposure or outcome (3)	Global score (10)	Interpretation[a]	Comments
Lee et al. [25]. Republic of Korea	4	1	3	8	High quality	Non-probabilistic school-based sampling limits representativeness. Limited adjustment for potential confounders, with no fully multivariable models assessing the independent association between burnout profiles and academic achievement.
Korhonen et al. [20], Finland	4	1	3	8	High quality	A sample drawn from a specific national context limits external validity. Limited control for potential confounders, with no fully adjusted multivariable models addressing socioeconomic or school-level factors.
Virtanen et al. [19]. Finland	3	2	1	6	Moderate quality	No a priori sample size or power calculation was reported; sample adequacy was inferred post hoc from CFA/SEM fit indices. Academic achievement was based on self-reported grades, which may introduce reporting bias despite acceptable internal consistency.
Usán-Supervía et al. [22], Spain	4	1	3	8	High quality	No sample size justification or statistical power calculation was reported. Regarding comparability, regression models did not explicitly adjust for key sociodemographic confounders, leaving room for residual confounding.
Usán-Supervía, Salavera Bordás and Mejías Abad [22], Spain	4	1	3	8	High quality	Although the sample was large and randomly selected, it was restricted to public secondary schools from a single Spanish province, which may limit the generalizability of the findings to other educational or socioeconomic contexts. In addition, the analyses did not explicitly adjust for relevant potential confounders.
Usán Supervía and Salavera Bordás [22]	3	2	3	8	High quality	No a priori sample size or power calculation was reported, despite the large sample (n = 2,652). Although schools were randomly selected, they were not representative of the city's social structure, as acknowledged by the authors, potentially introducing socioeconomic selection bias.
Atik and Özer (2020), Turkey	4	2	3	9	High quality	No formal priori sample size or power calculation specific to the primary outcomes was reported, despite justification based on SEM rules of thumb. The cross-sectional design prevents establishing temporal or causal relationships among trust in teachers, school attitudes, alienation, burnout, and academic achievement, even though mediation paths were tested using SEM.

Author and year	Selection (5)	Comparability (2)	Exposure or outcome (3)	Global score (10)	Interpretation[a]	Comments
Oyyo et al. [18]. Kenya	4	2	3	9	High quality	Although a relatively large random sample was drawn from 31 public secondary schools, participants were restricted to Form Four students from a single county, which may limit generalizability to other regions, grade levels, or private schools. No formal priori power calculation was conducted; sample size justification relied on rule-of-thumb proportions rather than outcome-specific statistical power
Altikulaç et al. [24], Finland	4	2	3	9	High quality	Although students were recruited from multiple schools, the sample was restricted to first-year secondary students from one country. No formal priori sample size or power calculation was reported; justification relied on latent profile analysis fit indices and conventions.
Teuber et al. [21]. Germany	3	1	1	6	Moderate quality	The study was explicitly designed as a pilot study. It included a relatively small convenience sample of upper secondary students (n = 395), limiting representativeness. No priori sample size or power calculation was conducted. Comparability was limited, as analyses did not clearly adjust for key sociodemographic confounders. Academic performance was assessed via self-reported grade point average, which may introduce reporting bias.
Özhan and Yüksel (2021), Turkey	4	2	3	9	High quality	Although stratified random sampling was used and multiple school types were included, the sample was restricted to public high schools in a single province, which may limit generalizability to other regions and to private schools.
Yedemie et al. (2025). Ethiopia	3	1	2	6	Moderate quality	This cross-sectional study used validated burnout measures and school-record grades. The sample was drawn from public secondary schools in a single city. Still, sampling procedures were not clearly reported, and analyses adjusted for a few confounders beyond basic demographics, which may limit representativeness and comparability.

[a]*Global score of the Newcastle-Ottawa Scale: ≥7, high quality; 4 to 6, moderate quality; and ≤3, low quality.*

Table 3.
Quality assessment of cross-sectional studies using the Newcastle–Ottawa Scale (NOS).

Across study designs and cultural contexts, the findings consistently indicate a negative association between academic burnout and academic performance. The majority of studies reported that higher levels of burnout were associated with poorer educational outcomes, including lower grades and reduced performance on standardized tests, suggesting that burnout represents a relevant correlate of academic functioning during adolescence.

Longitudinal studies added an essential layer of evidence by showing that the relationship between burnout and academic performance unfolds over time. Several studies found that higher burnout preceded later declines in educational achievement, while others suggested that poor academic performance increased the likelihood of subsequent burnout. Together, these findings support the idea of a reciprocal, potentially reinforcing process between burnout and academic outcomes during adolescence [26, 45, 46].

Some longitudinal studies also explored how this relationship operates. Their results suggest that the link between burnout and academic performance may be partly explained by intermediate factors, such as sleep problems or reduced academic engagement, and may vary depending on contextual influences, including parental support or peer-group dynamics[26, 27]. These findings highlight that burnout is embedded in a broader psychosocial and educational context.

Although the strength of the associations differed across studies, most reported small to moderate effects. Correlation coefficients generally fell within a weak-to-moderate range (approximately $r = -0.15$ to -0.40) and were consistently statistically significant. Taken together, these findings suggest that even relatively modest associations may translate into meaningful academic consequences when burnout persists over time.

Overall, the evidence reviewed here suggests that academic burnout is a relevant and consistent correlate of academic performance in adolescence, supported by both cross-sectional and longitudinal findings. At the same time, differences in study designs and analytical approaches point to areas where future research could further clarify the nature and mechanisms of this relationship.

6. Methodological challenges and research gaps

Despite the growing body of evidence linking academic burnout to academic performance, several methodological challenges and research gaps remain evident across the literature reviewed.

First, although longitudinal studies consistently showed higher methodological quality, their number remains limited compared with cross-sectional research. While cross-sectional designs have been helpful in establishing the presence of an association, they cannot clarify the temporal direction of effects. Hence, much of the available evidence still relies on designs that cannot distinguish whether burnout precedes poor academic performance, emerges because of it, or reflects a reciprocal process.

Second, even among longitudinal studies, there was substantial heterogeneity in analytical approaches. Some studies focused on direct associations, whereas others examined mediating or moderating mechanisms, making comparisons across these challenges. Furthermore, follow-up periods varied considerably, and relatively few studies extended beyond two or three measurement waves, limiting insight into longer-term developmental trajectories.

Third, adjustment for potential confounders was inconsistent, particularly in cross-sectional studies. While most longitudinal studies controlled for prior levels of burnout and academic performance, many cross-sectional studies adjusted only for basic sociodemographic variables. Critical contextual factors, such as school characteristics, classroom climate, and family-level variables, were often omitted or insufficiently detailed, potentially leading to residual confounding.

Another limitation concerns the measurement of academic burnout and academic performance. Although validated instruments such as the School Burnout Inventory and the Maslach Burnout Inventory–Student Survey were widely used, differences in scale versions, scoring procedures, and analytical treatment of burnout dimensions contributed to heterogeneity. Similarly, while many studies relied on objective indicators of academic performance, others used composite or context-specific measures, which may reduce comparability across educational systems.

Geographical representation also remains uneven. Most studies were conducted in European settings, with relatively limited evidence from low- and middle-income countries. This imbalance limits the generalizability of findings and underscores the need for research across a broader range of cultural and educational contexts.

Finally, few studies have explicitly addressed the mechanisms underlying the burnout–performance relationship. Although emerging evidence points to the role of factors such as sleep problems, academic engagement, and psychosocial context, these pathways remain underexplored. Greater emphasis on theoretically grounded models could help clarify how and under what conditions academic burnout affects students' educational outcomes.

Taken together, these challenges suggest that future research would benefit from more longitudinal designs with multiple waves, improved consistency in measurement and adjustment strategies, and broader geographic coverage. Addressing these gaps will be essential for advancing the understanding of academic burnout and for informing effective prevention and intervention strategies in educational settings.

7. Implications for educational practice and public health

The findings of this chapter have implications not only for educational practice but also for public health, given the close links between academic functioning, mental health, and later outcomes across the life course [3]. From this perspective, the evidence points to the importance of prevention and early intervention strategies during adolescence to support students' well-being, resilience, and sustained academic engagement across both educational and public health contexts.

At the school level, the association between academic burnout and poorer academic performance highlights the importance of strengthening protective factors within educational settings. Beyond early identification and prevention, schools play a central role in fostering students' resilience, understood as the capacity to adapt to academic demands, cope with stress, and maintain engagement in the face of challenges [47]. Academic approaches that promote resilience may include supportive teacher–student relationships, the development of adaptive coping and emotional regulation skills, realistic academic expectations, and school climates that value well-being alongside performance. Interventions aimed at reducing emotional exhaustion and cynicism, promoting engagement, and improving the school environment may help mitigate the negative academic consequences associated with burnout. Importantly, such efforts should extend beyond academic achievement and explicitly incorporate students.

In public health, academic burnout during adolescence can be understood as an early marker of vulnerability with potential long-term consequences. Poor academic performance linked to burnout may limit educational attainment, reduce future employment opportunities, and contribute to social and economic disadvantages later in life. Moreover, evidence from occupational health research suggests that individuals who experience burnout or related stress symptoms at younger ages are more likely to report burnout and mental health problems during their working lives, underscoring the relevance of early-life stress for adult health outcomes [48]. In this context, the evidence points to the importance of prevention and early intervention strategies, as risk factors present in early stages of life are predictive of vulnerability and adverse outcomes in adulthood [49]. Addressing these factors from childhood and adolescence may therefore help support students' well-being, resilience, and sustained academic engagement across the life course and across both educational and public health contexts.

These findings support the view that academic burnout is not only an educational issue but also a population health concern. Preventive efforts targeting burnout in school settings may, therefore, yield benefits beyond the classroom, contributing to healthier transitions into higher education and the labor market, and potentially reducing the burden of work-related burnout and mental health disorders in adulthood [50].

For future research, longitudinal studies with extended follow-up into early adulthood and working life are particularly needed to clarify how academic burnout trajectories relate to later occupational burnout, mental health, and labor market participation. It will be essential to understand the long-term implications of academic burnout better and to inform effective, cross-sectoral prevention strategies from educational, psychological, and public health perspectives.

8. Conclusions

This review brings together current evidence on the relationship between academic burnout and academic performance in adolescents. Across different educational systems, cultural contexts, and study designs, the findings point in the same direction: students who experience higher levels of academic burnout tend to perform more poorly academically. Although these associations are usually small to moderate in size, their consistency across studies suggests that burnout is a relevant factor in adolescents' academic functioning during a key developmental stage.

Findings from longitudinal studies add important nuance to this picture. Rather than a one-way association, the relationship between burnout and academic performance appears to be dynamic. In some cases, higher burnout precedes later declines in performance, while in others, academic difficulties increase the likelihood of subsequent burnout. This pattern suggests that burnout develops within an ongoing process shaped by students' educational demands and psychosocial contexts, rather than as an isolated experience.

The implications of these findings extend beyond school outcomes alone. From a public health perspective, academic burnout may have longer-term consequences by influencing educational attainment, access to employment opportunities, and future socioeconomic trajectories. There is also growing evidence that vulnerability to burnout earlier in life may carry forward into adulthood, increasing the risk of burnout or mental health problems during working life. This highlights the importance of considering burnout in adolescence within a broader life-course perspective.

Overall, the evidence supports viewing academic burnout as both an educational and a public health issue. Efforts to prevent or reduce burnout during adolescence may not only improve academic performance but also support healthier transitions into adulthood and the workforce. Future research would benefit from longitudinal designs that follow individuals across educational and occupational stages. At the same time, interventions and policies should aim to integrate academic and public health approaches that promote well-being, resilience, and sustainable engagement from an early age.

Acknowledgments

The authors acknowledge the use of Grammarly for English language editing, including grammar correction and sentence refinement. The authors take full responsibility for the chapter's content.

Acronyms and abbreviations

SBI	School Burnout Inventory
MBI-SS	Maslach Burnout Inventory–Student Survey
GPA	Grade Point Average

Conflict of Interest

The authors declare no conflict of interest.

Author details

José Ángel Hernández-Mariano[1]*, Erick Ordoñez-Villordo[1], Rocío Castilllo-Díaz[2], Fani Villa-Rivas[2], Nadia Velázquez-Hernández[3], Miguel Trujillo-Martínez[4], Edith Araceli Cano-Estrada[5], Dulce Milagros Razo-Blanco-Hernández[1], María Alicia Mejía-Blanquel[1] and Juan Carlos Fernando Sánchez-Velázquez[6]

1 Department of Research, Hospital Juarez of Mexico, Mexico City, Mexico

2 Faculty of Nursing and Midwifery, Juarez University of the State of Durango, Durango, Mexico

3 Scientific Research Institute, Juarez University of the State of Durango, Durango, Mexico

4 General Hospital with Family Medicine Unit Number 7, Mexican Social Security Institute, Cuautla, Mexico

5 Superior School of Tlahuelilpan, Autonomous University of Hidalgo State, Tlahuelilpan, Mexico

6 Nursing School, Hospital Juarez of Mexico, Mexico City, Mexico

*Address all correspondence to: jose.hernandezm@salud.gob.mx

References

[1] Steinberg L. Age of Opportunity: Lessons from the New Science of Adolescence; Age of Opportunity: Lessons from the New Science of Adolescence. Boston, MA: Houghton Mifflin Harcourt; 2014. p. 264

[2] Blakemore S-J, Mills KL. Is adolescence a sensitive period for sociocultural processing? Annual Review of Psychology. 2014;**65**:187–207. DOI: 10.1146/annurev-psych-010213-115202

[3] Eccles JS, Roeser RW. Schools as developmental contexts during adolescence. Journal of Research on Adolescence. 2011;**21**:225–241. DOI: 10.1111/j.1532-7795.2010.00725.x

[4] Patton GC, Sawyer SM, Santelli JS, Ross DA, Afifi R, Allen NB, Arora M, Azzopardi P, Baldwin W, Bonell C, et al Our future: A Lancet commission on adolescent health and wellbeing. The Lancet (London, England). 2016;**387**:2423–2478

[5] Salmela-Aro K, Savolainen H, Holopainen L. Depressive symptoms and school burnout during adolescence: Evidence from two cross-lagged longitudinal studies. Journal of Youth and Adolescence. 2009;**38**:1316–1327. DOI: 10.1007/s10964-008-9334-3

[6] Schaufeli M, Martínez I, Marqués-Pinto A, Salanova M, Bakker A. Burnout and engagement in University students. Journal of Cross-cultural Psychology. 2002;**33**:464–481. DOI: 10.1177/0022022102033005003

[7] Walburg V. Burnout among high school students: A literature review. Children and Youth Services Review. 2014;**42**:28–33. DOI: 10.1016/j.childyouth.2014.03.020

[8] May RW, Bauer KN, Fincham FD. School burnout: Diminished academic and cognitive performance. Learning and Individual Differences. 2015;**42**:126–131. DOI: 10.1016/j.lindif.2015.07.015

[9] Salmela-Aro K, Upadyaya K. School burnout and engagement in the context of demands-resources model. British Journal of Educational Psychology. 2014;**84**:137–151. DOI: 10.1111/bjep.12018

[10] Tuominen-Soini H, Salmela-Aro K. Schoolwork engagement and burnout among Finnish high school students and young adults: Profiles, progressions, and educational outcomes. Developmental Psychology. 2014;**50**:649–662. DOI: 10.1037/a0033898

[11] Bandura A. Self-efficacy: Toward a unifying theory of behavioral change. Psychological Review. 1977;**84**:191–215. DOI: 10.1037//0033-295x.84.2.191

[12] Salanova M, Schaufeli W, Martínez I, Bresó E. How obstacles and facilitators predict academic performance: The mediating role of study burnout and engagement. Anxiety, Stress, and Coping: An International Journal. 2010;**23**:53–70. DOI: 10.1080/10615800802609965

[13] Schaufeli WB, Martínez IM, Pinto AM, Salanova M, Barker AB. Burnout and engagement in university students a cross-national study. Journal of Cross-Cultural Psychology. 2002;**33**:464–481. DOI: 10.1177/0022022102033005003

[14] Hernández-Mariano JÁ, Hurtado-Salgado E, Velázquez-Núñez MDC, Cupul-Uicab LA. Prevalence of academic burnout among nursing students: A systematic review and meta-analysis. Journal of Nursing Education. 2024;**63**:533–539. DOI: 10.3928/01484834-20240502-04

[15] Kaggwa MM, Kajjimu J, Sserunkuma J, Najjuka SM, Atim LM, Olum R, Tagg A, Bongomin F. Prevalence of burnout among university students in low- and middle-income countries: A systematic review and meta-analysis. PLoS ONE. 2021;**16**: e0256402. DOI: 10.1371/journal.pone.0256402

[16] Consuelos-Sánchez KS, Cano-Estrada A, Castañeda-Márquez AC, Hernández-Mariano JÁ. Nursing training and its association with burnout syndrome among Mexican undergraduate students. Salud Mental. 2023;**46**:97–104. DOI: 10.17711/SM.0185-3325.2023.013

[17] Best O, Ban S. Adolescence: Physical changes and neurological development. British Journal of Nursing (Mark Allen Publishing). 2021;**30**:272–275. DOI: 10.12968/bjon.2021.30.5.272

[18] Oyoo S, Mwaura P, Kinai T, Mutua J. Academic burnout and academic achievement among secondary school students in Kenya. Education Research International. 2020;**2020**:6. DOI: 10.1155/2020/5347828

[19] Virtanen T, Kiuru N, Lerkkanen M-K, Poikkeus A, Kuorelahti M. Assessment of student engagement among junior high school students and associations with self-esteem, burnout, and academic achievement. Journal of Educational Research Online. 2016;**8**:137–157

[20] Korhonen J, Linnanmäki K, Aunio P. Learning difficulties, academic well-being and educational dropout: A person-centred approach. Learning and Individual Differences. 2014;**31**:1–10. DOI: 10.1016/j.lindif.2013.12.011

[21] Teuber Z, Nussbeck FW, Wild E. The bright side of grit in burnout-prevention: Exploring grit in the context of demands-resources model among Chinese high school students. Child Psychiatry and Human Development. 2021;**52**:464–476. DOI: 10.1007/s10578-020-01031-3

[22] Supervía PU, Bordás CS, Abad JJM, Orozco AM, Jarie L. Relaciones de la inteligencia emocional, burnout y compromiso académico con el rendimiento escolar de estudiantes adolescentes. Archivos de Medicina (Colombia). 2019;**19**:197–207

[23] Tuominen H, Niemivirta M, Lonka K, Salmela-Aro K. Motivation across a transition: Changes in achievement goal orientations and academic well-being from elementary to secondary school. Learning and Individual Differences. 2020;**79**:101854. DOI: 10.1016/j.lindif.2020.101854

[24] Altikulaç S, Janssen TWP, Yu J, Nieuwenhuis S, Van Atteveldt NM. Mindset profiles of secondary school students: Associations with academic achievement, motivation and school burnout symptoms. British Journal of Educational Psychology. 2024;**94**: 738–758. DOI: 10.1111/bjep.12676

[25] Lee J, Puig A, Kim Y-B, Shin H, Lee JH, Lee SM. Academic burnout profiles in Korean adolescents. Stress and Health: Journal of the International

Society for the Investigation of Stress. 2010;**26**:404–416. DOI: 10.1002/smi.1312

[26] Evers K, Chen S, Rothmann S, Dhir A, Pallesen S. Investigating the relation among disturbed sleep due to social media use, school burnout, and academic performance. Journal of Adolescence. 2020;**84**:156–164. DOI: 10.1016/j.adolescence.2020.08.011

[27] Li C, Tan X, Zhao Q, Ren P. Parental warmth may not always be beneficial: High parental warmth impairs victimized adolescents' academic achievement via elevated school burnout. Journal of Social and Personal Relationships. 2022;**39**: 1863–1884. DOI: 10.1177/02654075211068189

[28] Maslach C, Schaufeli WB, Leiter MPJB. Annu. Review of Psychology. 2001;**52**:397–422. DOI: 10.1146/annurev.psych.52.1.397

[29] Maslach C, Jackson S. The measurement of experienced burnout. Journal of Occupational Behavior. 1981;**2**:99–113

[30] Robotham D. Stress among higher education students: Towards a research agenda. Higher Education. 2008;**56**: 735–746. DOI: 10.1007/s10734-008-9137-1

[31] McCarthy ME, Pretty GM, Catano V. Psychological sense of community and student burnout. Journal of College Student Development. 1990;**31**:211–216

[32] Salmela-Aro K, Kiuru N, Leskinen E, Nurmi J-E. School burnout inventory (SBI). European Journal of Psychological Assessment. 2009;**25**: 48–57. DOI: 10.1027/1015-5759.25.1.48

[33] Maslach C, Jackson S, Leiter M. MBI: Maslach Burnout Inventory. Sunnyvale, CA: Consulting Psychologists Press; 1997

[34] Kristensen TS, Borritz M, Villadsen E, Christensen KB. The Copenhagen burnout inventory: A new tool for the assessment of burnout. Work and Stress. 2005;**19**:192–207. DOI: 10.1080/02678370500297720

[35] Bianchi R, Schonfeld IS, Laurent E. Burnout-depression overlap: A review. Clinical Psychology Review. 2015;**36**: 28–41. DOI: 10.1016/j.cpr.2015.01.004

[36] Walburg V. Burnout among high school students: A literature review. Children and Youth Services Review. 2014;**42**:28–33

[37] Tuominen-Soini H, Salmela-Aro K, Niemivirta M. Achievement goal orientations and subjective well-being: A person-centred analysis. Learning and Instruction. 2008;**18**:251–266. DOI: 10.1016/j.learninstruc.2007.05.003

[38] Lin S-H, Huang Y-C. Life stress and academic burnout. Active Learning in Higher Education. 2014;**15**:77–90. DOI: 10.1177/1469787413514651

[39] Kuncel NR, Credé M, Thomas LL. The validity of self-reported grade point averages, class ranks, and test scores: A meta-analysis and review of the literature. Review of Educational Research. 2005;**75**:63–82. DOI: 10.3102/00346543075001063

[40] Azeez NO, Adefabi RA, Ajasa FA. INSTITUTIONAL CAPACITY AND STUDENTS' ACADEMIC PERFORMANCE IN OYO STATE SECONDARY SCHOOLS. African Journal of Educational Practice. 2020;**6**:84–96

[41] Harlen W. Teachers' summative practices and assessment for learning – tensions and synergies. The Curriculum Journal. 2005;**16**:207–223. DOI: 10.1080/09585170500136093

[42] Harrell FE. Regression Modeling Strategies: With Applications to Linear Models, Logistic and Ordinal Regression, and Survival Analysis. Cham: Springer Series in Statistics; Springer International Publishing; 2015

[43] Page MJ, McKenzie JE, Bossuyt PM, Boutron I, Hoffmann TC, Mulrow CD, Shamseer L, Tetzlaff JM, Akl EA, Brennan SE, et al. The PRISMA 2020 statement: An updated guideline for reporting systematic reviews. British Medical Journal. 2021;**372**(n71). DOI: 10.1136/bmj.n71

[44] Stang A. Critical evaluation of the Newcastle-Ottawa scale for the assessment of the quality of nonrandomized studies in meta-analyses. European Journal of Epidemiology. 2010;**25**:603–605. DOI: 10.1007/s10654-010-9491-z

[45] Widlund A, Tuominen H, Korhonen J. Reciprocal effects of mathematics performance, school engagement and burnout during adolescence. British Journal of Educational Psychology. 2023;**93**: 183–197. DOI: 10.1111/bjep.12548

[46] Wang X, Zha W, Li C. The reciprocal dynamics of academic achievement and school burnout in middle schoolers: From individual and clique perspectives. Journal of Youth and Adolescence. 2025. DOI: 10.1007/s10964-025-02279-5

[47] Luthar SS, Cicchetti D, Becker B. The construct of resilience: A critical evaluation and guidelines for future work. Child Development. 2000;**71**: 543–562. DOI: 10.1111/1467-8624.00164

[48] Maslach C, Leiter MP. Understanding the burnout experience: Recent research and its implications for psychiatry. World Psychiatry. 2016;**15**:103–111. DOI: 10.1002/wps.20311

[49] Halfon N, Larson K, Lu M, Tullis E, Russ S. Lifecourse health development: Past, present and future. Maternal and Child Health Journal. 2014;**18**:344–365. DOI: 10.1007/s10995-013-1346-2

[50] Seidler A, Thinschmidt M, Deckert S, Then F, Hegewald J, Nieuwenhuijsen K, Riedel-Heller SG. The role of psychosocial working conditions on burnout and its core component emotional exhaustion – a systematic review. Journal of Occupational Medicine and Toxicology (London, England). 2014;**9**:10. DOI: 10.1186/1745-6673-9-10

Chapter 8

Sustaining the Vocational Teaching Workforce in Thailand: Burnout, Modernization Pressures and Technological Transformation

Nongluck Manowaluilou

Abstract

Burnout among teachers has emerged as a global occupational health concern, but vocational educators experience distinctive pressures arising from technological disruption, institutional performance demands, and rapidly shifting labor market expectations. This chapter examines burnout among Thailand's vocational teaching workforce through the lenses of modernization, digital transformation, and international benchmarking in technical and vocational education and training (TVET). Drawing on contemporary scholarship, empirical evidence, and international TVET comparisons, it argues that burnout is not merely an individual psychological state but a structural outcome of systemic misalignment between institutional demands, technological change, and teacher preparation. In Thailand, vocational teachers confront a convergence of pressures, including accelerated technological change, expanding administrative workloads, heightened student and parent expectations, national testing mandates, and cross-border competency frameworks associated with regional economic integration. At the same time, students frequently enter vocational pathways with lower academic preparation and higher socio-economic vulnerability, which increases teachers' emotional labor and instructional complexity – both recognized antecedents of burnout. The chapter demonstrates how Thailand's modernization and internationalization policies – while essential for future workforce competitiveness – have inadvertently shifted the burden of technological adaptation, performance accountability, and innovation mandates onto teachers. These responsibilities encompass continuous upskilling, student mentoring for innovation competitions, coordination with industry partners, and extensive documentation for evaluation and accountability systems – forms of "hidden labor" that remain undervalued in policy and compensation structures. Sustaining the vocational teaching workforce requires systemic reforms that close gaps in teacher preparation, technological self-efficacy, professional recognition, and institutional support, rather than relying on individual resilience alone.

Keywords: burnout, technology, sustaining, vocational teacher, professional development

IntechOpen

1. Introduction

The twenty-first century is marked by relentless technological disruption, accelerated socio-economic transitions, and expanded expectations placed on educational systems. While these pressures affect all levels of education, vocational education occupies a distinctive position – functioning simultaneously as a mechanism for national workforce development and as a bridge for lifelong learning during digital transformation. In Thailand, vocational teachers shoulder the responsibility of preparing students – many from non-academic or economically constrained backgrounds – for uncertain labor markets characterized by automation, platformized service economies, and rapid innovation cycles. The vocational teaching workforce is thus increasingly expected to (1) master emerging technical domains, (2) foster entrepreneurial mindsets, and (3) align with evolving industrial needs – often without adequate systemic support.

However, these escalating demands coincide with long-standing structural burdens across Thailand's education system: policy-driven performance metrics, student outcome pressures (including international benchmarking tests), institutional bureaucracy, and low public recognition of vocational pathways. The result is a heightened risk of burnout, emotional exhaustion, and workforce attrition among vocational teachers – an issue insufficiently examined in mainstream burnout literature, which historically centers on K–12 academic teachers.

This chapter highlights these dynamics and contributes three core insights:

(1) Technological disruption exacerbates burnout when teachers lack digital readiness, entrepreneurial literacy, or adaptive capacity to meet new, innovation-centered pedagogical expectations.

(2) Institutional demands, parental expectations, and global competitiveness pressures create structural stressors unique to the Thai vocational ecosystem.

(3) Generational asymmetries in innovation exposure (i.e., teachers not trained in entrepreneurial education or product innovation processes) intensify burnout during periods of rapid modernization.

Drawing on recent empirical findings from Thai teachers during COVID-19 – including significant correlations between self-efficacy, technology integration challenges, online teaching performance, and burnout – the chapter argues that sustaining the vocational teaching workforce requires policy interventions addressing both emotional well-being and workforce modernization.

2. Background: Thailand – Demography, education system, and vocational pathways

Thailand enjoys a generally favorable tropical climate with warm temperatures throughout the year, lacking harsh winters and experiencing less extreme seasonal variation compared to temperate countries. These conditions historically supported a strong agricultural base, enabling year-round cultivation of staple crops such as rice, fruits, and vegetables, and reinforcing agriculture and livestock as a central pillar of the national economy and rural livelihoods. While Bangkok developed into the nation's epicenter of political administration, commerce, and educational expansion, many other provinces experienced uneven development trajectories, with persistent disparities in infrastructure, economic opportunities, and access to qualified teachers.

In terms of vocational education, Thailand's formal vocational system is substantial and diverse, with hundreds of institutions serving nearly one million students across the country. These include both public and private vocational colleges that deliver technical and applied skills across a range of fields, including industry, commerce, agriculture, fisheries, hospitality, fine and applied arts, and information and communication technology [1].

These institutions are part of a nationwide network overseen by the Office of the Vocational Education Commission (OVEC), which administers hundreds of colleges – both public and private – across Thailand's provinces and aims to produce skilled workers and technologists aligned with labor market needs [2]. While none are formally designated as minority-specific vocational schools, their geographic distribution into more remote regions means that many ethnic minority students have access to vocational programs closer to home, especially when supported by local outreach and community education initiatives. The instructional burden is acutely felt in regional hubs like Chiang Mai Vocational College and Songkwae Technical College, which serve diverse populations, including ethnic minority learners (e.g., Hmong, Karen). Teachers here must navigate a structural mismatch, managing multigrade pedagogy and Thai as a Second Language (TSL) instruction without specialized training, adding layers of emotional and administrative labor to their roles.

2.1 Economic profile

Thailand is a sovereign nation in Southeast Asia, covering approximately 513120 square kilometers and administratively divided into 76 provinces, plus the Bangkok Metropolitan Area, clustered into six major regions (Northern, Western, Central, Northeastern, Eastern, and Southern) [1]. The country's capital and largest city is Bangkok (Krung Thep Maha Nakhon), a political, economic, and cultural hub with a metropolitan population of over 5.4 million residents, serving as the focal point in a wider urban region of more than 15 million people [2].

As of late 2024, Thailand's total population was estimated at around 66 million people, with an aging demographic profile – 15.6% aged 0–14 years, 57% aged 25–64, and over 13% aged 65 + – reflecting broader social transitions toward a "fully aged society", noting that over 13% of the population is aged 65 + while the primary labor bracket (25–64) stands at 57%. This context is vital to justify the urgent need for vocational workforce sustainability, with implications for workforce composition, labor demands, and education systems [1].

Thailand's economy is diversified, with key contributions from agriculture, tourism, and manufacturing. Agriculture is still a major source of employment and export earnings; it accounts for a substantial share of rural incomes, with rice, rubber, cassava, and aquaculture being significant contributors (data vary annually, but agriculture remains central to GDP and employment). Secondly, prior to the pandemic, tourism contributed roughly 12–20% of GDP through direct and indirect effects, with Thailand among the world's top destinations. Revenues have rebounded strongly since 2022 as international travel resumed. A majority of the income is also derived from industrial and services sectors, which underpin Thailand's participation in global value chains, including automotive production, electronics, and logistics. These economic structures shape labor market needs, especially for vocational and technical skills aligned with manufacturing, services, digital platforms, hospitality, and agritech [3].

2.2 Thailand's formal education structure

Thailand's formal education roots extend deep into its pre-modern past, when Buddhist temples served as the earliest centers of learning. In these *"dek wat"* systems, monks taught basic literacy, numeracy, moral conduct, and cultural knowledge long before state schooling existed, reflecting the integration of religion, community, and pedagogy in traditional Thai life. With the modernization drive under King Rama IV and King Rama V (mid- to late nineteenth century), the Siamese state began formalizing education to meet national development goals, establishing Western-style schools, normal teacher training, and a Ministry of Public Instruction in 1892 to centralize and professionalize schooling across the kingdom. This shift was not merely administrative; it marked the transition from informal learning spaces to structured classrooms with set curricula, schedules, and trained teachers.

The early twentieth century witnessed the emergence of specialized training schools alongside general academic education. In 1936, educational reforms under the National Education Plan formally introduced vocational education into the national system, establishing government regulations for its administration and expanding vocational schools into central and provincial areas. In the late 1930s and early 1940s, as Thailand became embroiled in the Greater East Asia War (World War II), vocational programs faced material shortages, disruptions, and shifting priorities as schools adapted to wartime conditions and reduced resources. Despite these challenges, the period deepened the nation's appreciation for practical and industrial skills, setting the stage for post-war reconstruction and the later expansion of vocational pathways. After the war, the Department of Vocational Education was formed with a clearer mandate to develop workforce-oriented training aligned with economic needs.

2.3 Formal and Non-formal school types in Thailand

Thailand's education system includes a range of formal and alternative learning environments. Public schools are government-funded and typically administered by the Ministry of Education or local administrative bodies; basic education, up to and including lower and upper secondary levels, is constitutionally mandated as tuition-free [4].

The formal education system in Thailand follows a sequential structure often described pedagogically as "3–3–3–4," though most official documents frame it as early childhood, primary, lower secondary, upper secondary, and higher education: Early childhood/Pre-primary: An optional stage for ages 3–5. Primary education (*Prathom* 1–6; ages 6–11): compulsory and tuition-free. – Lower secondary (*Mattayom* 1–3; ages 12–14): compulsory and tuition-free. – Upper secondary (*Mattayom* 4–6; ages 15–17/18): not compulsory but widely pursued, with both general and vocational tracks available. Higher education: Post-secondary programs typically extend for four years for bachelor's degrees in most fields, with some profession-specific longer programs (e.g., medicine, teacher education was five years but was later shortened to four years. While Thai teacher education was historically anchored in a mandatory five-year baccalaureate model to ensure rigorous professional mastery, the system has recently transitioned to a standardized four-year degree program – a strategic realignment intended to synchronize teacher production with broader higher education frameworks and the accelerating demands of the modern labor market [4]. Notably, basic education through *Mattayom* 3 (grade 9) is legally compulsory, while tuition-free education effectively covers up to 15 years of learning (pre-primary through upper secondary), as mandated by Thailand's constitution and education law [4].

In contrast, private schools are independently funded and operated, encompassing international schools, English-medium programs, and historically rooted religious or mission schools (such as Catholic and other faith-based institutions), which often command higher tuition and competitive admissions. Beyond the formal school environment, the education system also incorporates Non-Formal and Alternative Learning Centers, which provide vocational training, adult education, and community-based skills development opportunities outside the formal schooling structure. These pathways are particularly important for lifelong learners, workforce retraining, and individuals who require flexible, practice-oriented learning opportunities beyond the traditional classroom.

2.4 Vocational education in Thailand: Tracks and frameworks

There are two main student tracks starting at the upper secondary level (Mattayom 4–6). Thai students typically choose between either the general academic track, which is mainly a preparation for university and broader academic pathways, or the vocational track (lower and upper Secondary Vocational Education). The vocational education track aims to build technical skills, employability, and industry engagement; it operates across formal, non-formal, and informal systems. Vocational education is thus focused on work-ready competencies, industry skills, and technical professions.

2.4.1 Formal vocational education

The aftermath of World War II (1941–1945) marked a turning point in the evolution of vocational education in Thailand. During the war, vocational programs suffered from material shortages and reduced student and teacher participation as national resources were redirected to the war effort. The disruption highlighted the fragility of early vocational training and underscored the need for a more resilient and purpose-driven system. After World War II, Thailand reorganized vocational education to support national reconstruction and industrial growth, establishing the Department of Vocational Education and expanding technical and commercial schools to produce mechanics, technicians, and clerical workers for a modernizing economy. Foreign partnerships during the 1950s, particularly with Germany, introduced more practice-oriented training models and eventually laid the foundation for Thailand's contemporary dual vocational education system.

Students in institutions like the School of Ten Divisions of Traditional Thai Crafts or the College of Dramatic Arts learn through apprenticeship-style pedagogy that bridges artisanal knowledge and formal certification. However, despite their cultural and economic contributions, vocational teachers continue to occupy a socially liminal position, expected to train the nation's workforce and preserve its cultural capital while working in institutions that struggle with insufficient personnel, uneven funding, and weak public recognition. Consequently, the post-war legacy of economic reliance combined with institutional underinvestment contributes to contemporary burnout among vocational teachers, who are expected to support national workforce development while operating in a system burdened by historical instability and persistent structural constraints.

These schools, therefore, demonstrate that vocational education in Thailand extends beyond industrial and technical trades, encompassing heritage arts, craftsmanship, and creative performance as recognized professional pathways. Formal vocational education is administered largely by the OVEC [5] and engages students in competency-based, skill-based, and work-based learning. Program levels include:

(1) Vocational Certificates (*Por Wor Chor*): upper-secondary level qualifications emphasizing practical skills mastery.

(2) Diplomas and higher diplomas: post-secondary and professional practice levels with deeper specialization.

(3) Higher vocational qualifications and degrees, including degree programs linked to technology and applied sciences [6].

Crucially, this is not a uniquely Thai problem but a global pattern observed across developed and developing economies alike, where vocational teachers are burdened with rapidly expanding roles, insufficient preparation pipelines, and inadequate systemic support. If these structural conditions persist, shortages of qualified vocational educators are likely to accelerate, triggering a chain reaction in which weakened vocational institutions struggle to produce a future-ready workforce, thereby undermining national innovation capacity, labor market competitiveness, and broader economic resilience.

2.4.2 Formal vocational education is delivered by public and private institutions

Across Thailand's provinces, Technical Colleges and Industrial and Community Education Colleges form the backbone of the formal vocational education system, offering students industry-relevant training and nationally recognized credentials in technical and applied fields. In addition to these mainstream institutions, Thailand also operates specialized vocational institutes modeled after Japan's KOSEN-style Technical Engineering Programs, which provide focused five-year pathways integrating theoretical study with applied practice to develop highly skilled engineering technicians for industry [7]. Complementing these technical pathways are creative and cultural vocational schools, including institutes specializing in music and performing arts, culinary arts, fine and applied arts, and traditional craftwork, which support both cultural preservation and creative industry development.

A prominent organizational feature of Thailand's vocational landscape is its Dual Vocational Education System, an industry-embedded training approach whereby students alternate between workplace environments and classroom instruction under structured agreements between schools and employers. Under this system, vocational institutions collaborate directly with companies to deliver work-linked learning and skills development. The dual system is widespread: nearly 95% of vocational institutions participate in some form of industry-linked training, collectively serving hundreds of thousands of learners and forging partnerships across manufacturing, services, and emerging sectors [5].

2.4.3 Non-Formal and informal vocational pathways

Beyond the formal vocational system, Thailand also supports non-formal vocational learning, which is delivered through adult education centers, community learning hubs, and short skill-development courses aimed at workforce upskilling and reskilling. In parallel, informal vocational training occurs in everyday settings through apprenticeships, family businesses, and employer-led in-house training, where skills are gained through participation and hands-on experience rather than structured coursework. Together, these non-formal and informal pathways complement the formal education system and play an important role in supporting lifelong learning for workers at different stages of their careers.

3. Professional qualifications

Thailand's qualification framework includes the Thailand Professional Qualification Institute (TPQI) system, which aligns occupational standards with competency certification for learners and workers. TPQI [8] develops professional qualifications, occupational standards, and competency assessments recognized nationally and compatible with ASEAN frameworks, facilitating micro-credentials and lifelong learning recognition outside traditional degree paths [5]. The TPQI system supports several mechanisms for skill validation, competency portfolios, and professional recognition that help bridge formal education, workplace requirements, and learner mobility.

Teachers in Thailand are governed by the Teachers' Council of Thailand (*Khurusapha*), the statutory body responsible for professional standards, licensing, and ethical codes. To teach in formal educational institutions (public and private schools delivering the Thai curriculum), educators must obtain a professional teaching license issued by *Khurusapha* [9]. There are two main categories: (1) Provisional Teaching License (P-License), which is valid for two years, is issued when the candidate meets basic qualifications but has not completed professional competency assessments; it is renewable and intended to allow early service while competencies are developed [10], and (2) Basic Teaching License (B-License), which is valid for five years from issuance, is recognized as the standard professional credential for school teachers; its renewal supports ongoing professional development [9].

4. Burnouts causes and effects

Burnout literature recognizes that uncertainty amplifies stress responses, especially under neoliberal performance regimes, where workers are judged through metrics, competition, and continuous improvement discourses. In education, neoliberalization operates through standardized testing, output-based funding, performance indicators, and benchmarking, producing pressure for constant optimization and accountability. Under these conditions, uncertainty is not an anomaly but a structurally embedded condition that shapes teachers' experiences. When modernization reforms layer rapid technological change on top of existing accountability cultures, uncertainty becomes chronic rather than episodic – transforming from a short-term stressor into a long-term structural driver of burnout [11, 12].

Within vocational education systems, this transformation intersects with the distinctive nature of Technical and Vocational Education and Training (TVET), which is more tightly coupled to labor market volatility than general education. Across OECD countries, vocational teachers are recognized as needing both pedagogical and occupational expertise, yet they are challenged by digitalization, shifting student demand patterns, and evolving labor market requirements that necessitate continuous skill renewal and professional adaptability [13–15]. UNESCO-UNEVOC and CEDEFOP reports similarly note that TVET systems globally must respond to rapidly evolving work environments, digital transitions, and lifelong learning imperatives, while teacher training infrastructure remains uneven and insufficient in many contexts [16–19]. TVET Asia further emphasizes that the acceleration of digital and green skills agendas across ASEAN amplifies institutional stress in systems where teacher capacity development lags behind policy ambition [20].

In Thailand, according to Manowaluilou and Thanarachataphoom (2023), modernization triggers a triple uncertainty framework, producing three interlocking stress pathways for vocational teachers [21].

The first, economic uncertainty, concerns the durability and employability of taught skills. Automation, artificial intelligence, platform economies, and Industry 4.0 technologies destabilize occupational forecasts in fields such as automotive mechanics, electrical trades, and hospitality services. For vocational teachers, this produces anticipatory anxiety: they must continuously future-proof curricula without authoritative predictive frameworks or robust institutional support, while still being evaluated on student employability outcomes. Economic uncertainty thus becomes a cognitive burden, where teachers question the relevance of their content within shifting labor markets, reflecting a phenomenon reported in both national and international TVET systems [13, 14, 16].

The second form, pedagogical uncertainty, arises from disruptions to how learning is expected to occur. Modern reforms introduce blended learning, digital simulations, competency-based assessment, entrepreneurial project cycles, and industry-embedded apprenticeships – practices that diverge from traditional vocational instruction. UNESCO-UNEVOC analyses emphasize that many vocational teachers globally were trained primarily as technicians rather than pedagogues, creating gaps in instructional self-efficacy when new modalities are introduced without adequate training [16, 17]. In Thailand, curriculum reforms introducing innovation and entrepreneurship compound this challenge, as professional development lags behind the speed of reform, increasing emotional exhaustion and diminishing perceived instructional competence [21, 22].

The third dimension, identity uncertainty, concerns the question, “Am I still competent in my role?” Teacher identity in vocational sectors has historically been built on technical mastery and role legitimacy. However, modernization alters these criteria of expertise: mechanical drafting yields to CAD/CAM systems, machining yields to CNC automation, and traditional instruction yields to innovation mentorship and entrepreneurial coaching. Senior teachers – whose professional identities formed around industrial-era skill models – may experience generational displacement as younger colleagues demonstrate stronger digital fluency. Burnout theory links such identity threats to depersonalization, functioning as a defensive detachment strategy when teachers feel their expertise is no longer valued [11, 12].

These forms of uncertainty accumulate within broader performance cultures. Teacher shortages and retention issues, documented across OECD education systems, indicate that teaching remains under strain due to workload pressures, limited professional autonomy, and high attrition rates [13, 14]. TVET systems in Asia and Europe report similar pressures, as they are expected to support digitalization, green transitions, and industrial modernization while ensuring quality, relevance, and equity [17, 18, 20]. These expectations intensify stress for vocational teachers, who must balance instructional, technological, administrative, and industry liaison responsibilities.

The consequences extend beyond individual well-being. Persistent burnout among vocational teachers erodes instructional quality, weakens industry links, reduces the attractiveness of the profession, and exacerbates shortages in critical technical fields. International reports warn that teacher shortages – aggravated by burnout and attrition – pose systemic risks to educational sustainability and economic competitiveness [13, 16, 18]. In this sense, vocational teacher burnout is not merely an occupational health concern but a structural outcome of intersecting pressures across modernization, policy reform, and labor market demands.

5. Conceptual and theoretical framework

This chapter proposes a Triple Uncertainty Framework of Vocational Burnout to analyze burnout as a socio-technical phenomenon. This model integrates Economic Uncertainty (skill durability), Pedagogical Uncertainty (digital disruption), and Identity Uncertainty as shown in **Figure 1**. The latter is particularly salient for the *"Kru Chang"* – traditional masters of craft whose professional identities are being reconfigured into innovation mentors and entrepreneurial coaches. This shift often leads to generational displacement, where senior educators feel their technical mastery is undervalued in the face of mandated digital fluency. The crisis of vocational teacher burnout in Thailand is fundamentally socio-technical in origin, necessitating a shift from purely psychological perspectives toward a Triple Uncertainty Framework. This model illustrates how educators are caught in the interlocking pressures of economic uncertainty regarding the durability of taught skills, pedagogical uncertainty stemming from new digital modalities, and identity uncertainty as traditional mastery is challenged. This exhaustion is exacerbated by a "multi-speed temporal architecture", where the accelerated cycles of industrial innovation (moving in quarters) clash with the slower bureaucratic rhythms of institutional reform (moving in years).

Within this mismatch, the teacher functions as a "human buffer", absorbing the friction between state-driven innovation mandates and the reality of outdated infrastructure. This burden triggers a profound identity reconfiguration; the traditional *"Kru Chang"* – once revered for technical craftsmanship – is now forced to navigate the unfamiliar terrains of innovation mentorship and entrepreneurial coaching.

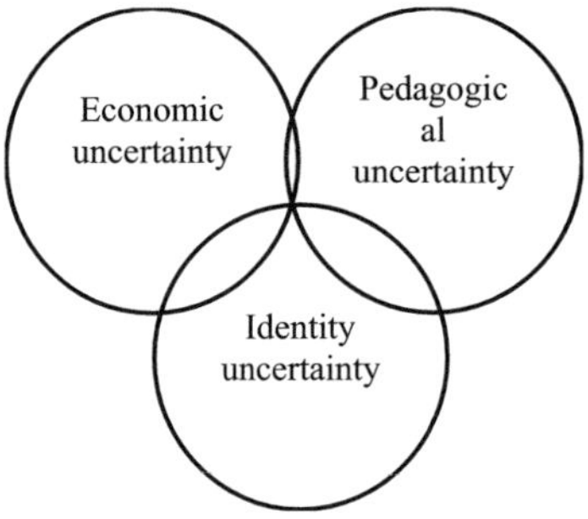

Figure 1.
The Triple Uncertainty Framework of Vocational burnout.

6. Modernization pressures and structural burnout drivers in vocational teaching

Historically, the Thai vocational sector was structured to supply an industrial-era workforce – servicing mechanical trades, electrical maintenance, hospitality, tourism, marine, automotive, and other practice-oriented domains. However, the emergence of the digital economy and creative economy has transformed labor market expectations, requiring competencies such as data-driven decision-making, digital fabrication, platform-based entrepreneurship, agile product development, and sustainability-oriented innovation aligned with the Sustainable Development Goals (SDGs).

This rapid shift has generated a structural mismatch between what vocational institutions were designed to produce and what contemporary industries demand. The consequences of this mismatch are twofold and particularly consequential for teacher burnout:

(1) Learners remain insufficiently prepared for digitally mediated work environments, lacking exposure to emerging technologies, innovation frameworks, and entrepreneurial mindsets.

(2) Vocational teachers themselves lack formal training in entrepreneurial and innovation-based education, as these frameworks only recently entered the Thai curriculum, leaving many in-service educators without the technological fluency or pedagogical preparation required for digital transformation.

Since these transitions and transformations unfolded while vocational teachers were already in-service – rather than being pre-integrated into teacher preparation pipelines – many vocational educators must upskill under high time pressure, with limited institutional support and continuous performance expectations.

According to Manowaluilou [16], research on entrepreneurial and innovation-centered learning emphasizes that innovation can only flourish when adequate structural supports are in place and when pressures on vocational educators are appropriately mediated by administrative systems and professional environments.

In practice, this means that vocational institutions must provide sufficient instructional resources, policy clarity, psychological support, and collaborative spaces for vocational teachers. At the same time, vocational students must be well-prepared – cognitively, emotionally, and structurally – before entering the classroom. When these preconditions are met, the phenomenon of *proactive innovation lesson design* becomes far more likely to emerge, as vocational educators are no longer operating under unmanaged burnout, excessive uncertainty, or pedagogical overload.

Globally, entrepreneurial and innovation-oriented frameworks initially emerged within higher education – particularly within teacher education programs, design schools, and startup ecosystems – rather than within traditional vocational training pathways. As a result, Thailand's older vocational teacher cohorts, who were trained during the industrial-era model of vocational education, rarely encountered entrepreneurial education, business model innovation, or product development processes during their preparation. When national reforms later introduced entrepreneurship and innovation modules into vocational curricula, these in-service teachers faced substantial pressure to teach concepts they had never experienced firsthand. Lacking experiential grounding and institutional scaffolding, many vocational educators reported heightened stress, reduced self-efficacy, and burnout symptoms as they attempted to "retrofit" entrepreneurial innovation into existing teaching identities and workloads [23].

Drawing on Maslach and Leiter's [14, 15] work, burnout manifests when persistent job demands coincide with inadequate resources, leading to emotional exhaustion, depersonalization, and reduced personal accomplishment. In the vocational context, these dimensions map onto teachers' lived experiences in distinct ways:

(1) **Emotional exhaustion** arises as teachers attempt to continuously upskill – often outside paid working hours – with limited institutional scaffolding. The burden of mastering unfamiliar technologies or entrepreneurial frameworks depletes emotional and cognitive resources.

(2) **Depersonalization** can emerge as a coping mechanism when teachers feel overwhelmed by innovation mandates. Detached or cynical attitudes toward "innovation reforms" are not signs of resistance per se but are adaptive responses to structural overload, aligning with Maslach's characterization of depersonalization as a defensive strategy to manage excessive demands.

(3) **Reduced personal accomplishment** becomes salient when teachers perceive a misalignment between institutional expectations and their actual capacity to deliver new forms of pedagogy. When entrepreneurial outcomes, competitions, or innovation outputs become metrics of success, teachers lacking experiential knowledge may internalize a sense of failure or incompetence, despite their expertise in traditional vocational domains.

Leiter and Maslach's Areas of Worklife Model (1999) further helps explain why this burden is structural and not individual. Burnout arises not merely from "hard work," but from chronic mismatches in key domains such as Workload (continuous upskilling and innovation tasks), Control (limited influence over curricula or reform pacing), Reward (low recognition for innovation coaching), Community (fragmented peer support for new pedagogies), Fairness (uneven training opportunities), and Values (misalignment between traditional vocational values and entrepreneurial mandates).

Each domain is readily observable within Thai vocational modernization efforts. Teachers are required to adopt innovative roles without adequate professional development, technological infrastructure, or policy clarity – producing systemic mismatches that intensify burnout risk. In this essence, burnout among vocational teachers is not merely a psychological reaction, but an outcome of institutional modernization without synchronized teacher preparation. The vocational teacher becomes the "interface layer" between state-driven innovation agendas and classroom realities – responsible for translating emerging economic priorities into pedagogical practice while absorbing the emotional costs of structural transition.

7. Technological disruption as a burnout catalyst

7.1 Digital competency pressures

Teachers' technological self-efficacy is now central to educational performance. Recent Thai data show that teachers with higher technology-related self-efficacy demonstrate stronger online performance, while those lacking confidence are at greater risk of burnout. During COVID-19 lockdowns, many experienced emotional exhaustion due to technology-oriented instructional demands, especially when digital pedagogy conflicted with established classroom practices [23].

International literature corroborates this: technology integration correlates with increased teacher workload, stress, and self-efficacy challenges [24, 34]. In Thailand, this dynamic was intensified by uneven digital infrastructure across provinces and socioeconomic inequalities among students, forcing teachers to assume new roles in troubleshooting, platform customization, and digital classroom management.

7.2 Innovation exposure and cognitive overload

Entrepreneurial education introduces cognitive domains foreign to many teachers: idea validation, product development cycles, prototyping, market feasibility, scalability, and innovation ecosystems. Without supportive professional development, teachers encounter cognitive overload, which is strongly associated with burnout conditions such as emotional depletion and reduced personal accomplishment.

Moreover, Thai vocational students increasingly expect instructors to provide mentoring for entrepreneurship competitions, innovation showcases, and project-based learning. These expectations are magnified by prestigious contests, inter-school competitions, and national skill challenges – turning teachers into de facto innovation coaches, often without compensation or release time. This aligns with burnout scholarship, which associates high job demands with emotional exhaustion. In the Thai context, these job demands are not merely administrative but epistemic – teachers must continuously acquire new knowledge domains to maintain relevance in a rapidly modernizing society.

8. Institutional and societal stressors in Thai vocational education

These temporal burdens intersect with Thailand's geographic and social landscape of vocational education. Vocational programs are disproportionately popular among students from rural provinces and peri-urban regions outside Bangkok, where families often prioritize rapid workforce entry and stable employment over university pathways. Despite lingering stereotypes that vocational tracks attract underprivileged youth or those with lower academic achievement, vocational education retains strong labor-market value in many technical and service sectors, with graduates frequently securing employment faster than their university counterparts. Yet, this mix of pragmatic appeal and social stigma creates its own tension: vocational colleges must reconcile their role as engines of regional employability with a national narrative that still valorizes academic pathways.

Compounding this is the existence of high-performing vocational institutions that have built international reputations in niche areas – ranging from mechanical craftsmanship to culinary arts, hospitality, or creative arts – where Thai vocational students have earned distinctions and world awards. Such recognition elevates institutional prestige, but it also generates performance expectations that reverberate through administration and teaching staff. Maintaining competitive status becomes an implicit mandate; teachers are expected not only to meet routine instructional duties but also to train students for competitions, exhibitions, or international showcases. This reputational pressure operates alongside modernization demands, adding another layer of accountability that is rarely acknowledged in policy documents but is deeply felt within school cultures.

8.1 Administrative, pedagogical, and performance pressures in Thai vocational teaching

Administrative workload has become a defining burden for Thai vocational teachers. In daily practice, teachers must manage documentation for student records, evaluation reports, accreditation and audit compliance, quality assurance paperwork, teacher licensing requirements, and various reporting systems mandated by multiple administrative layers. These tasks compete directly with instructional time, lesson preparation, and student mentoring, thereby increasing emotional exhaustion and reducing the capacity for pedagogical innovation. During the pandemic era, this administrative load intensified as online teaching introduced new communication channels, digital platforms, tracking systems, and technical troubleshooting demands, layering logistical complexity onto an already saturated workload.

Beyond paperwork, vocational teachers frequently engage in interdisciplinary and multi-grade instruction. In many provincial institutions, staffing shortages require teachers to cover subjects across multiple trades or academic domains, even when they are not formally trained in those fields. Multi-grade or cross-cohort teaching further complicates lesson planning, since students may vary widely in academic readiness, trade specialization, or practical experience. The burden is greater in vocational systems that combine academic subjects, practical workshops, cooperative education, and dual-training components within the same program.

A unique vocational challenge in Thailand emerges from the dual vocational education funding model, where institutions count student enrollment to secure operating budgets. To maintain enrollment numbers, some schools operate parallel programs – regular vocational schooling and dual-system workplace placements – requiring teachers to advise students, negotiate schedules, and retain learners in both tracks. Teachers become informal counselors and recruitment agents, responsible not just for teaching but also for persuading students to persist in the program so that the school retains funding. This retention responsibility adds relational, emotional, and administrative labor that is rarely reflected in official job descriptions.

Quality assurance systems introduce another layer of institutional pressure. Educational evaluations – intended to demonstrate instructional quality and institutional legitimacy – often emphasize documented evidence rather than sustained pedagogical practice. Schools prepare extensive portfolios, binders, photographic evidence, and compliance reports to satisfy evaluation frameworks. In some cases, events, competitions, or showcases are organized partly to generate evidence of student achievement, school reputation, or "best practice" demonstrations. Vocational teachers are thus expected to prepare students for competitions, exhibitions, or innovation contests, not only for the sake of learning outcomes but also to enhance institutional visibility and satisfy evaluators.

Taken together, administrative overload, interdisciplinary teaching, multi-cohort management, performance assessment cultures, and labor-market alignment responsibilities form a complex ecosystem of pressures. These pressures do not merely increase workload but reshape the identity of vocational teachers – expanding their roles beyond instruction into bureaucracy, public relations, career counseling, and institutional survival. The cumulative effect is a form of occupational overload that drains the time, attention, and emotional resources necessary for high-quality vocational teaching and mentorship.

8.2 Student and parent expectations

Vocational education carries unique social perceptions in Thailand. Families often view vocational schooling as a pathway to rapid employability, and many students enter vocational programs not out of intrinsic interest but due to competitive exam tracking, academic pressures, or limited access to general education pathways. This creates a differentiated expectation landscape: parents expect swift transitions into work, students hope for marketable skills without excessive academic burden, and schools must demonstrate placement success to maintain legitimacy. Vocational teachers, therefore, shoulder responsibilities that extend beyond instruction. They must mediate student and parent expectations, secure internship or cooperative placements, and provide informal career counseling and emotional support – functions that remain absent from formal workload calculations. Teachers become intermediaries between schools, families, and industries, negotiating not only technical competencies but also aspirations, anxieties, and employment trajectories.

Geographic context deepens this complexity. Each province or region has distinct economic strengths – such as automotive and manufacturing clusters in the Eastern Economic Corridor, hospitality and tourism in the South, traditional crafts and textiles in the North, agriculture and food processing in the Northeast, and fisheries in coastal provinces. These local economic ecosystems shape labor-market expectations and skill demands. However, teacher preparation in Thailand remains largely uniform, with limited specialization aligned to provincial industries, local craftsmanship traditions, or emerging technological niches. As a result, vocational teachers may arrive well-qualified in general pedagogy or trade fundamentals but underprepared for region-specific skill needs, whether that involves high-end machining, heritage crafts, artisanal production, or digital tourism platforms.

In contrast, several countries explicitly connect regional industry identities with vocational teacher preparation and youth skill pipelines. Japan's "Cool Japan" strategy promotes cultural and creative industries – including animation, traditional arts, gaming, fashion, and cuisine – by integrating niche vocational programs with regional cultural economies and export-oriented creative clusters [25]. China's "Made in China 2025" links vocational training to advanced manufacturing, robotics, and smart factories, with provinces developing specialized technical colleges and apprenticeship pathways aligned to their industrial bases [26]. South Korea's Creative Economy initiative similarly connects vocational and polytechnic institutions to digital media, design, and cultural production ecosystems clustered around cities like Seoul, Busan, and Daegu [27]. These models illustrate how aligning vocational ecosystems with territorial strengths can elevate both the prestige and effectiveness of vocational pathways.

Thailand's vocational system, by comparison, aims to serve diverse regional economies but lacks a coordinated mechanism that connects provincial industry clusters to teacher preparation, curricular specialization, or cultural-economic branding. The result is a structural gap: while regions possess strong economic identities, vocational teachers often lack the localized training, cultural knowledge, or technological specialization needed to fully leverage those identities for workforce development. This mismatch has implications not only for student outcomes but also for national competitiveness in emerging cultural, technological, and creative economies. This mismatch intensifies individualized teaching demands. Teachers must adapt national curricula to provincial economies, customize training for learners with varied expectations, and compensate for gaps in industry exposure – often through self-initiated learning or informal networking with local enterprises.

8.3 PISA, National Tests, and International Benchmarking

While PISA and academic testing dominate public discourse, vocational education operates under different assessment logics centered on competency, employability, and certification rather than standardized academic scores. Thai vocational qualifications emphasize skills demonstration, workplace performance, and competency standards aligned with the TPQI and the Office of the OVEC. Assessments often include practical exams, cooperative education evaluations, and dual-training performance reports from employers. These systems aim to verify that learners can perform in real environments, but they also require teachers to coordinate with industry partners, supervise workplace training, and align classroom instruction to evolving occupational standards – tasks that demand substantial administrative coordination and professional judgment.

Internationally, benchmarking pressures manifest differently depending on national TVET models. Countries like Germany, Switzerland, and Austria integrate dual training systems with strong employer participation and clear certification pathways, resulting in high vocational prestige and smoother school-to-work transitions. In Japan and South Korea, continuous investment in technological innovation and industry-school partnerships has positioned vocational tracks as engines of national modernization rather than as second-tier options.

8.4 Paperwork, Competitions, and Performance cultures

Thailand is not unique in burdening teachers with paperwork; international data show administrative tasks are a substantial source of stress across education systems. According to the OECD's Teaching and Learning International Survey (TALIS), roughly half of teachers across OECD countries identify general administrative work [28] – such as forms, reports, attendance records, communication logs, and compliance requirements – as a significant source of work-related stress, with experienced teachers reporting administrative burden more often than novices [29]. Although the average time spent on such tasks may vary, the perception that paperwork interferes with core instructional work is widespread and culturally salient, reflecting how bureaucratic accountability systems can displace pedagogical focus and erode teacher well-being [30].

In the Thai vocational context, paperwork intersects with a pervasive culture of competition and performance validation. Schools are expected to compile extensive documentation for quality assurance, accreditation audits, external evaluations, and teacher licensing processes. The creation of portfolios, compliance binders, evidence files, and bureaucratic submissions often dominates teachers' time, limiting their capacity to engage deeply with students' individualized learning needs or to develop rich, practice-oriented instruction. At the same time, competition culture imposes additional performance expectations that extend well beyond routine instruction. Vocational teachers are routinely tasked with identifying, preparing, and mentoring students for innovation fairs, technical skill tests, startup challenges, robotics exhibitions, and inter-school competitions designed to boost institutional prestige. Success in these arenas contributes to school reputation, attracts partnerships, and can influence administrative evaluations, yet the labor involved is rarely acknowledged in formal workload models or salary structures.

The combined effect of administrative overload and competitive coaching functions contributes to burnout through multiple mechanisms. First, the time burden of paperwork reduces available hours for lesson planning, individualized support, and reflective practice, heightening emotional exhaustion. Second, the symbolic burden of building institutional prestige through competitions adds identity pressure, especially in environments that valorize measurable success. Third, the friction between administrative demands and instructional ideals can lead to depersonalization as teachers detach affectively to cope with relentless procedural obligations.

Comparative evidence from Japan illustrates how performance and paperwork pressures can intensify teacher strain, even in high-attaining systems. TALIS 2024 data indicate that a majority of Japanese teachers report excessive administrative work as a primary source of stress, and many also cite responsibilities related to parent communication and changing mandates as substantial stressors, contributing to long weekly hours and reduced opportunities for classroom engagement [30]. In Japan, full-time teachers report total working hours far above the OECD average, with a significant share of non-instructional time devoted to administrative and extracurricular duties, indicating that the pressures of accountability and institutional performance can drive overload, even in contexts with strong educational outcomes [30].

8.5 The Global–Local Burden: Continuous industrial updating and cross-border pressures

Vocational teachers worldwide shoulder a distinctive burden: unlike general subject teachers, who teach relatively stable knowledge domains, vocational instructors must continually update their expertise to keep pace with industries defined by rapid technological, economic, and organizational change. This challenge is visible internationally. In Germany's dual system, teachers must remain aligned with advanced manufacturing; in Japan, technical instructors must track robotics and automation; in South Korea and Singapore, vocational educators are expected to integrate AI, digitalization, and innovation ecosystems into their teaching. Even in countries with strong TVET systems, teachers describe a constant struggle to remain current with fast-moving industrial standards.

Cross-border educational influences amplify these pressures. Thai policymakers routinely benchmark Thailand against high-performing vocational systems in Singapore, China, Japan, and South Korea, whose TVET ecosystems are supported by strong industrial partnerships, research institutes, and sustained public investment. These nations have become aspirational models – Singapore's "SkillsFuture," Japan's "KOSEN," South Korea's "Meister schools," and China's "Made in China 2025" all serve as reference points for reform. While such international orientation is common in globalized education policy, it creates a cascading expectation that Thai teachers must rapidly adopt foreign pedagogies – project-based learning, competency frameworks, systems thinking, maker education, startup methodologies, and dual-training models – often without adequate systemic scaffolding.

Thailand's vocational sector operates in an 'Asymmetrical Reform' environment. While policy benchmarks are drawn from global models like Japan's KOSEN, China's Made in China 2025, and South Korea's Creative Economy, the necessary localized resources often lag behind. This creates a temporal mismatch, where global expectations travel easily across borders, but the institutional scaffolding required for teachers to succeed remains constrained.

When combined with other systemic burdens – paperwork, competitions, skill assessment demands, student diversity, and region-specific labor market expectations – these global-local pressures make vocational teachers particularly vulnerable to burnout. The profession demands continuous industrial relevance without offering continuous industrial support. The pace of technological progress, coupled with the symbolic weight of regional competition, positions vocational teachers at the frontline of national economic modernization while simultaneously leaving them underprepared and overstretched. In this sense, burnout in vocational education is not merely an individual psychological condition but a structural outcome of globalization, technological acceleration, and policy borrowing. It reflects the mismatch between what the global economy demands from vocational teachers and what national systems provide to sustain them. The result is a multi-layered pressure system in which global benchmarking becomes internalized at the school level, contributing to identity-based stress and institutional burnout.

9. Empirical insights from the Thai context

Recent empirical research on Thai teachers during the COVID-19 era offers valuable evidence for understanding burnout antecedents and moderating factors. A national study involving 243 Thai teachers across elementary, secondary, and vocational levels found clear differences between teachers with high burnout and low burnout risk [23]. Key findings relevant to this chapter include:

Teachers with a low risk of burnout demonstrated higher levels of self-efficacy and better online teaching performance than those at high risk [23].

- Burnout correlated negatively with self-efficacy, especially in the emotional exhaustion and depersonalization dimensions [23].

- Technology challenges intensified burnout, particularly among teachers lacking prior digital pedagogy experience [23].

- Teaching experience did not guarantee better performance or lower burnout; more experienced teachers reported higher emotional stress during online transitions [23].

These findings reinforce the role of self-efficacy as a key moderator between technology integration demands and burnout. This aligns with international evidence demonstrating that online teaching competence and teacher self-efficacy are inversely associated with digital burnout and emotional dysregulation, indicating that technological confidence protects teachers from stress and exhaustion [31].

Large comparative surveys reinforce this pattern. Analyses from the OECD TALIS indicate that higher teacher self-efficacy correlates with lower burnout, higher job satisfaction, and improved professional resilience across multiple national contexts [32]. Crucially, this relationship appears largely independent of demographic factors such as age or years of service, suggesting that self-efficacy operates as a cross-cultural psychological buffer against occupational stress.

10. Generational asymmetry and entrepreneurial innovation gaps

Entrepreneurial education represents a paradigmatic shift from teacher-centered content delivery toward innovation-driven, problem-based, and entrepreneurial learning. This transition introduces a generational asymmetry within Thailand's vocational teaching workforce. Younger vocational teachers tend to be more digitally fluent and have often been exposed to innovation ecosystems through university incubators, startup competitions, hackathons, and digital platforms [14]. By contrast, older vocational teachers were trained during an era when Thai education lacked entrepreneurial, innovation-based, or digital-ecosystem frameworks, resulting in substantial gaps in digital readiness, innovation literacy, and adaptive capacity [15].

The consequence is a two-speed vocational workforce in which digital and entrepreneurial capacities are unevenly distributed across generations. Older teachers face burnout when institutional rhetoric demands "innovation-driven teaching," while system-level professional development remains fragmented or insufficient [16]. This dynamic aligns with a core burnout mechanism: stress emerges when environmental demands escalate faster than individuals' adaptive resources, coping mechanisms, or opportunities for skill renewal – a relationship widely recognized in burnout theory [11, 12]. The innovation pipeline – from problem framing → ideation → prototyping → testing → commercialization – requires technical expertise, managerial decision-making, and design thinking competencies [17]. When teachers are expected to guide students through these cycles without prior experiential grounding, burnout manifests through defensive detachment (depersonalization), reduced personal accomplishment (professional self-doubt), and emotional exhaustion from continuous self-training [11, 23].

Moreover, technology amplifies generational asymmetry through at least three distinct stress pathways:

(1) Pedagogical Tech Stress (Online Teaching Tools): The shift toward LMS platforms, asynchronous instruction, digital submissions, and reduced face-to-face interaction undermines teachers' perceived instructional control and feedback capacity, contributing to emotional exhaustion and lower efficacy [23, 33].

(2) Technological Upheaval Stress (AI, Automation, Digital Fluency): The rapid introduction of AI tools, automated assessment systems, and data dashboards requires digital fluency that older teachers may not possess. OECD TALIS data indicates that teachers experiencing low digital self-efficacy report higher stress and lower job satisfaction across multiple countries [22].

(3) Tech-Specific Occupational Stress (Industry Tools & Sector Technologies): Vocational teachers must keep pace with evolving occupational technologies (e.g., PLC controllers, CAD/CAM platforms, hotel PMS systems) that update on industry cycles rather than academic cycles, a trend well-documented in UNESCO-UNEVOC reports on digital TVET modernization [13].

Taken together, these forces create a vocational teaching environment where modernization expectations outpace institutional supports, producing structurally induced burnout rather than individual failure. Systemic solutions – such as continuous industry-linked training, cross-generational mentorship, and strengthened PD ecosystems – are therefore essential to sustaining workforce capacity rather than expecting individual teachers to self-correct under escalating pressures.

11. Modernization, pace disparities, and the temporal burden on vocational educators

Modernization has not only transformed Thailand's economic and technological landscape – it has also altered the tempo at which institutions are expected to operate. Digital industries refresh products and workflows according to accelerated cycles measured in quarters or even weeks. Innovations in software, platform business models, and automation technologies are released, updated, and replaced in rapid succession. By contrast, educational systems operate under slower bureaucratic rhythms: curriculum reforms move through multi-year approval and accreditation cycles, procurement processes require annual budget cycles, and teacher training infrastructures are designed for gradual rather than immediate adaptation. Individual teachers occupy a third temporal layer altogether, acquiring new competencies through sporadic in-service trainings, informal peer exchanges, or self-funded upskilling – none of which synchronize neatly with state reforms or industry innovation timelines.

Thailand's digital transformation brings pace disparities into sharper focus, generating a series of temporal pressures that vocational educators must navigate simultaneously, as shown here:

The first pressure concerns obsolescence fear, where the rapid evolution of production technologies, smart manufacturing systems, and AI-driven operations creates an environment of constant revision. Teachers are aware that a tool or method mastered today may be eclipsed within a few innovation cycles. The emotional charge here differs from general uncertainty: it is not a question of *"Will this be relevant?"* but *"How long until this becomes outdated?"* – producing continuous temporal vigilance rather than episodic anxiety.

The second pressure involves role displacement, where modernization reconfigures what counts as authoritative knowledge. Traditional vocational expertise – rooted in manual skill, craftsmanship, or equipment-based diagnostics – is increasingly supplemented or superseded by data literacy, systems thinking, and innovation orchestration. This positions teachers paradoxically: they are responsible for preparing students for jobs evolving faster than their own training pathways, while their accumulated tacit knowledge risks being recast as "legacy skills." The challenge here is not only pedagogical but also intergenerational and inter-temporal, as identities formed during slower industrial cycles collide with the cadence of digital economies.

A third pressure emerges from institutional lag, referring to the structural inability of education systems to synchronize with the velocity of external change. Even when reform is politically prioritized, implementation is slowed by procurement cycles, infrastructure unevenness, provincial disparities, and credentialing rigidity. Technologies such as CAD/CAM platforms, collaborative robots, or IoT monitoring may be standard in industry for years before vocational institutions can acquire equipment, train staff, and certify curricula. Teachers, therefore, operate within temporally mismatched environments, where what is taught, what is needed, and what is possible rarely align in the same timeframe.

In Thailand, these temporal strains are further intensified by cultural and institutional expectations around image, prestige, and performance [33]. Thai society places a strong emphasis on *face-saving* and institutional image; therefore, vocational schools frequently rely on competitions, showcases, innovation fairs, and public award systems to signal modernization, capability, and competitiveness to stakeholders – including parents, employers, policymakers, and prospective students. These events serve as visible evidence of progress in contexts where underlying instructional or infrastructural gaps are less easily displayed. Consequently, teachers are tasked with organizing exhibitions, coaching students for competitions, producing documentation for awards, and curating public-facing success narratives – activities that may function as institutional defensive mechanisms to maintain legitimacy in competitive educational markets.

Taken together, these dynamics produce a form of temporal strain distinct from psychological uncertainty: vocational educators are required to bridge past, present, and future simultaneously – preserving foundational competencies rooted in industrial-era craftsmanship, gesturing toward emergent digital practices, and performing modernization for public consumption – all without synchronized institutional mechanisms to reconcile these time horizons. Modernization, therefore, burdens educators not only with new content but also with new temporal expectations, requiring responsiveness to external rhythms they did not choose and cannot control.

12. Policy implications and pathways to sustaining the vocational teaching workforce

Recent international scholarship emphasizes that sustaining the vocational education workforce requires coordinated systemic reform rather than reliance on individual resilience or short-term professional development initiatives [12, 13, 17]. The challenges identified in this chapter – namely sustaining the vocational education workforce, strengthening teacher preparation, enhancing technological self-sufficiency, improving professional recognition, and reinforcing institutional support – are widely documented across global TVET systems, suggesting that Thailand's experience reflects a broader structural pattern rather than a context-specific anomaly.

First, workforce sustainability literature highlights that vocational teachers are particularly vulnerable to burnout and attrition when innovation mandates, industry coordination, and student mentoring are layered onto existing workloads without formal recognition or workload adjustment [13, 19]. Evidence from OECD and UNESCO-UNEVOC reports suggests that recalibrating workload models – by formally recognizing innovation coaching, dual-training coordination, and pastoral support as core professional duties – can significantly improve retention and professional commitment.

Second, studies on teacher preparation consistently report a structural gap between vocational teachers' occupational expertise and their preparedness for digital pedagogy, entrepreneurial education, and innovation-oriented instruction [13, 19]. International models recommend longitudinal professional learning systems that integrate pedagogy, industry exposure, and ongoing in-service development, rather than fragmented, tool-based workshops. Such systemic preparation reduces cognitive overload and strengthens professional self-efficacy.

Third, technological self-sufficiency has emerged as a critical protective factor against burnout. Empirical research shows that low technological self-efficacy is strongly associated with emotional exhaustion and reduced instructional confidence [31]. The literature stresses that technological capacity must be institutionally scaffolded through shared infrastructure, technical support staff, and stable digital ecosystems, rather than being left to individual teachers to self-manage.

Fourth, professional recognition plays a decisive role in sustaining vocational teacher identity. Comparative studies indicate that vocational educators often experience symbolic devaluation relative to academic teachers, despite their central role in workforce development [27]. Policy-oriented research recommends expanding definitions of professional excellence to include mentoring, industry collaboration, and student support, alongside formal career pathways and recognition mechanisms that reinforce vocational teaching as a high-status profession.

Finally, institutional support and governance structures shape how these pressures are experienced in practice. Excessive administrative demands and compliance-oriented accountability systems have been repeatedly linked to burnout across education systems [17]. Streamlining reporting requirements, providing clerical support, and involving teachers in reform design are widely recommended strategies for reducing emotional exhaustion and restoring professional agency [12].

Taken together, the literature underscores that these five dimensions are interdependent. Addressing deficiencies in one area without corresponding reforms in others risks reproducing burnout through systemic misalignment. Sustainable vocational education reform, therefore, depends on synchronized interventions that align institutional expectations, teacher capacity, technological infrastructure, and professional recognition.

Ensuring the sustainability of Thailand's vocational teaching workforce demands more than incremental reforms. It requires a reconfiguration of how the nation understands vocational teachers: not merely as instructional technicians but as knowledge brokers, industrial translators, pastoral caregivers, competition coaches, and community responders [33]. This multidimensional labor cannot be stabilized through salary adjustments alone; it must be supported through structural redesigns that address technological, institutional, cultural, and emotional pressures simultaneously.

One of the most urgent priorities is the strengthening of technological and pedagogical self-efficacy. In the current landscape, professional development remains heavily oriented toward tool-based training – brief workshops on platforms, software, or digital devices – rather than cultivating fluency in digital pedagogy [23]. Vocational teachers need to be equipped to interpret learning analytics, manage online engagement, scaffold hybrid instructional models, innovate in TVET [21], and mentor students through innovation cycles. The COVID-19 period revealed, through national empirical research on 243 Thai teachers, that self-efficacy acted as a buffering variable: those with higher technological and pedagogical confidence demonstrated significantly lower burnout, even under conditions of online workload intensification [23]. These findings mirror international patterns captured by OECD TALIS data [28] and digital-burnout studies across higher education: confidence in one's technological and instructional competence is one of the few modifiable predictors of teacher resilience.

Yet competence alone cannot shield teachers from exhaustion when their most time-consuming functions remain invisible. Vocational educators carry what policy documents rarely acknowledge: vast volumes of hidden labor. They supervise innovation teams, accompany students to skill Olympiads, negotiate cooperative education placements with industries, write entrepreneurship mentorship reports, and prepare students for startup showcases or robotic competitions that become institutional currency in image-conscious systems. In Thai society, where *face-saving* and institutional prestige matter profoundly, these competitions serve as powerful legitimacy signals for vocational schools. They demonstrate that vocational students can innovate, compete, and win – shifting public perception in ways that formal curricula alone cannot. But the burden falls squarely on teachers, who must rapidly elevate student skills under constraints of outdated equipment, insufficient budgets, and students who often work part-time to support their families. International literature frequently observes that students with strong family support excel academically, yet in Thai vocational education the inverse is common: students navigating economic hardship are expected to cultivate high-level technical and entrepreneurial competencies under conditions that would cripple learners in more privileged systems. Teachers absorb the emotional load of this paradox, oscillating between coach, counselor, and surrogate guardian, a role configuration that accelerates emotional exhaustion and depersonalization if left unsupported.

Administrative burden compounds these pressures further. Vocational teachers devote increasing portions of their workday to producing evaluation documents, accreditation portfolios, compliance evidence, quality assurance reports, and licensing dossiers. These bureaucratic expectations align with international modernization agendas but often displace instructional and mentoring time, creating what scholars call "productive inefficiency," where institutional legitimacy is pursued at the expense of pedagogical depth. Digital paperwork consolidation, automated reporting pipelines, and clerical support could relieve this bottleneck, redirecting scarce cognitive resources back to core instructional and innovation work. Countries that have implemented such systems – including parts of Europe and East Asia – report improved teacher satisfaction and reduced attrition, not through increased salary but through reduced administrative friction.

If Thailand aspires to produce a future-ready workforce, entrepreneurial and innovation-oriented teacher preparation must be institutionalized rather than improvised. Entrepreneurial education demands familiarity with the product and startup lifecycle – from problem framing and customer discovery to prototyping, business model design, and commercialization. International vocational excellence models illustrate this clearly. Germany's dual system embeds industry tutors directly into learning, China's applied technology universities operate under state innovation mandates, South Korea's Meister schools align tightly with strategic sectors, and Japan's KOSEN institutes once stood as a global benchmark for engineering-oriented vocational training. Even as some struggle with demographic decline or reputation drift, these models share one principle: teachers are trained systemically for the economies they serve.

Mental health and social support infrastructures form the final, often neglected, pillar of workforce sustainability. Vocational teachers encounter forms of emotional labor rarely acknowledged in general education: they mediate student crises, navigate family dysfunction, respond to community emergencies, and maintain institutional image under scrutiny. During floods in Thailand, vocational colleges deploy teams to repair household electrical systems for affected communities, much like KOSEN institutions in Japan transform into disaster response hubs during earthquakes and tsunamis. These acts strengthen civic identity and institutional legitimacy, but they also rely on teacher stamina and altruism – traits that burnout erodes fastest. Money alone cannot renew these capacities. Teachers require reflective peer communities, counseling pathways, burnout screening, and policies that allow temporary workload adjustments. Without such infrastructures, burnout becomes a pipeline to professional detachment, reduced instructional quality, and premature exit from the field.

12.1 Toward a sustainable future for vocational educators: A Pain–Gain Model for systemic relief

Sustaining the vocational teaching workforce requires shifting from compliance-driven reform to capacity-driven reform. The Pain–Gain Model helps illustrate how "administrative congestion" can be converted into "cognitive space" for innovation. At the core of this transition is the 3E Doctrine – Empowerment, Equity, and Equality, which provides a conceptual anchor for ensuring that teachers remain "whole" while the nation modernizes.

The preceding analyses show that vocational teachers in Thailand operate at the intersection of multiple systemic forces: technological acceleration, industrial uncertainty, bureaucratic expansion, competition-driven prestige cultures, cross-national benchmarking, and shifting student demographics. Through a PESTEL lens, these forces appear not as isolated frictions but as structural determinants of well-being:

- **Political** decentralization and accreditation regimes
- **Economic** industrial upgrading and labor-market volatility
- **Sociocultural** hierarchies and face-saving norms
- **Technological** disruption and digital asymmetry
- **Environmental** crises requiring school-based emergency responses
- **Legal** frameworks governing licensing and compliance

The Pain–Gain Transition Roadmap through the 3E Doctrine (**Figure 2**) shows how these pressures converge on the individual teacher, producing a daily experience defined more by interruption than intention, and more by obligation than innovation.

To chart a path forward, vocational teaching can be reframed through the Pain–Gain Model. Core pain points are now well-documented: emotional exhaustion from unrecognized innovation coaching; administrative congestion that erodes instructional time; knowledge insecurity due to rapid industrial change; intergenerational tension over digital and entrepreneurial skills; and pastoral labor supporting students facing poverty, family instability, and stigma. Yet each pain point contains latent systemic gains if addressed through institutional rather than individual solutions. Reducing administrative overload yields cognitive space for curriculum design; formalizing competition mentorship converts invisible burdens into prestige pathways; structured entrepreneurial training enhances national innovation capacity; and mental-health infrastructure preserves expertise, stabilizes retention, and lowers recruitment costs. The problem is not that gains are unattainable, but that the current system extracts them from teachers without compensatory protection, creating an unsustainable exchange.

Thus, easing teachers' pain and enabling systemic gain requires a triple shift in how the vocational education ecosystem is governed and supported:

First, modernization must move from compliance-driven reform to capacity-driven reform. Policies should not merely demand digital pedagogy, innovation mentoring, entrepreneurship teaching, or international benchmarking – they must build the competencies and infrastructures that make those demands humanly and professionally feasible. Second, prestige must be reallocated. In a face-conscious society where institutional image is guarded through competitions, documentation, and public relations, vocational teachers are routinely positioned as the custodians of reputational legitimacy. A sustainable system must redistribute prestige so that instructional quality, pastoral care, and industry collaboration are valued alongside medals and paperwork. Third, accountability must become reciprocal. If teachers are accountable to national goals, institutions must be accountable for teacher

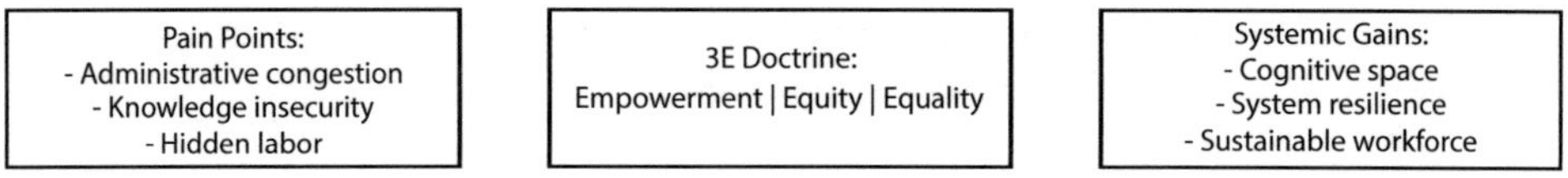

Figure 2.
The Pain–Gain Transition Roadmap Through 3E doctrine.

well-being; if teachers are asked to innovate, governments must guarantee the tools to innovate; if teachers are evaluated, evaluation must recognize the full spectrum of vocational labor rather than its narrow outputs.

At the philosophical core of this transformation lies the 3E Doctrine – Empowerment, Equity, and Equality – which offers a conceptual anchor for vocational education reform. Empowerment demands the reallocation of prestige in a face-conscious context where competitions and documentation guard institutional image; prestige must also recognize instructional quality, pastoral care, and industry collaboration. In addition, reciprocal accountability, where teachers possess agency, autonomy, competencies, and a voice in decisions that shape their work, replaces passive compliance with active participation. Equity ensures differentiated support according to need – recognizing that rural schools, high-poverty student populations, and resource-constrained provinces require more than uniform teacher training modules. Equality affirms that vocational teachers deserve the same societal respect, professional status, and developmental opportunities afforded to other education sectors; without such recognition, vocational education will continue to fight upstream against cultural stigma.

13. Policy and Executive-audience version (positive framing)

Vocational educators are central to Thailand's long-term competitiveness, especially in an era of industrial upgrading and digital transformation. Ensuring the sustainability of this workforce requires a shift from reform strategies that emphasize compliance toward strategies that build system-wide capacity and professional resilience. Thailand's vocational teachers operate within a dynamic ecosystem shaped by global technological acceleration, shifting labor-market demand, and evolving student profiles. When analyzed through a PESTEL perspective, the landscape reveals a range of external drivers – economic restructuring, technological innovation, sociocultural expectations, political decentralization, environmental challenges, and legal accreditation frameworks. These forces present not only pressures but also opportunities for modernization, collaboration, and systemic innovation.

Within this context, the Pain–Gain Model provides a useful reframing tool. It identifies core burdens that limit instructional and innovative capacity, while also highlighting the potential gains that become attainable through strategic intervention. For example, streamlining administrative processes creates room for inquiry-based pedagogy; recognizing mentoring and industry collaboration as professional work elevates vocational education's strategic value; and structured support for students strengthens both retention and equity outcomes. In this framing, the system does not "blame" teachers for constraints but rather acknowledges them as critical contributors whose effectiveness depends on institutional design.

Moving toward sustainable modernization requires three strategic shifts:

(1) **Capacity-centered modernization.** Investments in digital tools, curriculum development, industry partnerships, and innovation training ensure that reform creates capability rather than merely compliance.

(2) **Prestige diversification.** Expanding the definition of vocational excellence beyond competitions to include teaching quality, student support, and employer engagement strengthens legitimacy and broadens recognition.

(3) **Reciprocal accountability.** Clear standards for performance, paired with system-level support mechanisms, incentivize innovation while protecting educator well-being.

The 3E Doctrine – Empowerment, Equity, and Equality – offers a forward-looking framework for guiding this transition. Empowerment ensures that teachers have agency and voice; Equity ensures that resources reflect contextual needs; and Equality ensures that vocational educators enjoy professional status consistent with their contribution to national development. By applying these principles with coherence and fidelity, Thailand can transform vocational education into an engine for innovation, social mobility, and resilient workforce preparation. The future of vocational education depends not on extracting more effort from teachers but on designing systems that enable them to excel, collaborate, and remain committed over the long term. Such a trajectory aligns with international best practices and positions Thailand to compete and thrive in a rapidly changing global economy [34].

14. Conclusion

The evidence presented in this chapter demonstrates that vocational teacher burnout in Thailand cannot be reduced to individual weakness, personality traits, or temporal pandemic disruption. Rather, it constitutes the cumulative expression of modernization pressures, international competitiveness discourses, structural mismatches between school capacity and industrial expectations, and longstanding cultural narratives surrounding vocational education. The vocational teacher occupies a uniquely strained position: accountable to industry but employed by schools, expected to teach for today while anticipating tomorrow, evaluated through prestige-driven competitions while under-resourced for basic instructional work, and asked to support marginalized students despite inadequate professional preparation for multilingual, multi-level, and socioeconomically complex classrooms.

These tensions are not uniquely Thai. Across OECD countries, Japan, South Korea, China, the EU, and Southeast Asia, vocational teachers increasingly face the paradox of accelerated innovation coupled with institutional stagnation. Teachers are required to update knowledge across three domains – digital pedagogy, industry technologies, and entrepreneurial innovation – while simultaneously absorbing administrative burdens, emotional labor, and performance cultures that reward visibility over sustainability. When reframed through this global comparative lens, Thai vocational teacher burnout becomes both a national workforce risk and an international policy challenge. Without structural intervention, nations may soon experience parallel crises: teacher shortages, curriculum stagnation, and weakened pipelines of future-ready skilled labor.

Addressing this crisis requires an approach anchored in empowerment, equity, and equality. Empowerment demands that vocational teachers gain agency through digital fluency, industry exposure, and recognized innovation work – not as unpaid extra labor but as legitimate professional practice. Equity requires redistributing institutional resources to account for regional industrial variation, equipment disparities, and access gaps between urban and rural schools. Equality demands that vocational teachers receive the same legitimacy, public respect, and developmental opportunities as their academic counterparts, closing the symbolic and material divide that has historically devalued vocational pathways.

Finally, sustaining the vocational teaching workforce must be viewed not as an educational issue alone but as an economic imperative. Teachers are the mediators between national development strategies and human capital formation. When they burn out, detach, or exit the profession, the consequences cascade: reduced instructional quality, weakened innovation ecosystems, and declining competitiveness in the global skills economy. Conversely, when teachers are supported – emotionally, structurally, and professionally – they become multipliers of national capacity, enabling students to transition from local competencies to global mobility.

Thailand's vocational system sits at a pivotal juncture. If strategic attention is directed toward relieving structural burdens, recognizing hidden labor, synchronizing institutional pace with industrial change, and elevating vocational identity, then vocational teachers can lead rather than merely survive modernization. The question is not whether change is possible, but whether reform will align with the lived realities of those who carry the system. The future of the workforce depends on the future of its teachers – and sustaining them is both the starting point and the necessary condition for any country aspiring to thrive in the next economic era.

Acknowledgments

The author acknowledges the use of ChatGPT (OpenAI, https://www.openai.com) for language polishing and clarity improvement of the manuscript. The tool was used solely to enhance readability and linguistic quality; all scholarly arguments, data collection, interpretations, and conclusions remain the author's own.

I would like to express my deepest gratitude to the Department of Vocational Education, Faculty of Education, Kasetsart University, for providing the scholarly foundation and institutional support that made this research possible.

A special note of thanks is extended to the administrators, staff, and educators at the vocational colleges I visited during my fieldwork. The lived experiences shared by the teachers in these institutions – who daily navigate the complexities of acting as a "human buffer" between the rapid velocity of industry and the slower rhythms of bureaucracy – were instrumental in refining the core arguments of this work.

I am profoundly indebted to my collaborator researchers and the esteemed professors whose mentorship and critical feedback have been invaluable. Their guidance has been essential in helping me move beyond a psychological view of burnout toward a more robust "Triple Uncertainty Framework". Through our shared dialogs, my understanding of the vocational landscape has been significantly sharpened, particularly regarding the identity reconfiguration of the traditional "Kru Chang" into a modern innovation mentor.

Finally, I am grateful for the intellectual support that helped clarify the path from compliance-driven reform to capacity-driven reform. The insights gained from these collaborators and institutions have ensured that the vision for a sustainable future for vocational educators – anchored in the 3E Doctrine of Empowerment, Equity, and Equality – is now clear and focused. This work is a testament to our collective effort to transform vocational modernization from mere performance into true progress.

Author details

Nongluck Manowaluilou
Department of Vocational Education, Faculty of Education, Kasetsart University, Bangkok, Thailand

*Address all correspondence to: fedunlm@ku.ac.th

References

[1] Office of the Education Council. Thailand Education Statistics 2023 Bangkok, Thailand. Office of the Education Council, Ministry of Education; 2023. https://www.nso.go.th/public/e-book/Statistical-Yearbook/SYB-2023/185/

[2] Bangkok Metropolitan Administration. About Bangkok. n d. Available from: https://bmc.go.th/en/ [Accessed: 2026-Febraury-14]

[3] UN Tourism. Tourism Statistics: Thailand Country Profile. 2025. Available from: https://www.untourism.int/tourism-statistics [Accessed: 2026-January-14]

[4] Education in Thailand. n d. Available from: http://backoffice.onec.go.th/uploads/Book/2057-file.pdf [Accessed: 2026-March-18]

[5] Office of the Vocational Education Commission (OVEC). Dual Vocational Education System. Ministry of Education Thailand; n d. Available from: https://www.vec.go.th/Portals/43/fileDocument/pr_Dvec.pdf [Accessed: 2026-July-04]

[6] Teachers' Council of Thailand. English Version – Professional License Information. Bangkok: Teachers' Council of Thailand (Khurusapha); 2023. Available from: https://www.ksp.or.th/wp-content/uploads/2024/10/Eng-Regulation-of-TCT-on-Professional-Knowledge-and-Experience-Certification.pdf [Accessed: 2026-March-04]

[7] National Institute of Technology Thai National College of Technology Project. Thai National College of Technology Project. n d. Available from: https://www.kosen-k.go.jp/en/global/thai_kosen [Accessed: 2025-April-04]

[8] Thailand Professional Qualification Institute (TPQI). About TPQI – Background. n d. Available from: https://www.tpqi.go.th/en/home [Accessed: 2025-March-05]

[9] Teachers' Council of Thailand. Professional Licensing Information Portal. Teachers': Council of Thailand (Khurusapha); 2023. Available from: https://www.ksp.or.th/wp-content/uploads/2023/11/English-Version-P-license.pdf

[10] Equitable Education Fund (EEF). Thai Vocational Education and Training Overview. 2023, May 17. Available from: https://en.eef.or.th/2023/05/17/thai-vocational-education-and-training-overview/ [Accessed: 2026-February-14]

[11] Leiter MP, Maslach C. Burnout and engagement in the workplace: A contextual analysis. Advances in Motivation and Achievement. 1999;**11**(11):275–301. https://www.researchgate.net/publication/277476888_Burnout_and_engagement_in_the_workplace_A_contextual_analysis#fullTextFileContent

[12] Maslach C, Leiter MP. Burnout. In: Fink G, editor. Stress: Concepts, Cognition, Emotion, and Behavior. Elsevier Academic Press; 2016. p. 351–357

[13] OECD. Teachers and Leaders in Vocational Education and Training. OECD Publishing; 2021. Available from: https://www.oecd.org/content/da

m/oecd/en/publications/reports/2021/03/teachers-and-leaders-in-vocational-education-and-training_5641deea/59d4fbb1-en.pdf [Accessed: 2026-January-01]

[14] OECD. Education at a Glance 2023: OECD Indicators. OECD Publishing; 2023. Available from: https://www.oecd.org/en/publications/2023/09/education-at-a-glance-2023_581c9602.html [Accessed: 2025-December-31]

[15] OECD. The Future of Education and Skills: Education 2030. OECD Publishing; 2020. Available from: https://www.oecd.org/en/about/projects/future-of-education-and-skills-2030.html [Accessed: 2024-April-04]

[16] UNESCO-UNEVOC. Trends Mapping: Digital Skills Development in TVET Systems. UNESCO-UNEVOC International Centre; 2020. Available from: https://unevoc.unesco.org/pub/trends_mapping_study_digital_skills_development_in_tvet_teacher_training.pdf [Accessed: 2025-February-04]

[17] UNESCO-UNEVOC. Greening TVET: Trends, Opportunities and Challenges. UNESCO-UNEVOC International Centre; 2022. Available form: https://unevoc.unesco.org/home/SDGs+and+Greening+TVET [Accessed: 2025-March-06]

[18] European Centre for the Development of Vocational Training (CEDEFOP). Preparing for 2040: Four AI-powered scenarios for the future of continuing skills development. CEDEFOP. 2022. Available form: https://www.cedefop.europa.eu/en/news/preparing-2040-four-ai-powered-scenarios-future-continuing-skills-development [Accessed: 2025-June-05]

[19] CEDEFOP. The Changing Nature and Role of Vocational Education and Training in Europe. CEDEFOP Research Paper Series Volume 2 Results of a survey among European VET experts Luxembourg; 2017. Available from: https://www.cedefop.europa.eu/files/5564_en.pdf

[20] TVET Asia Secretariat. Regional Report of ASEAN-ROK Technical and Vocational Education and Training Mobility (TEAM) Programme – Component 1: 'Enhancing the Competitiveness of Human Resources through Responsive TVET Curriculum Supported by Involvement of Industries and Labor Market Information' Integrating the Case Studies of 10 AMS. TVET Asia Regional Report. 2021. Available from: https://asean.org/wp-content/uploads/2022/10/20220927-0.Regional-Report-1.pdf [Accessed: 2025-September-01]

[21] Manowaluilou N. Development of an instructional system design as a guideline for nursepreneur mastery learning: Elevating healthcare through design thinking and InnoTVET approach. Journal of Infrastructure, Policy and Development. 2024;**8**(15):10236. DOI: 10.24294/jipd10236

[22] Manowaluilou N, Thanarachataphoom T, Pimthong P, Ugsornkid S, Ketkosan N. Digital literacy and fluency in education: Enhancing teacher education preparedness policy. Journal of Infrastructure, Policy and Development. 2024;**8**(8):4415. DOI: 10.24294/jipd.v8i8.4415

[23] Manowaluilou N, Thanarachataphoom T. Digital frontiers: Investigating the impact of online teaching engagement on Thai

teachers' self-efficacy and burnout amid the COVID-19 pandemic. International Education Studies. 2023;**16**(6):1–13. DOI: 10.5539/ies.v16n6p33

[24] Ertmer PA, Ottenbreit-Leftwich AT, Sadik O, Sendurur E, Sendurur P. Teacher beliefs and technology integration practices: A critical relationship. Computers and Education. 2014;**59**(2):423–435. DOI: 10.1016/j.compedu.2012.02.001

[25] Ministry of Economy, Trade and Industry (METI). Cool Japan Initiative Policy Report. Government of Japan; 2013. Available from: https://www.meti.go.jp/english/policy/mono_info_service/creative_industries/creative_industries.html [Accessed: 2026-March-01]

[26] State Council of the People's Republic of China. Made in China 2025 Strategic Plan. Beijing: 2015. Available from: https://cset.georgetown.edu/wp-content/uploads/t0432_made_in_china_2025_EN.pdf [Accessed: 2026-March-04]

[27] Ministry of Economy and Finance. Creative Economy Action Plan and Measures to Establish a Creative Economy Ecosystem. Government of South Korea; 2013. Available from: https://english.moef.go.kr/pc/selectTbPressCenterDtl.do?boardCd=N0001&seq=3289 [Accessed: 2024-March-02]

[28] OECD. Results from TALIS 2024: The State of Teaching — Administrative workload as stressor across OECD. 2025. Available from: https://www.oecd.org/en/publications/results-from-talis-2024_90df6235-en/full-report/the-demands-of-teaching_0e941e2f.html [Accessed: 2026-July-04]

[29] OECD. TALIS 2024 Country Note: Japan — Stress sources including administrative work. 2025. Available from: https://www.oecd.org/en/publications/results-from-talis-2024_90df6235-en/full-report/the-demands-of-teaching_0e941e2f.html [Accessed: 2026-June-02]

[30] Jerrimm J, Sims S. Teacher workload and well-being. New international evidence from the OECD TALIS study. 2020. Available from: https://johnjerrim.com/wp-content/uploads/2020/11/working_paper_workload_wellbeing_november_2020.pdf [Accessed: 2025-March-04]

[31] Yang X, Du J. The effect of teacher self-efficacy, online pedagogical and content knowledge, and emotion regulation on teacher digital burnout: A mediation model. BMC Psychology. 2024;**12**:51. DOI: 10.1186/s40359-024-01540-z

[32] Bing H, Sadjadi B, Afzali M, Fathi J. Self-efficacy, emotion regulation as predictors of teacher burnout among English as a forieng language teachers: A structural Equation Modeling approach. Frontiers. 2022;**13**. DOI: 10.3389/fpsyg.2022.900417

[33] Manowaluilou N, Nilsook P, Buasuwan P. Perceptions and the new paradigm of Thai vocational education. International Journal of Innovation and Learning. 2022;**33**(3):344–365. DOI: 10.1504/IJIL.2023.130101

[34] World Bank. Thailand Economic Monitor: The Road to Economic Recovery. World Bank Group; 2022. Available from: https://documents1.worldbank.org/curated/en/099505112112129099/pdf/P1774810eff81c0030b22f0874a695a491d.pdf [Accessed: 2026-May-01]

Chapter 9

The Missing Link in Burnout Research: Teacher Wellness and Systemic Recovery across Six Continents

Helena H. Heydenreich

Abstract

Teacher burnout has intensified worldwide, yet research and policy efforts continue to overlook the underlying forces driving the crisis. Building on five decades of scholarship, from early warnings about occupational burnout to its later recognition as a global workplace phenomenon, this chapter exposes a persistent gap: the neglect of educator wellness within public health and education systems. Drawing on evidence from six continents, it integrates eight theoretical frameworks, including positive psychology, psychological capital, Maslow's sailboat metaphor, posttraumatic growth, spiritual resilience, ecological systems theory, transformative learning, and sociocultural theory. These perspectives converge in the Teacher Wellness Program (TWP), a systemic model designed to reposition teacher well-being at the center of educational reform and global development goals. The chapter argues that teacher well-being constitutes critical infrastructure for sustainable learning systems and represents a moral imperative for educational recovery worldwide.

Keywords: teacher burnout, educator well-being, systemic recovery, posttraumatic growth (PTG), PERMA model, psychological capital (PsyCap), Maslow's sailboat model, spiritual resilience (Ortberg), transformative learning (Mezirow), sociocultural theory (Vygotsky), ecological systems theory (Bronfenbrenner), sustainable development goals (SDG 3 and SDG 4), moral injury, chronic workplace stress, policy frameworks, collective well-being, professional efficacy, psychosocial stressors, public health strategies

1. Introduction

Half a century ago, Freudenberger [1] described burnout as the exhaustion experienced by those who care deeply and give relentlessly. His early work identified a pattern among care professionals whose compassion became their source of depletion – a paradox that education has since inherited. When World Health Organization (WHO) [2] classified burnout as an occupational phenomenon, it confirmed Freudenberger's insight on a global scale: burnout is not a fleeting stress condition but an institutional and public-health crisis [3].

This chapter draws exclusively on *secondary data analysis*, a synthesis of international research, meta-studies, and institutional reports published across six continents. Its findings are interpretive rather than empirical, integrating existing global evidence to identify converging patterns and propose a unified framework for systemic recovery [4].

The argument is simple but urgent: teacher wellness represents the missing link in burnout research and public-health strategy. Education systems worldwide continue to rely on the moral endurance of teachers while neglecting the structural reforms required for sustainable well-being [9]. Through a synthesis of theory, global evidence, and systemic frameworks, this chapter calls for a new understanding of wellness as shared responsibility and institutional design [5].

2. A brief history of burnout research

The study of burnout began in 1974 when the American psychologist Herbert Freudenberger used the term to describe the gradual depletion of energy and motivation among professionals in human service fields. Working in a free clinic for people in crisis, he observed that those who cared the most often collapsed first. Freudenberger's description of burnout as a state of emotional and physical exhaustion caused by excessive demands on one's energy and strength remains one of the most cited foundations of the concept [3].

During the late 1970s and early 1980s, Christina Maslach and Susan Jackson expanded the construct through their research on emotional labor. They identified three primary dimensions of burnout: emotional exhaustion, depersonalization, and a reduced sense of personal accomplishment [6, 7]. This multidimensional model shifted the focus from individual fatigue to the relational and organizational contexts in which burnout occurs. By the 1990s, burnout was recognized not only as a psychological experience but as a social and occupational phenomenon that affected both performance and moral purpose [4].

Over the past five decades, scholars have refined and extended Freudenberger's and Maslach's work to include the physiological, systemic, and moral aspects of exhaustion. The term "moral injury," often used in health and education contexts, reflects the deep conflict professionals experience when their values are violated by the systems they serve. These developments underscore that burnout is not a symptom of weakness but a signal of structural imbalance [5].

The World Health Organization's classification of burnout as an occupational phenomenon in the International Classification of Diseases (ICD-11) was, therefore, not a new discovery but an institutional confirmation of what researchers had long documented. It formally recognized that chronic workplace stress, left unmanaged, can lead to a state of depletion that undermines both health and professional integrity, while situating burnout within organizational and policy responsibility rather than individual pathology. Despite this recognition, burnout prevention continues to receive limited attention in education policy frameworks and public-health strategies. Historical evidence suggests that while definitions of burnout have evolved, systemic responses remain inadequate [5].

This chapter builds upon that historical foundation by situating burnout within the education sector, where care, meaning, and moral purpose intersect. Teachers, like healthcare workers, are part of the social infrastructure that sustains collective well-being. When their energy collapses, entire learning ecosystems falter. Understanding how burnout has been defined, ignored, and rediscovered over 50 years provides the necessary context for addressing what may be the most overlooked public-health challenge in global education [5].

3. Burnout as a public-health concern

Burnout is no longer a marginal psychological topic or a private occupational struggle. It has become a matter of public health that affects not only individual well-being but also the functioning of entire institutions and societies. The WHO[2] defines burnout as a syndrome resulting from chronic workplace stress that has not been successfully managed, characterized by exhaustion, cynicism, and reduced professional efficacy. When applied to education, this definition reveals the collective implications of teacher distress: compromised instructional quality, student disengagement, and the erosion of professional communities [3].

In many countries, burnout has reached epidemic proportions among teachers, paralleling rates previously seen in emergency medicine and social work. The phenomenon undermines national goals for learning outcomes, teacher retention, and psychological well-being. The cost is measurable not only in human terms but also in economic productivity. Studies in the United States, Europe, and Asia estimate that teacher attrition and absenteeism caused by burnout account for billions in lost expenditure annually [3, 4]. The impact on developing regions is even more severe, as resource scarcity compounds stress and reduces recovery capacity.

Viewing burnout through a public-health lens transforms how societies respond to it. Instead of treating it as an individual pathology, it must be understood as a systemic exposure to chronic psychosocial stressors. Public-health approaches focus on prevention, capacity building, and community resilience rather than reacting after collapse. In this sense, schools can be viewed as ecological microcosms of health: spaces where prevention, care, and recovery intersect. When teacher well-being declines, the entire school ecosystem experiences a cascade of secondary effects, from reduced collaboration to lower student performance.

The health implications of teacher burnout extend beyond the classroom. Psychological strain, insomnia, and chronic fatigue among educators have been linked to increased risks of cardiovascular disease, depression, and anxiety disorders [8]. These outcomes mirror the same physiological and neurological effects documented in other high-burden professions, confirming that burnout is a legitimate occupational hazard. Recent teacher well-being analyses report corresponding increases in chronic stress and fatigue [9].

From a policy perspective, integrating wellness into education is not an optional initiative but a matter of population health. The sustainable development goals (SDGs) provide the framework for this alignment. SDG 3 calls for ensuring healthy lives and promoting well-being for all at all ages, while SDG 4 emphasizes inclusive and equitable quality education. These goals intersect at the point of teacher wellness. Without healthy teachers, the pursuit of quality education becomes unsustainable [10]. Notably, the SDGs committed the global community to health and quality education in 2015, yet it was only in 2019 that burnout was formally recognized within the international health classification system. This lag reflects a broader pattern in which teacher well-being has been rhetorically valued but institutionally under-addressed.

In practice, addressing burnout as a public-health concern requires collaboration between health, education, and labor sectors. Governments must recognize teacher well-being as a public investment in human capital. Programs that embed wellness into school systems through leadership training, workload regulation, and psychological support serve the same preventive function as vaccination campaigns or nutrition policies. They safeguard not only those who teach but also the generations who learn from them.

This chapter, therefore, situates teacher wellness within the broader discipline of public health. The focus shifts from individual resilience to institutional design. If health systems can prevent epidemic disease, education systems can prevent systemic burnout [5]. The following theoretical framework offers an integrative model for doing so.

4. Theoretical and conceptual framework

The TWP integrates eight complementary theories, each illuminating a dimension of recovery and human flourishing in education.

- **PERMA model of well-being** [11] – Positive emotion, engagement, relationships, meaning, and accomplishment represent the five core pillars of sustainable well-being. In the context of education, PERMA reframes wellness as a collective culture rather than individual self-care.

- **Psychological capital** [12] – The HERO model (hope, efficacy, resilience, optimism) provides the psychological resources educators need to persist through adversity. PsyCap highlights that well-being is a capacity that can be developed, not a fixed trait.

- **Maslow's sailboat model** [13] – Expanding Maslow's hierarchy, this model visualizes growth and safety as interdependent. Teachers cannot self-actualize while their basic professional and emotional needs remain unmet. Wellness, therefore, requires structural stability as a foundation for growth.

- **Posttraumatic growth** [14, 15] – PTG explores how adversity can lead to transformation, not merely recovery. It positions burnout as a catalyst for renewed meaning and strength when systems enable reflection, connection, and reinvention.

- **Ortberg's anchor and compass** [16] – Spiritual resilience and moral purpose anchor the educator's identity. Wellness becomes a matter of soul-keeping, caring for the inner life that sustains outward service.

- **Bronfenbrenner's ecological systems theory** [17] – Burnout is not an isolated experience; it emerges from the interaction of multiple systems. Teacher well-being must, therefore, be viewed within the broader ecology of school culture, policy, community, and society.

- **Mezirow's transformative learning theory** [18, 19] – True learning arises from disorienting dilemmas that force a re-examination of meaning. For educators, burnout can become a turning point – a moment that invites reflection, reframing, and transformation.

- **Vygotsky's sociocultural theory** [20] – Growth occurs through collaboration and support. The Zone of Proximal Development reminds us that wellness is relational; recovery happens within a community, not in isolation.

Together, these theories form the scaffolding for the TWP: a model that views burnout and recovery as systemic, psychological, and spiritual processes of human development.

Although burnout presents with overwhelming global severity, educators also demonstrate a remarkable capacity for transformation and reconstruction. The concept of posttraumatic growth provides a way to understand this trajectory, particularly when teachers move from depletion toward renewed purpose and identity. Empirical research also confirms that PTG can occur in high-stress educational environments when reflection and support are present [15]. This process is illustrated in **Figure 1**, which visualizes how teachers may progress through stages of internal collapse, reflection, reintegration, and renewed strength.

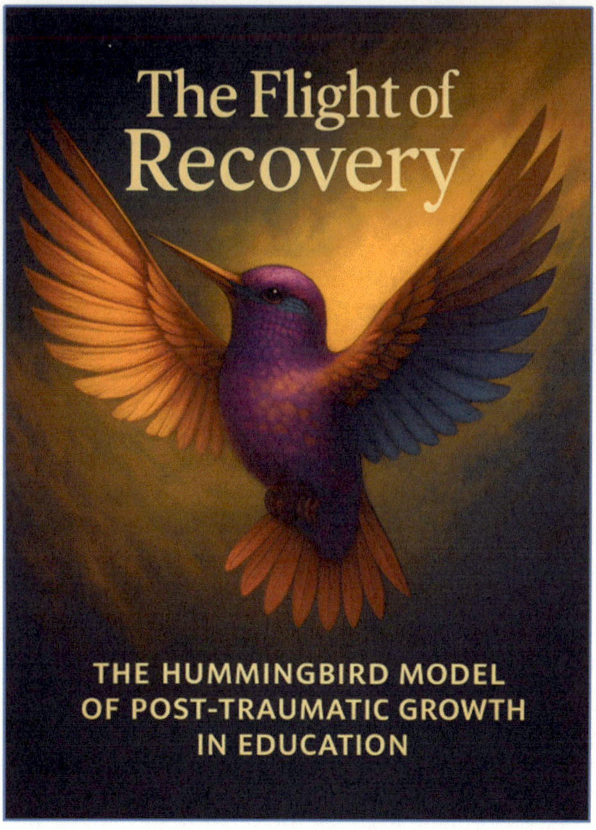

Figure 1.
The hummingbird model of post-traumatic growth in education (created by the author using Image Generator Pro (2025)).

As shown in **Figure 1**, the posttraumatic growth hummingbird model illustrates how teachers can evolve from emotional depletion toward renewed purpose and professional identity. The model highlights five interrelated domains of growth commonly observed after periods of intense strain: strengthened relationships, deeper appreciation of life, increased personal resilience, expanded possibilities, and renewed meaning. By visually mapping this transformation, the figure emphasizes that recovery is neither linear nor passive. Instead, it reflects an active process in which educators reinterpret adversity, reconnect with their core values, and rebuild a sense of inner stability.

5. Global context and research evidence

Burnout is no longer confined to high-stress professions like healthcare or emergency response; it has become a defining feature of education across every continent. While first identified by [1] and validated by [2], global analyses over the past decade document scale, persistence, and systemic drivers of this crisis accross education systems worldwide [40].

Across six continents, similar trends emerge. In sub-Saharan Africa, recent UNESCO–Teacher Task Force analyses highlight widespread psychological strain and high attrition risk among teachers, driven by instability, workload pressure, and limited support structures [5]. In Europe, OECD monitoring shows that workload intensity and administrative burden remain the strongest predictors of stress and reduced job satisfaction among teachers [4]. In Asia, empirical studies in China and India report chronic overwork and emotional exhaustion as major contributors to burnout among teachers [21, 22]. In the United States, a national survey by RAND found that large numbers of teachers report frequent job-related stress and considerable intentions to leave the profession [9]. In Latin America, regional monitoring from Fundación SM and empirical studies [23] show that burnout is pervasive, intensified by postpandemic instability and resource disparities. In Australia (Oceania), Black Dog Institute [24] reports that psychological distress among Australian teachers is almost double that of the general population, with many educators considering leaving due to chronic stress and emotional fatigue.

6. The hidden suffering of teachers worldwide

A global perspective on teacher burnout highlights the urgency of intervention. The following data, compiled from international sources such as the RAND Corporation, UNESCO, the OECD, and peer-reviewed research, reveal the staggering burnout rates affecting educators worldwide:

As shown in **Table 1**, these numbers are not abstract; they are a mirror held up to a profession that has been told for decades that burnout is a personal weakness. But when large proportions of teachers across multiple regions report high levels of stress, burnout, or intent to leave, the evidence is no longer up for debate. This is not a failure of character; it is a failure of design.

These numbers tell a story far louder than any policy memo or staff meeting ever could. Behind every percentage is a classroom, a teacher, a life. From the United States to sub-Saharan Africa, the picture is the same: educators are exhausted, disillusioned, and burning out. This is not a regional glitch; it is a global crisis. And to

Region	Country/ area	Burnout rate	Source
North America	United States	53% report burnout; 16% intend to leave.	[9, 25]
Europe [General]	Regional	Over 90% of the region's teacher shortage – equal to about 4.8 million posts – results from attrition rather than a lack of qualified teachers.	[5]
Europe [General]	Spain	Two in five teachers report burnout, anxiety, or depression; 47% are neutral or open to leaving.	[3, 5]
Europe [General]	United Kingdom	69% of teachers are considering leaving the profession; workload is the main reason.	[26]
Australia	Australia	Australian teachers report depression, anxiety, and stress levels three times the national average, indicating extreme psychological strain.	[27]
Asia	China	66.6% of primary school teachers experience burnout, with 45.7% showing depressive symptoms under the national "Double Reduction" policy, which has increased teacher workload.	[22]
Sub-Saharan Africa	Regional [SSA]	Annual attrition ranges between 5–30%; 55% of South African teachers would leave if they could; UNESCO projects that 15 million teachers will be needed by 2030.	[3, 28, 29
Latin America	Regional	Over 30% report high-to-very high burnout.	[23]

Table 1.
Teacher burnout rates by region.

those who still insist, "The problem lies somewhere else," the answer is simple: It is not. It is right here – in every school and every system that refuses to listen.

As illustrated in **Figure 2**, this map represents reported burnout, high-stress levels, or intention-to-leave rates among teachers across six continents between 2022 and 2025. Data were compiled from [9] and [25] for the United States; [4] and [26] for Europe and the United Kingdom; [24] and the Australian Teacher Workforce Data National Report [39] for Australia; [22] for China; [23] for Latin America; and [28, 29] the HSRC [30], and [31] for sub-Saharan Africa. In Australia, recent national datasets indicate that more than 50% of teachers report clinically significant symptoms of anxiety or depression, nearly 60% experience high emotional exhaustion, and one in three early-career teachers plans to leave the profession within five years [24, 39]. Although South Africa has not conducted a publicly released national educator-health survey since 2005, more recent labor-force analyses [31] show rising attrition, instability, retirement-related outflows, and widening qualification gaps. Combined with regional UNESCO monitoring, this suggests that current levels of burnout and intent to leave are likely to be higher than earlier national estimates. The color scale (0–25%, 26–45%, 46–60%, 61 +) indicates the proportion of teachers reporting burnout, high stress, or intention to leave.

Despite increased global awareness of teacher burnout following the COVID-19 pandemic, recent evidence indicates that the crisis is worsening rather than stabilizing in several regions. In North America, the proportion of teachers reporting burnout rose sharply from 44% in 2022 [32] to 53% in 2025, with 16% intending to leave the profession [9, 25]. This upward trend stands in stark contrast to the assumption that postpandemic recovery would relieve pressure on the profession. Conversely, in sub-Saharan Africa, the crisis is intensified by the absence of updated

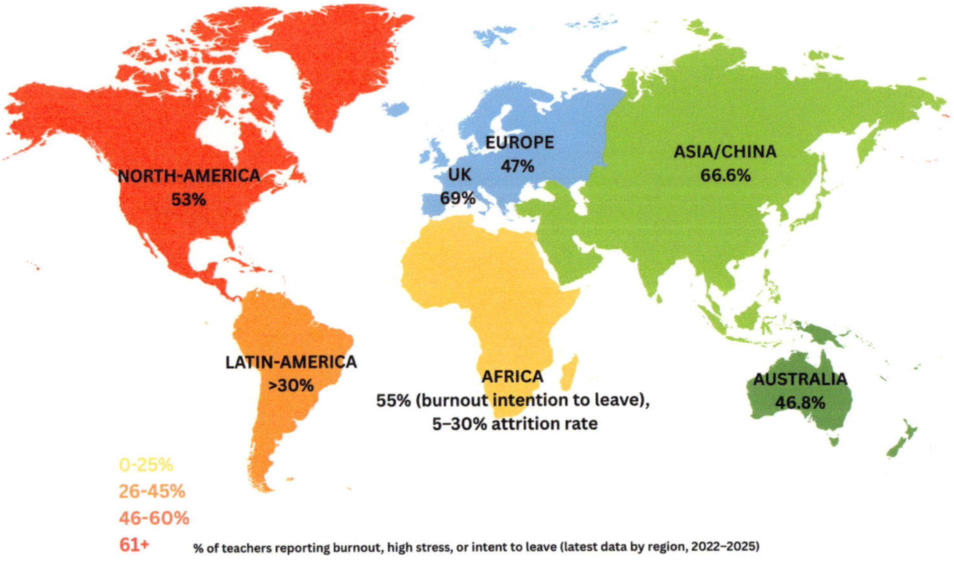

Figure 2.
Global distribution of teacher burnout rates by region (created by the author using Image Generator Pro (2025)).

national data. With the last comprehensive educator-health survey conducted in 2005 and only fragmented labor-force evidence available since, the region faces a blind spot in monitoring teacher well-being [41].

This lack of contemporary data reflects a deeper systemic neglect: burnout cannot be addressed when it is not measured, and the absence of surveillance itself signals a structural failure to protect the workforce [38]. Australia shows an equally troubling escalation. A 2025 study by UNSW Sydney reports that Australian teachers now experience depression, anxiety, and stress levels approximately three times higher than the national average, signaling psychological strain far beyond typical occupational stress and pointing to a workforce operating under unsustainable conditions [39]. Even as this manuscript is being revised, newly released data continue to reveal rising burnout rates and worsening conditions for teachers worldwide, underscoring the urgency of systemic intervention and reinforcing the central argument of this study.

When the same syndrome occurs under different conditions, it ceases to be a cultural phenomenon; it becomes structural. Burnout is, therefore, best understood as a failure of system design rather than a reflection of individual devotion. Addressing it requires systemic frameworks that position teacher wellness as public infrastructure, not personal luxury.

To visualize this concept, the following figure reinterprets Abraham Maslow's hierarchy of needs as an interdependent model of safety and growth. Originally proposed by [13], the *Sailboat Model* replaces the fixed pyramid with a dynamic metaphor in which growth and security must coexist. Within education, this means that teachers cannot pursue creativity, purpose, or excellence when foundational conditions, such as professional respect, manageable workloads, and psychological safety, remain unstable. Just as a sailboat cannot move forward without a steady hull, teachers cannot thrive without systems that safeguard their well-being.

Recent international monitoring reinforces this interpretation, showing that teacher burnout follows nearly identical patterns across regions with very different cultures, indicating systemic rather than individual origins [5].

As shown in **Figure 3**, this visual reimagines Maslow's hierarchy as a sailboat, where safety (the hull) and growth (the sail) function interdependently. The model illustrates that teachers require professional stability, emotional safety, and clear direction to sustain meaningful development and resilience within their institutions.

This reimagined model provides a bridge from global evidence to systemic response. It positions teacher wellness not as an act of personal perseverance but as a product of organizational design. The next section introduces the TWP, a recovery framework grounded in these principles and informed by psychological, ecological, and spiritual theories that support long-term flourishing.

7. Case snapshots across continents

While global statistics reveal striking convergence, the lived experience of burnout and recovery differs across cultural and economic contexts. The following snapshots from Finland, India, and Rwanda illustrate how systemic wellness can be interpreted and applied in diverse educational ecosystems. Each reflects a unique way of

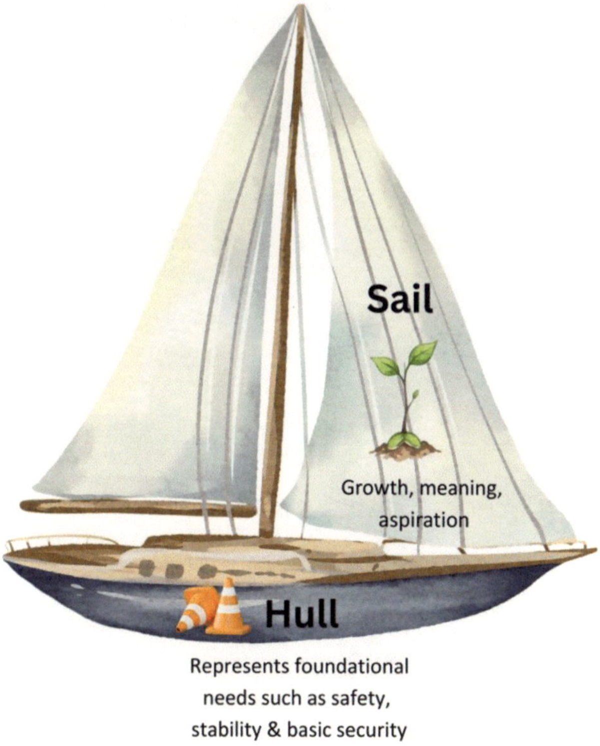

Figure 3.
Maslow's sailboat model of integrated growth and stability (created by the author using Canva Pro (2025)).

translating theory into practice and demonstrates that teacher wellness is not bound by geography but by shared human conditions of meaning, purpose, and balance.

7.1 Finland: Trust and the PERMA culture

Finland's education system is often described as one of the most trusted in the world. Teachers operate within a professional culture that values autonomy, reflection, and intrinsic motivation. These characteristics align closely with PERMA model of well-being, in which positive emotion, engagement, relationships, meaning, and accomplishment are nurtured through authentic professional agency [11].

This conceptual model forms a bridge from global evidence to systemic response. It reframes teacher wellness not as an act of *personal perseverance* but as a product of *organizational design* in action. The next logical question is: *What does flourishing look like when the system itself begins to heal?*

Seligman (2011), *PERMA Model of Well-being,* provides one answer [11]. It identifies five elements that define authentic flourishing: p*ositive emotion, engagement, relationships, meaning, and accomplishment.* In the TWP, these elements are visualized through *the PERMA Bloom*, symbolizing that when trust, balance, and connection are nurtured, wellness expands organically across individuals and communities.

As illustrated in **Figure 4**, this visual represents Seligman's five pillars of well-being: positive emotion, engagement, relationships, meaning, and accomplishment. It

Figure 4.
The PERMA bloom: flourishing in real time (created by the author using Canva Pro (2025)).

illustrates that when teachers are supported by trust-based environments, they not only survive but flourish. This creates a culture of sustained growth and relational vitality.

In this framework, flourishing is not a personal luxury; it is the natural outcome of systems that prioritize humanity over compliance. A healthy school culture is not built through policy alone but through relationships that protect, empower, and inspire those within them.

Well-being in Finnish schools is not treated as an auxiliary activity but as a fundamental condition for learning. Collaborative planning, professional dialog, and a balanced curriculum structure enable teachers to find purpose within their practice rather than outside it. Leadership models reinforce trust rather than surveillance, and policies discourage competitive performance metrics that erode morale. As a result, Finnish teachers report higher levels of job satisfaction, stronger collegial ties, and a deeper sense of belonging than their international counterparts [4]. These patterns are highlighted in the recent OECD analysis, including the TALIS 2024 Overview, [36] which documents Finland's high levels of teacher trust, autonomy, and job satisfaction. The Finnish case demonstrates how wellness can be structurally embedded through professional respect, sustainable workload design, and a culture of relational leadership.

7.2 Case illustration: India – stability and the sailboat of growth

In India, the Tata Trusts' educator development projects illustrate the value of systemic stability for teacher wellness. Drawing on Kaufman's [13] reinterpretation of Maslow's sailboat model, these initiatives recognize that growth and safety function interdependently. Teachers who are provided with emotional security, professional mentorship, and ongoing training can navigate uncertainty more effectively and sustain personal growth.

The Tata Trusts' model emphasizes *mentorship rather than top-down evaluation*, giving educators the psychological and social scaffolding to reflect, experiment, and innovate. This approach aligns with both Seligman's PERMA framework and Luthans' Psychological Capital (PsyCap), particularly the dimensions of *hope* and *efficacy*. Independent analyses of the Tata Trusts' initiatives highlight that teachers participating in these programs report increased confidence, stronger professional identity, and improved instructional innovation, particularly through the Digital Infrastructure for Knowledge Sharing integration and preservice mentoring pathways [33]. As teachers gain a sense of professional security and trust, they are more willing to engage in creative pedagogy and community collaboration.

As shown in **Figure 5**, this visual is inspired by India's Tata Trusts' educator development projects and reflects the three-tiered approach to sustainable reform: local pilots, regional partnerships, and national implementation. It illustrates that the goal of pilot programs is not performance, but partnership between vision and reality. The Indian example highlights that, in resource-variable contexts, structural support and a stable professional environment can act as the keel that keeps the educational sailboat balanced during systemic storms.

7.3 Rwanda: Leadership as scaffolding

Rwanda's School Leadership Professional Development Program (SLPDP) offers a model of leadership grounded in community and shared responsibility. Rooted in the concept of the Zone of Proximal Development [20], the program

Figure 5.
India's grounded approach to piloting change – from local to national impact (created by the author using Image Generator Pro (2025)).

views leadership not as hierarchical oversight but as the facilitation of collective growth. Principals are trained to support teachers through reflective dialog, emotional regulation, and peer mentoring. This creates a professional environment in which growth becomes a shared, supported process rather than an isolated burden.

Figure 6 illustrates the collaborative structure of Rwanda's SLPDP, where wellness is shared among teachers, leaders, unions, and curriculum teams. The circular design reflects a relational ecosystem of support and shows how leadership becomes the catalyst for collective recovery and reform.

Early evaluations of the SLPDP revealed marked improvements in teacher engagement and student performance, particularly in rural schools where professional isolation was most severe [34]. Teachers reported feeling supported rather than inspected, describing their principals as allies in well-being rather than administrators of compliance. This shift from supervision to scaffolding reflects the heart of Vygotsky's theory: growth occurs through connection. The Rwandan example underscores that wellness is not a product of individual strength but of relational leadership and systemic empathy.

Together, these three contexts demonstrate that, while burnout is global, recovery is local. Each system draws upon universal principles of human flourishing, trust, safety, and relational support to design wellness frameworks that respect cultural and economic realities. The lessons from Finland, India, and Rwanda affirm that the TWP can adapt across continents without losing its moral and theoretical coherence.

Figure 6.
Stakeholder buy-in in Rwanda's SLPDP (created by the author using Image Generator Pro (2025)).

8. The Teacher Wellness Program: A systemic recovery framework

The TWP was developed through secondary data analysis of international research, policy reports, and institutional documentation. It synthesizes recurring patterns in burnout causation and recovery across global contexts. The framework reframes wellness as shared accountability between individuals, institutions, and governments.

Among the countries studied, Finland stands out as a living example of what systemic wellness looks like in practice. In Finnish schools, well-being is not an additional initiative but an integrated component of school culture and policy. Collaborative leadership, workload autonomy, and access to psychological support are not considered optional; they are embedded in the daily operational DNA of the education system. Teacher wellness in Finland is not decorative; it is structural, forming the backbone of a sustainable, high-trust learning environment.

Figure 7 presents a visual inspired by Finland's education system, where teacher wellness is integrated into structural design rather than treated as an external initiative. The DNA metaphor symbolizes the systemic interdependence of workload autonomy, psychological support, collaborative leadership, and wellness as a policy

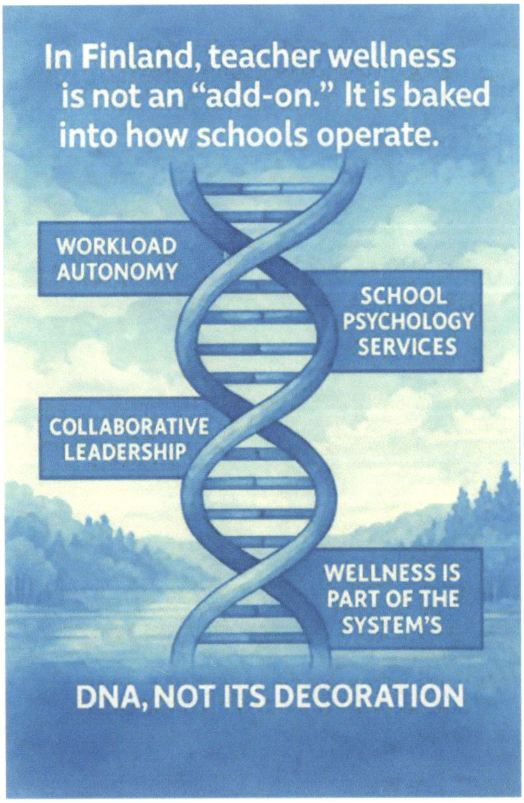

Figure 7.
Teacher wellness embedded in system design: the Finnish model (created by the author using Image Generator Pro (2025)).

foundation. This reflects international evidence showing that structural protections, not isolated initiatives, produce long-term workforce stability [4].

This model reinforces the core principle of the TWP: Recovery must be institutionalized, not improvised. Sustainable wellness begins when systemic design aligns with human needs. When the system shifts, teachers can recover without relying on personal endurance alone.

The TWP consists of six interconnected modules, forming a continuum of transformation:

- **Naming the burnout** – recognition of systemic rather than personal causes.
- **Reclaiming identity and purpose** – reconnecting with intrinsic motivation (PERMA, Mezirow).
- **Restoring boundaries and energy** – establishing limits and renewal (Maslow's sailboat).
- **Building resilience and psychological strength** – cultivating hope, efficacy, resilience, and optimism (PsyCap).

- **Reclaiming voice and embedding wellness** – turning reflection into advocacy (PTG, Vygotsky).

- **Embedding wellness into policy and culture** – institutionalizing care (Ortberg, Bronfenbrenner).

Each module integrates reflection, relational practice, and systemic application. Together, they shift wellness from a personal coping mechanism to an organizational mindset.

The TWP operates at three levels: school, leadership, and policy, aligning with SDG 3 (good health and well-being) and SDG 4 (quality education). Case illustrations from Finland, India, and Rwanda demonstrate how contextual adaptation can sustain the same foundational principles of trust, purpose, and human dignity. This multi-level design ensures that wellness becomes a structural expectation rather than an individual responsibility.

This diagram visualizes the six interconnected stages of recovery in the TWP, a process shown in **Figure 8** as a sequence that moves from personal awareness to institutional transformation. These stages include naming the burnout, reclaiming identity and purpose, restoring boundaries and energy, building resilience and psychological strength, reclaiming voice and embedding wellness, and leading for wellness through systemic responsibility. Together, they reflect a cyclical path of renewal within the educational ecosystem.

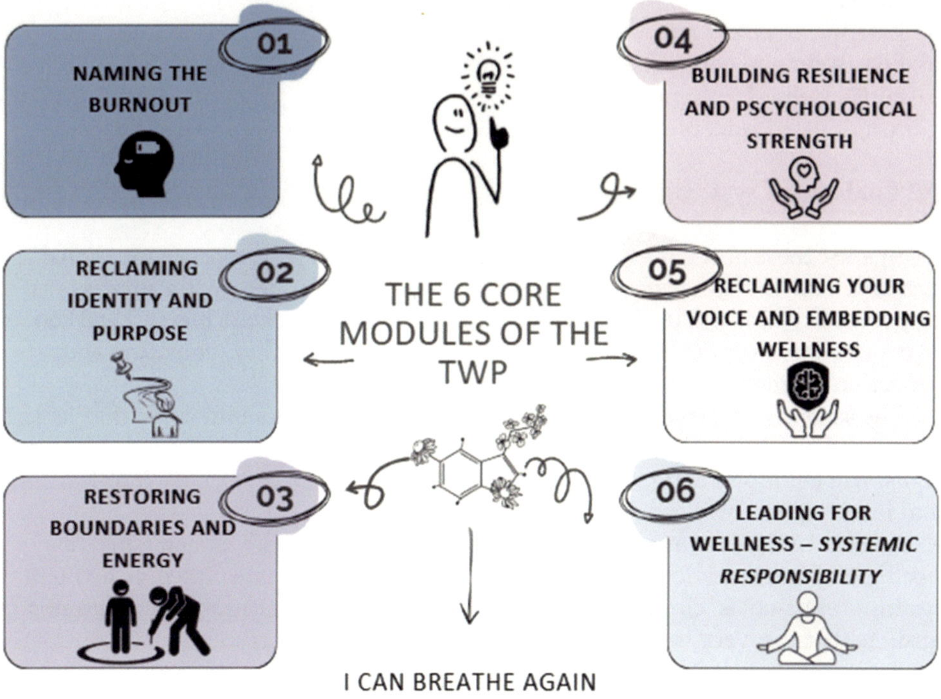

Figure 8.
The six core modules of the TWP – from burnout to embracing wellness (created by the author using Canva Pro (2025)).

9. Barriers and enablers of systemic wellness

Implementing wellness as a systemic priority in education is neither a technical task nor a short-term initiative. It requires cultural transformation, policy coherence, and courageous leadership. Across contexts, two forces consistently shape outcomes: the barriers that maintain burnout and the enablers that make recovery possible.

9.1 Barriers to systemic wellness

The first barrier is *policy inertia*. Although burnout is widely recognized, few ministries of education have formal wellness frameworks integrated into school governance. Existing policies tend to isolate teacher well-being within employee assistance programs or short-term wellness campaigns, rather than embedding it into professional development or leadership structures.

A second barrier is *the misplacement of responsibility.* In many systems, teachers are encouraged to manage their wellness through self-care initiatives, while the organizational pressures that create exhaustion remain unchanged. This imbalance reinforces the illusion that burnout is a personal failure rather than a design flaw in the system.

A third barrier lies in *cultural stigma.* In several regions, particularly within collectivist or high-performance cultures, admitting emotional distress is perceived as a weakness. Teachers may fear professional judgment or job insecurity if they disclose burnout symptoms. This silence allows systemic dysfunction to persist unchallenged.

Finally, *resource inequity* remains a persistent obstacle. Schools in low- and middle-income regions often lack the material and human capital to implement sustained wellness programs. Without external support or policy alignment, even the most motivated leaders struggle to maintain momentum beyond the pilot phase.

9.2 Enablers of systemic wellness

Against these obstacles, promising enablers are emerging across educational systems. The first is *distributed leadership.* When wellness becomes a shared responsibility rather than an individual task, schools evolve from hierarchical control to collaborative stewardship. Leaders who model vulnerability, empathy, and reflection normalize care as part of the professional culture.

The second enabler is *reflective practice.* Teacher-wellness initiatives that include structured reflection sessions, peer coaching, or journaling exercises help educators transform emotional fatigue into insight. Reflection turns experience into learning, and learning into resilience.

A third enabler is *intersectoral collaboration.* Partnerships between education, health, and social services extend wellness beyond school walls. Integrating mental-health professionals, counselors, and wellness facilitators into school ecosystems ensures that recovery is supported, not outsourced.

A final enabler is *policy alignment with the SDGs.* SDG 3 (good health and well-being) and SDG 4 (quality education) converge around the moral imperative to sustain the people who sustain learning. Systems that measure educational success solely through academic outcomes overlook the human foundations on which those outcomes depend. Embedding wellness indicators into school evaluation frameworks transforms well-being from aspiration to accountability.

Collectively, these enablers demonstrate that systemic wellness is not a luxury but a leadership practice grounded in evidence, empathy, and ethical design. The TWP synthesizes these insights into a coherent recovery model that can be contextualized across regions. By addressing barriers and amplifying enablers, education systems can move from burnout to balance, from reaction to prevention, and from survival to transformation.

The data confirm that teacher burnout is a systemic issue requiring institutional reform. Where wellness efforts fail, they do so because responsibility has been misplaced – from the system to the individual. The TWP addresses this imbalance by positioning wellness as a shared moral and structural duty.

This synthesis reveals that burnout is not simply a psychological condition but a mirror of how systems allocate care and power. When the ecology of education is redesigned to protect well-being, recovery becomes both a personal and institutional outcome. The evidence across six continents suggests that wellness cannot be sustained through temporary interventions; it must be governed through structure, leadership, and culture.

Its interdisciplinary foundation brings together eight theories into a single ecology of transformation. Seligman's PERMA defines the destination: flourishing. Luthans, Youssef, and Avolio's PsyCap provides the inner tools. Kaufman's reinterpretation of Maslow's sailboat offers direction through balance. Tedeschi and Calhoun's PTG reframes crisis as a catalyst, while Ortberg's spiritual model roots recovery in purpose. Bronfenbrenner, Mezirow, and Vygotsky connect wellness to the environment, transformation, and community.

Together, they reveal that teacher wellness is not a psychological luxury; it is the moral and operational infrastructure of sustainable education. Viewing schools as public-health ecosystems reframes teacher well-being as preventive architecture. Every act of institutional care becomes an investment in collective resilience.

10. Conclusion

Half a century has passed since Freudenberger [1] warned that those who care most are most at risk of burning out. When the WHO [2] formally recognized burnout as an occupational phenomenon, it confirmed what educators had long known. Yet, awareness has not led to decisive action. The global rise in burnout since the COVID-19 pandemic is particularly troubling. In North America, rates have climbed from 44% in 2022 to 53% in 2025. Similar patterns appear across Europe, Asia, Latin America, and Australia. In sub-Saharan Africa, the absence of updated national teacher-well-being data since 2005 reveals a different crisis: systems are operating without reliable indicators, even as instability, attrition, and projected shortages intensify.

This erosion of teacher well-being places SDG 3 (good health and well-being) and SDG 4 (quality education) at risk. A global education system cannot claim to pursue SDG 4 while ignoring the workforce upon which it depends. Nor can it uphold SDG 3 when the very professionals responsible for children's development experience chronic stress, depression, and exhaustion at levels far exceeding those of comparable occupations.

The evidence has never been missing; it has been scattered. Fragmented datasets, outdated national surveys, inconsistent policy monitoring, and the absence of integrated wellness frameworks have collectively allowed burnout to become normalized. Even after COVID-19 exposed systemic vulnerabilities and pushed educators to a breaking point, most systems returned to prepandemic structures without addressing the fundamental design flaws that caused the collapse. The question is not whether lessons were available; this is why they were not learned.

The TWP bridges this gap by offering a multi-theoretical, systemic framework that unites psychology, leadership, organizational design, and spiritual grounding. It reframes wellness as infrastructure rather than intervention. As [35, 37] observes, tending to the inner life forms the foundation for all other forms of care. Systems that neglect the inner life of their people eventually collapse under their own weight. When institutions nurture both the structural and the spiritual, they rediscover balance: the point where compassion becomes a form of governance.

Teacher wellness is not optional; it is the operating core of sustainable development, social cohesion, and educational quality. When we heal the people who hold the system together, the system heals itself. The rising global burnout rates, the absence of coherent policy responses, and the widening gaps in data all point to the same conclusion: education cannot be reformed without protecting the educators who carry it. The TWP offers a path forward, grounded in global evidence and human dignity, for a world that can no longer afford to ignore the cost of inaction.

Figure 9 brings together the core wellness frameworks discussed in this chapter, providing a final integrative visual that reflects how recovery progresses across personal, relational, and systemic dimensions of education. It symbolizes how teachers move from depletion to renewal when systems align purpose and possibility. Sustaining teachers is not merely an educational reform; it is a global public-health imperative for the next generation.

Figure 9 presents the final reflective composition of the TWP, bringing together the model's core visual metaphors in a single integrated image. This composition unites Maslow's sailboat, the PERMA Tree, the hummingbird model of posttraumatic growth, the Compass of direction, and the Anchor of grounding. Together, they symbolize holistic recovery and transformation in education, showing how teachers move from fragmentation toward clarity, stability, renewed purpose, and integrated well-being. The candle represents vulnerability and the recognition of burnout, while the cape reflects the psychological strengths of hope, efficacy, resilience, and optimism developed through PsyCap. Positioned within a horizon of stars, the teacher stands oriented toward possibility, illustrating that recovery is not linear but guided by meaning, connection, and systemic support.

11. Practical solutions across levels of the education system

A global review of burnout data reveals that teacher well-being cannot be restored through isolated initiatives. The rise in burnout across regions with vastly different economies and cultures indicates a structural failure. Recent evidence from North America shows burnout increasing from 44% in 2022 to 53% in 2025, despite widespread postpandemic awareness campaigns. In sub-Saharan Africa, the absence of a national educator health survey since 2005, combined with 2016 workload and stress indicators and subsequent UNESCO monitoring, suggests that

Figure 9.
The final mirror – integrating theories of recovery and transformation (created by the author using Image Generator Pro (2025)).

current burnout levels are likely higher than earlier estimates. These gaps in measurement and accountability place both **SDG** 3 (good health and well-being) and Goal 4 (quality education) at risk. Against this backdrop, practical solutions must operate at multiple levels of the education system to address both resource gaps and structural causes.

At the individual level, teachers benefit from structured opportunities to rebuild psychological resources such as autonomy, competence, hope, and resilience. Evidence-based practices include guided reflection, boundary-setting tools, strengths-based coaching, and access to mental-health support. When teachers can name their stressors and access stable recovery pathways, their well-being and professional agency increase.

At the professional level, leadership has the strongest influence. Supportive principals who prioritize relational trust, collaborative problem-solving, and realistic workload management significantly reduce burnout risk. Professional learning communities, mentoring structures, and shared decision-making processes strengthen collective efficacy and create environments where teachers feel valued rather than surveilled. Leadership that models vulnerability and reflection normalizes wellness as part of professional culture.

At the public level, national policies shape the working conditions in which burnout occurs. Governments influence teacher well-being through class-size regulations, workload expectations, mental-health provision, competitive compensation, and retention-focused workforce planning. Investment in teacher recruitment, initial preparation, and leadership training remains essential for stabilizing schools in high-pressure contexts. Countries that treat wellness as part of workforce planning demonstrate higher retention and greater instructional stability.

At the systemic level, sustainable change requires embedding wellness into the design of education systems themselves. This includes integrating teacher well-being into accountability frameworks, curriculum reforms, institutional cultures, and long-term budget priorities. When wellness becomes a structural expectation rather than a peripheral initiative, schools are better able to renew themselves and support teachers in meaningful, lasting ways. International analyses show that high-performing systems increasingly treat teacher wellness as foundational to educational quality rather than supplementary to it.

Across these levels, one barrier remains clear: the missing link in most global systems is the integration of teacher well-being into the core of educational policy. Without this anchor, reforms lose coherence, burnout becomes chronic, and inequities deepen. Recognizing wellness as a public obligation – central to workforce stability, professional dignity, and equitable learning outcomes – provides a way forward. When the responsibility for wellness shifts from the individual to the system, sustainable and just education becomes possible.

AI use disclosure

The author acknowledges the use of OpenAI's ChatGPT-5.2 for language polishing and manuscript refinement. The figures used in the chapter were created by the author using Canva Pro and Image Generator Pro, 2025.

Author details

Helena H. Heydenreich
Independent Researcher, Vredenburg, South Africa

*Address all correspondence to: hheyd@yahoo.com

References

[1] Freudenberger HJ. Staff burn-out. Journal of Social Issues. 1974;**30**(1): 159–165. DOI: 10.1111/j.1540-4560.1974. tb00706.x

[2] World Health Organization. (2019, May 28). Burn-out an "occupational phenomenon": International Classification of Diseases. World Health Organization. Available from: https://www.who.int/news/item/28-05-2019-burn-out-an-occupational-phenomenon-international-classification-of-diseases [Accessed: 2025-August-12]

[3] UNESCO. (2024). Global Education Monitoring Report 2024: A lifelong learning culture for inclusive, sustainable societies. UNESCO. Available from: https://www.unesco.org/reports/gem-report/en/2024

[4] OECD. Education at a Glance 2024: OECD Indicators. Paris, France: OECD Publishing; 2024. DOI: 10.1787/c00ca d36-en

[5] UNESCO, International Task Force on Teachers for Education 2030; Fundación SM. Informe Mundial Sobre El Profesorado 2025: Afrontar la Escasez de Docentes Y Transformar la Profesión. Parice, France: UNESCO; 2025. DOI: 10.54675/DMNB3339

[6] Maslach C, Jackson SE. The measurement of experienced burnout. Journal of Organizational Behavior. 1981;**2**(2):99–113. DOI: 10.1002/job.4030020205

[7] Maslach C, Leiter MP. The Truth about Burnout: How Organizations Cause Personal Stress and What to Do about It. San Francisco, CA, USA: Jossey-Bass; 1997

[8] Maslach C, Leiter MP. The Burnout Challenge: Managing People's Relationships with Their Jobs. Cambridge, MA, USA: Harvard University Press; 2022

[9] Doan S, Steiner ED, Pandey R, Woo A. Teacher Well-being and Intentions to Leave: Findings from the 2023 State of the American Teacher Survey. Santa Monica, CA, USA: RAND Corporation; 2023. DOI: 10.7249/RR A1108-8

[10] United Nations; Department of Economic and Social Affairs, New York, NY, USA. Sustainable Development Goals (SDG 3 and SDG 4). 2015. https://sdgs.un.org/goals [Accessed: 2025-August-15]

[11] Seligman MEP. Flourish: A Visionary New Understanding of Happiness and Well-being. New York, NY, USA: Free Press; 2011

[12] Luthans F, Youssef CM, Avolio BJ. Psychological Capital: Developing the Human Competitive Edge. Oxford, United Kingdom: Oxford University Press; 2006

[13] Kaufman SB. Transcend: The New Science of Self-actualization. Perigee, New York, NY, USA: TarcherPerigee; 2020

[14] Tedeschi RG, Calhoun LG. The posttraumatic growth inventory: Measuring the positive legacy of trauma. Journal of Traumatic Stress. 1996;**9**(3):455–471. DOI: 10.1007/BF02103658

[15] Tedeschi RG, Calhoun LG. Posttraumatic growth: Conceptual

foundations and empirical evidence. Psychological Inquiry. 2004;**15**(1):1–18. DOI: 10.1207/s15327965pli1501_01

[16] Ortberg J. The Me I Want to Be: Becoming God's Best Version of You. Grand Rapids, MI, USA: Zondervan; 2009

[17] Bronfenbrenner U. The Ecology of Human Development: Experiments by Nature and Design. Cambridge, MA, USA: Harvard University Press; 1979

[18] Mezirow J. Transformative Dimensions of Adult Learning. San Francisco, CA, USA: Jossey-Bass; 1991

[19] Mezirow J. Learning as Transformation: Critical Perspectives on a Theory in Progress. San Francisco, CA, USA: Jossey-Bass; 2000

[20] Vygotsky LS. Mind in Society: The Development of Higher Psychological Processes. Cambridge, MA, USA: Harvard University Press; 1978

[21] Pandey S, Sayed S. Burnout among school teachers in India: A review of the literature. Shodh Sari-An International Multidisciplinary Journal. 2024;**3**(4):308–320. DOI: 10.59231/SARI7764

[22] Zhong Y, Lai S, Li Y, Yang K, Tang H, Zhang X-Y. Burnout and its relationship with depressive symptoms in primary school teachers under the "Double Reduction" policy in China. Frontiers in Public Health. 2024;**12**:1420452. DOI: 10.3389/fpubh.2024.1420452

[23] Marsollier R, Expósito CD, Varela JJ, Miranda R, Guzmán P, López-Orellana C. Burnout syndrome prevalence among Latin American teachers during the pandemic. Mental Health & Prevention. 2024;**34**:200346. DOI: 10.1016/j.mhp.2024.200346

[24] Black Dog Institute. (2023). National Teacher Survey – Summary (Preliminary Data). Black Dog Institute. Available from: https://www.blackdoginstitute.org.au/wp-content/uploads/2021/08/National-Teacher-Survey_Summary_FEB_2023_final.pdf [Accessed: 2025-August-27]

[25] Chambers C (2025). What a new survey says about teachers' plans to leave their jobs: Despite some signs of progress, well-being and low pay are still major challenges. NEA Today. Available from: https://www.nea.org/nea-today/all-news-articles/what-new-survey-says-about-teachers-plans-leave-their-jobs

[26] NASUWT. The Big Question: Teachers' Workload and Well-being Survey. Birmingham, United Kingdom: NASUWT Teachers' Union; 2023. Available from: https://www.nasuwt.org.uk

[27] UNSW Sydney. (2025). Teachers' depression, anxiety and stress at three times the national norm. UNSW Newsroom. Available from: https://www.unsw.edu.au/newsroom/news/2025/08/teachers-depression-anxiety-and-stress-three-times-national-norm [Accessed: 2025-August-03]

[28] Pitsoe VJ, Machaisa PR. Teacher attrition catastrophe in Sub-Saharan Africa: A hurdle in the achievement of UPE, EFA policy goals and MDGs. Science Journal of Sociology and Anthropology. 2012;**2012**: sjsa-215

[29] Shisana O, Peltzer K, Zungu-Dirwayi N, Louw J, editors. The Health of Our Educators: A Focus on HIV/AIDS in South African Public Schools, 2004/5 Survey. Capte Town, South Africa: HSRC Press; 2005. Available from:

https://www.hsrcpress.ac.za/books/the-health-of-our-educators

[30] Educator Survey II Study Team. Zuma K, Simbayi LC, Rehle T, Mbelle N, Zungu NP, Mthembu J, North A, Van Zyl J, Jooste S, Moyo S, Wabiri N, Maduna V, Mabaso M, Naidoo I, Chasela C, Chikovore J. The Health of Educators in Public Schools in South Africa, 2016 (Commissioned by the Department of Basic Education). Cape Town, South Africa: Human Sciences Research Council; 2016. Available from: https://hdl.handle.net/20.500.11910/10971

[31] Shepherd D (2022). Teachers' level of education and employment over the last two decades: What can be learnt from labour force survey data (Teacher Demographic Dividend Working Paper). Teacher Demographic Dividend (TDD), Southern Africa Labour and Development Research Unit (SALDRU). Available from: https://tdd.sun.ac.za/downloads/C.-Shepherd-2022-Teacher-Education-and-Employment-TDD-10-Nov-2022.pdf

[32] Gallup. (2022). State of the global workplace: 2022 report. Gallup Press. Available from: https://www.gallup.com/workplace/349484/state-of-the-global-workplace-2022-report.aspx

[33] Tata Trusts. Education Portfolio: Annual Review 2022–2023. Mumbai, India: Tata Trusts; 2023. Available from: https://www.tatatrusts.org

[34] Ministry of Education (Rwanda). Education Sector Strategic Plan (ESSP) 2024–2029. Kigali, Rwanda: Government of Rwanda; 2024

[35] Ortberg J. Soul Keeping: Caring for the Most Important Part of You. Grand Rapits, MI, USA: Zondervan; 2014

[36] OECD. Results from TALIS 2024: The State of Teaching. Paris, France: OECD Publishing; 2025. DOI: 10.1787/90df6235-en

[37] Ortberg J. If You Want to Walk on Water, You've Got to Get Out of the Boat. Grand Rapids, Michigan, USA: Zondervan; 2001

[38] Henderson C (2025). Teacher wellbeing and the shaping of teacher shortages in crisis-affected contexts (Background paper commissioned by the International Task Force on Teachers for Education 2030 for the 2024 Global Report on Teachers). International Task Force on Teachers for Education 2030

[39] Australian Institute for Teaching and School Leadership. (2025). National trends: Teacher workforce (June 2025 edition). AITSL. Available from: https://www.aitsl.edu.au/research/australian-teacher-workforce-data/atwd-reports/national-trends-teacher-workforce-jun2025

[40] World Bank. (2024). Implementation Status & Results Report: Rwanda Quality Basic Education for Human Capital Project (P168551). World Bank. Available from: https://projects.worldbank.org/en/projects-operations/project-detail/P168551

[41] Human Sciences Research Council. (2005). Educator supply and demand in the South African public education system: Integrated report. HSRC Press. Available from: https://www.hsrcpress.ac.za/books/educator-supply-and-demand-in-the-south-african-public-education-system